ALSO BY PAUL NEWELL

Victorian Portsmouth
1860-1869

Victorian Portsmouth 1860-1869

by
Paul Newell

Moyhill Publishing

© Copyright 2021 Paul Newell.

All rights reserved. This book, or any portion thereof, may not be reproduced or used in any manner whatsoever without the express written permission of the author except for the use of brief quotations in a book review.
The moral right of the author has been asserted.

First Published in 2021 by Moyhill Publishing.
ISBN 978-1-913529-80-2

A CIP catalogue record for this book is available from the British Library.

Printed in UK.

Transcripts and Images have been created by myself with thanks to
The British Newspaper archive (www.britishnewspaperarchive.co.uk),
or from my own private collection.

Book Design by *Moyhill* Publishing.

Cover image courtesy of Julian Colander
Own work, CC BY-SA 3.0
https://commons.wikimedia.org/w/index.php?curid=28210534

The papers used in this book were produced in an environmentally friendly way from sustainable forests.

Moyhill Publishing,
1965 Davenport House, 261 Bolton Rd, Bury, Gtr. Manchester BL8 2NZ. UK

Contents

INTRODUCTION 1
1860 – LANDPORT RAGGED SCHOOLS 2
1860 – LAUNCH OF THE PRINCE OF WALES 2
1860 – LAYING THE FIRST STONE OF THE PORTSMOUTH DOCK 2
1860 – THE STATE OF THE GAOL 4
1860 – WHAT IS DOING AT PORTSMOUTH? 5
1861 – A NEW TRANSPORT CARRIAGE 5
1861 – GREAT FIRE AT PORTSMOUTH 6
1861 - THE PARADE OF VICE 7
1861 – CHURCH EXTENSION IN THE PARISH OF PORTSEA 7
1861 – BLONDIN AT PORTCHESTER 9
1861 – LAST PORTSDOWN FAIR 11
1861 – DANGEROUS NUISANCE IN EAST STREET 11
1861 – LAUNCH OF H.M.S. GLASGOW 12
1861 – DEATH OF THE PRINCE CONSORT 12
1861 – IMPROVEMENTS TO LUMPS FORT 12
1861 – THE ARRIVAL OF THE WARRIOR 13
1861 – NAVAL AND MILITARY PREPARATIONS 13
1861 – NEW DRINKING FOUNTAIN ON SOUTHSEA COMMON 14
1861 – SOUTHSEA PIER AND THE CABMEN 14
1861 – VISITS TO THE WARRIOR 15
1862 – MURDEROUS ATTACK ON A CONVICT WARDER AT PORTSMOUTH DOCKYARD 15
1862 – THE NEW DEFENCES OF PORTSMOUTH 15
1862 – THE TUSCARORA 22
1862 – EAST HANTS CRICKET GROUND 22
1862 – SOLDIERS' INSTITUTES 22
1862 – REDUCTION OF THE FLEET 24
1862 – THE PORTSMOUTH FORTIFICATIONS 24
1863 – BALL AT THE PORTLAND HALL 24
1863 – INSPECTION OF THE GARRISON OF PORTSMOUTH BY THE DUKE OF CAMBRIDGE 25
1863 – MEMORIAL CROSS OF THE 8TH (KING'S) REGIMENT 26
1863 – RURAL FETE AT EAST COSHAM 27
1863 – CELEBRATION OF THE PRINCE OF WALES MARRIAGE 29
1863 – THE TOWN AND HARBOUR OF PORTSMOUTH 38
1863 – THE SPITHEAD FORTS 44
1863 – PRINCE ALFRED AT A SAILOR'S FUNERAL 45
1863 – MONUMENT TO ADMIRAL SIR CHARLES NAPIER 45
1863 – VISIT OF PRINCE & PRINCESS LOUIS OF HESSE TO THE DOCKYARD 45
1863 – THE GARRISON CHURCH AND FONT 47
1863 – WORK IN PORTSMOUTH DOCKYARD 47
1863 – THE CHESAPEAKE MEMORIAL 48
1863 – DEFENCES OF THE ISLE OF WIGHT 49
1864 – EASTNEY BARRACKS AND THE EXTENSION OF PORTSMOUTH DOCKYARD 50
1864 – CHRISTMAS TREAT TO RAGGED SCHOOL CHILDREN 52
1864 – OPENING OF THE NEW CIRCUS AT LANDPORT 53
1864 – EMPLOYMENT OF CONVICTS IN THE DOCKYARD 53
1864 – GARIBALDI'S VISIT TO PORTSMOUTH 54
1864 – GUNPOWDER AT PORTSMOUTH 55
1864 – ADDITIONS TO OUR IRONCLAD FLEET 55

Contents

1864 – LAUNCH OF THE ROYAL ALFRED	57
1864 – THE CORONATION HOLIDAY	60
1864 – SUSPENDING OPERATIONS	60
1864 – THE WARRIOR DECOMMISSIONED	60
1864 – YACHTING SEASON AT RYDE	61
1865 – THE SOUTHSEA BEACH MANSION	62
1865 – THE NAVAL FESTIVAL AT PORTSMOUTH	63
1865 – THE PURIFICATION OF PORTSMOUTH	71
1865 – CENTENARY FESTIVAL OF NELSON'S SHIP, THE VICTORY	71
1865 – PRESENTATION OF THE VICTORIA CROSS ON SOUTHSEA COMMON	72
1865 – THE GREAT TEA QUESTION	73
1866 – EXPERIMENTAL FIRING AT THE ROYAL SOVEREIGN	74
1864 – SWEDISH BRIG WRECK AT SANDOWN	76
1864 – THE CHURCH BELLS OF PORTSMOUTH	77
1866 – PORTSMOUTH AND GENERAL STEAM BISCUIT COMPANY	78
1866 – OYSTER CULTURE IN THE AREA	78
1867 – A MUCH NEEDED IMPROVEMENT	80
1867 – IMPROVEMENT OF THE NAVY	80
1867 – THE NAVAL REVIEW	80
1867 – TELFORD'S REMINISCENCES OF PORTSMOUTH	83
1867 – THE EMPRESS OF THE FRENCH	84
1867 – UNFOUNDED RUMOURS	84
1867 – COMPETITION IN THE DOCKYARDS	84
1867 – THE CONDITION OF THE KINGSTON BURIAL GROUND	85
1867 – THE PORTSMOUTH PANTOMIME	87
1867 – STATE OF THE ROADS AT FRATTON	87
1867 – SOUTHSEA IMPROVEMENTS	88
1867 – THE PORTSMOUTH FEMALE PENITENTIARY AND SOCIETY FOR THE REFORMATION OF FALLEN WOMEN	89
1867 – CONVICT LIFE IN PORTSMOUTH PRISON	94
1867 – SALE OF A BREWERY	98
1867 – VISIT OF PRINCE MINBUTAIHO	99
1868 – THE GRAND VOLUNTEER REVIEW AT PORTSMOUTH	101
1868 – PORTSMOUTH BOROUGH GAOL	105
1868 – THE POST REFORM ACT GENERAL ELECTION AT PORTSMOUTH	107
1868 – THE VOLUNTEER REVIEW AT PORTSMOUTH PART II	113
1868 – THE MILITARY REVIEW AS SEEN FROM WIDLEY FORT	115
1868 – A NEW STAINED-GLASS WINDOW	117
1868 – QUEEN'S INSPECTION OF H.M.S GALATEA	117
1868 – THE PORTSMOUTH GUARDIAN	118
1868 – DEATH OF THE VICAR OF PORTSMOUTH	118
1868 – IMPROVEMENTS TO THE FORTS AT PORTSMOUTH	118
1868 – LIFE AT SOUTHSEA	119
1868 – OPENING OF ST. MARK'S TEMPORARY CHURCH	120
1868 – A POEM TO CAPTAIN KENNICOTT	121
1868 – PROJECTED IMPROVEMENTS IN SOUTSEA	121
1868 – ARRIVAL OF TROOPS FROM ABYSSINIA	122
1868 – LANDPORT DRAPERY BAZAAR	122
1868 – ALBERT COTTAGES AT LANDPORT	122
1868 – THE ELECTION OF GOVERNOR AT THE WORKHOUSE	123

Contents

1868 – HAMPSHIRE AND ISLE OF WIGHT BLIND SCHOOL AND HOME 124
1868 – THE FENIAN CONSPIRACY 127
1869 – TEMPERANCE DEMONSTRATION AT NORTH END 129
1869 – PORTSMOUTH CHIMES 131
1869 – OPENING OF THE NEW MILITARY GYMNASIUM AT PORTSMOUTH 132
1869 – OPENING OF THE NEW THEATRE AT EASTNEY BARRACKS 134
1869 – THE FUNERAL OF MR. PEABODY 135
1869 – SANGER'S CIRCUS 138
1869 – FUNERAL OF ADMIRAL WARDEN 138
1869 – THE EASTNEY FLOWER SHOW 139
1869 – THE HILSEA LINES 140
1869 – THE REDUCTIONS IN THE GOVERNMENT DOCKYARDS 143
1869 – THE PORTSMOUTH VOLUNTEER REVIEW 146
1869 – WELFARE OF THE PORTSMOUTH EMIGRANTS 149
1869 – FUNERAL OF CAPTAIN COLIN ARTHUR CAMPBELL 151
1869 – HER MAJESTY'S BIRTHDAY 152

INTRODUCTION

Following the horrors of the Crimean War in the 1850's, the 1860's were a time of relative peace for Great Britain in contrast to their European counterparts who were undergoing territorial disputes and unification of principalities such as in Italy and Prussia. However, the paranoia of a French invasion, which never came, led to the Defence Act of 1860 and an unprecedented defensive building programme which was no more apparent than in Portsmouth.

The Palmerston Follies (as they were known as) were constructed along the ridge of Portsdown Hill to deter invaders from the North entering the city. The Hilsea Lines were also erected as a second line of defence and forts were constructed in the Solent to repel ships trying to enter the Channel. There were also modifications to the existing forts along the seafront such as Lumps Fort. None of these fortifications have ever been put to the test but Volunteer exercises were carried out with regularity during this decade.

Ironically, the threat had passed sufficiently for the French navy to be welcomed to Portsmouth in 1865 with much pomp and circumstance!

In addition to defensive strengthening, Portsmouth underwent other modifications, especially in Southsea which emerged as a seaside resort becoming popular with day trippers who arrived by railway.

The Dockyard continued to produce ships for the Navy but it also saw, towards the end of the decade, a downturn in work which led to the first emigrations to the new dominion of Canada from the port. High vigilance had to be maintained for fear of sabotage by the Fenians. Rumours were common but again, nothing materialised.

Sanitation improved and it was then that the first drainage system was laid and the first steps towards social modernisation were slowly taken.

Experience events in Portsmouth in the 1860's as reported by the newspapers of the time in this second volume of Victorian Portsmouth.

1860 – LANDPORT RAGGED SCHOOLS.

The proposition to establish ragged free schools, for poor children at Landport, has been partially carried out. On Thursday, the first of the two schools proposed to be founded was opened. It is situated in Oxford Street, Landport, a low neighbourhood, containing a number of ragged children who might be possibly reclaimed from the streets, and the succeeding results, by means of the school. A store has been boarded and converted into a comfortable schoolroom, which opened with about 30 scholars. The committee announced that the schools are conducted on entirely unsectarian principles, and earnestly ask the public for assistance to enable them to carry out the remaining portion of their intention - the founding of another school in Marylebone. On behalf of so good a cause, the appeal will not, we believe, be made in vain.

1860 – LAUNCH OF THE PRINCE OF WALES.

The launching of the *Prince of Wales*, screw three-decker, took place at Portsmouth on Wednesday with the most complete success. For some days previous the weather had been unpropitious in the extreme, and on Wednesday morning broke dark and lowering, with a cold N.N.W. wind, promising little pleasure to the visitors at the launch. As the morning wore on the sky became clearer, with glimpses of sunshine, and as enthusiasm on such occasions never flags with the inhabitants of Portsmouth, some thousands of people had assembled on every point whence a view of the proceedings could be obtained by the time the ship was launched.

Among those present on the platform erected under the bows of the vessel were Admiral W. Bowles, C.B., Rear-Admiral the Hon. G. Grey with Flag-Lieuts. Robinson and Swinburn; Captains Farquhar and Hamilton; Commanders His Serene Highness the Prince of Leiningen, Cator, &c.; Her Serene Highness the Princess of Leiningen and Miss Bowles; His Serene Highness Prince Edward of Saxe Weimar, &c. The band of her Majesty's ship *Victory* was in attendance, and played a variety of airs during the proceedings preliminary to the launching of the vessel. At 12.25 p.m. the master builder, Mr. Abethell, placed the bottle of wine, which was suspended in the usual manner, in the hands of the Princess of Leiningen, who broke it against the ship's bows amid the cheering of all present, and the ceremony of christening the *Prince of Wales* was complete.

The workmen immediately commenced splitting away the blocks remaining under the ship's keel, and at 12.30 p.m. the cord being cut which held suspended the pigs of ballast, these descended in their channels and liberated the vessel from the dogshores. A few minutes more and she began to move, gliding easily into the water, accompanied by cheering from the crowds of people present, and the grains of the National Anthem from the *Victory*'s band. The ship was no sooner clear of the shed under which she had been constructed, than flag staffs rose as if by magic from her decks, displaying the Royal Standard, the Admiralty Ensign and the Union Jack. She was checked further before being taken in tow by steam tugs, she was berthed for the present alongside the *Victorious* hulk in the harbour, and will be placed in the steam basin on the next spring tide for the purpose of docking and receiving her machinery &c.

The *Prince of Wales* was laid down on the 10th June 1848 from designs approved by the then surveyor of the Navy, Sir Wm. Symonds, and intended for a sailing three-decker. It was, however, subsequently determined that, with several others then on the stocks, she should undergo considerable alterations, necessary to adopt her to the screw and for this purpose she was cut asunder amidships and lengthened about 50 feet; her stern was also lengthened as much as was necessary to enable her to receive her outer stern-post for her screw-shafting and rudder. The figurehead of the ship is a bust of His Royal Highness the Prince of Wales, and has been executed by Messrs. Hellyer, of Cosham and Southampton. Her burden in tons is 3,994. Her propelling power consists of a pair of 400 horsepower (nominal) trunk engines, by Messrs. Penn and Sons.

1860 – LAYING THE FIRST STONE OF THE PORTSMOUTH DOCK.

The ceremony of laying the first stone of the New Camber Dock took place on Thursday last, by the Worshipful Mayor, W.H. Garrington, Esq., in presence of the various civic functionaries of the Corporation in their robes of office, several of the naval and military authorities, and a large concourse of the principal gentry, tradespeople, and inhabitants of the town and neighbourhood. The event was to have been celebrated on Tuesday, but was prevented by the inclemency of the weather, notwithstanding that nearly all the necessary arrangements had been completed.

Before attempting to describe the scene, we deem it best to give our readers some idea of the spot on which it took place, for we believe that many were hitherto ignorant of the exact whereabouts of the site. The proposed new dock, the dimensions of which are 370 feet in length, 36 feet wide, and 23 feet 6 inches greatest depth, will run in a direction from west to east, its entrance being about midway in the obliquity of the outer Camber (which runs inwards from south-west to north-east) and the bridge, its eastern end extending nearly to the road which passes from the Custom House to Portsea. The north side of the dock is flanked by the Artillery Barracks, the south the Custom House quay and the Camber. The materials required for the work are enumerated as follows:—Cornwall granite, 10,700 cubic feet; Roach Portland stone, 101,000 ditto; Purbeck ditto, 12,000; Memel timber, 300 loads; excavation to be removed, 25,000 cubic yards; clay for dam, 1,700 ditto. The blocks of stone, which vary in weight from six tons downwards, are conveyed from the vessels in the Camber along "travellers," or "gantry's," and lowered into the dock by means of chains and pulleys. The bottom will be formed of concrete, the foundation of the same to be about 4 feet thick; not more than two-thirds of the dock have been excavated at present, although there are about 200 tons of stone upon the ground, and the stonework will now proceed with vigour, under the able hands of Mr. William Hanson, the contractor, who has reported progress some time since, the whole being, as is well known, under the superintendence Mr. C.W.E. Pineo, C.E., engineer to the Corporation.

With regard to the preparations for the occasion, the Dock was decorated from side to side by rows of suspended banners and national ensigns, amongst which were a silk flag surmounted by the royal arms, and another having on it the borough arms. Seats were erected at the east end, for the accommodation of about 600 persons, admitted by ticket. Seats were also arranged on the north side for the convenience of the public, who likewise thronged the excavations and stone work around. A platform was also erected under the gallery at the east end for photographic apparatus.

At about two o'clock, the various gentlemen to take part in the ceremony made their appearance. The band of the 1st battalion of the 11th Regiment entered first, and took a position on the south side of the dock. Then came the members of the Corporation headed by the Mayor, followed by most of the Aldermen and Councillors, and amongst the company we also noticed—Vice Admiral H.W. Bruce, Naval Commander-in-Chief; Col. Anderson, R.M.; Major Sturdee, of the Civil Service Artillery Volunteers; Major Hall and Captain Galt, of the 2nd Hants Artillery Volunteers, &c., &c.

The first thing accomplished was a photograph of the scene, by Mr. Poates, before the laying of the stone, all the members of the Council, the naval and military authorities being present at the bottom of the Dock, and the public in large numbers all around, but high up on the stones and embankments.

The Mayor then said, "Gentlemen of the Town Council, you are met here today to lay the new site of the Camber Dock, under the provisions of an Act of Parliament passed the year before last. For the satisfaction of the public, I may as well first state that the reason the ceremony was postponed last Tuesday, was on account of the wet weather and the consequent dampness of the ground, which was considered to have rendered it unsafe to proceed then, it was therefore deferred until today in order to avoid the possibility of accident; and whatever may have been thought to the propriety or impropriety of that course, I think the present fine weather will amply repay for the trouble and annoyance that has been consequently occasioned. I had intended to enter somewhat largely upon the circumstances that had led to the construction of this dock, and its importance to the borough and the public; but I feel too unwell to stand here long enough to enable me to do so now, which I therefore hope you will excuse. I cannot however, pass it over, whatever the differences of opinion on the subject may have been, without observing, that I think no one can deny that this borough requires such an important addition to its public works. It was only yesterday that I was informed that some time since, five ships came here for the purpose of being docked for repairs, and in consequence of there not being sufficient accommodation at this port they were obliged to be sent to Southampton, where they laid for the space of one month undergoing the necessary repairs. Now I think you will readily see that the money which must have been spent for the purpose would have made a most desirable addition to our resources in this borough. I am aware that a great deal was said at the time of our starting this project, in reference to our large undertaking, and that it must be a losing speculation, and never would pay. Gentlemen, will however bear with me when I state as my firm conviction, that I believe it will prove a profitable speculation, and that we shall be able to pay off the amount of principal and interest of the money borrowed, and also save a few pounds to be placed to the credit of the public funds. I do indeed see that the undertaking may be made remunerative, and I do hope that you all may not only look at it in the same light, but that all will be determined to do their best towards promoting its interests, which will, I have not the slightest doubt, ultimately prove a benefit to this borough."

Mr. Pineo then informed his worship that the hermetically sealed tin case then held in his hand, contained a copy of the Act of Parliament authorising the construction of the dock, one each of the current coins of the present reign, a list of the members of the Town Council, a copy each of the *Portsmouth Times, Hants Telegraph, Hants Advertiser, Portsmouth Guardian,* and *West Sussex Gazette,* which, with his permission, were then placed in the concrete cavity, and which was then embedded in cement, spread the Mayor and again by the Engineer. The band then struck up, and the signal was given for removing the suspended stone, which weighed 4 tons, 3 cwt., immediately over the spot, on which it was to be laid. The stone was then lowered by the workmen upon the "traveller" above, and the Mayor taking the silver trowel, kindly lent by the Messrs. Emanuel for the occasion, with the assistance of the Engineer, his assistant, and the Contractor, fixed it in the place assigned for it, when the necessary levels and squares having been accurately ascertained, the Mayor, striking the stone three times with a mallet, said, "I declare this stone to be truly laid, and my sincere wish is that God may bless the undertaking, and that it may ultimately prove a source of gratification and benefit to the borough, and to its representatives."

Another photograph was then taken representing the act of laying the stone.

Three cheers were then given for the Queen and also for the Mayor, the band striking up "Hearts of Oak." The company then retired from the dock, and the guests proceeded to the Queen's Warehouse, at the Custom House for dinner.

1860 – THE STATE OF THE GAOL.

The Epiphany Sessions for this Borough were held yesterday before J.D. Coleridge, Esq., Recorder. There were 16 prisoners for trial, but none of the cases were of more than ordinary importance. The Recorder, in charging the grand jury, said, "I am happy to tell you that the calendar is unusually light, and I do not know that any of the cases present any features for observation, and therefore it would be my duty at once to dismiss you to your duties, was there not a matter intimately connected with me as recorder, and with you as inhabitants of this borough, - I mean the state of the gaol in this town, and the condition of the prisoners in it. Some time ago, soon after I was appointed to the office which it is still a pride to fill, I drew your attention to the subject. At that time, I must confess, rather arguing from what I knew must take place under the circumstances, than from any practical examination of the facts of the case, but since that time, I have, from time to time, made enquiries, and put questions upon the subject, and the result is that I am pained and sorry to say that I have found that the gaol, beyond all doubt and dispute, is not such a gaol as it ought to be.

In the first place it is not large enough. As the population of the Borough increases, and as the naval and military establishments of a place like this increase, it must of necessity be, that the gaol accommodation must be more wanted. There are not cells enough, to give each prisoner, as a matter of average, a separate cell. The last time I made enquiries, not long ago, I found that there were three prisoners in one cell, one sleeping on the bedstead and two on the cell floor. I need not point out to you the inconvenience, the unhealthiness, the indecency, and the inconsistency of this with gaol discipline. The general arrangements are bad and defective. It is almost impossible to separate and classify the prisoners. This is a matter fatal to prison discipline, and which, too often turns a gaol into a breeding place for crime. There is scarcely an important place in the country where there are not better means for classifying prisoners then in Portsmouth. This is a state of things discreditable to us, and which you ought to set about improving.

I need not refer to the economy of making the gaol what it ought to be. Unless we make punishment effective, and the gaol really a matter of dread and avoidance, we shall keep the gaol full, multiply criminals, encourage crime, and waste large sums of money annually. I do assure you that it adds greatly to the difficulty of my administering justice, as Criminal Judge of this borough, and, although I know that all is done that can be done by the excellent and zealous persons who fill offices, superior and inferior, in this gaol, yet I never feel certain that I am doing good when I am sentencing a prisoner. Short imprisonments seldom do any good and on giving long terms, in the present state of the gaol, I am not sure that I am not corrupting the criminal. It is not my function to enter into matters of finance; it is not my province to enter into them; I don't pretend to understand them but any man of common sense may see that the present gaol is insufficient for this borough.

It is a question whether, if by making the gaol effective, we shall not have a considerable annual reduction of expenditure. This is a matter which no questions of mere finance ought to keep you back from considering. I make no apology for bringing this subject forward, neither am I in the habit of wasting your time with dissertations upon statements of timings in general; but this is a matter which intimately interests us all, you as inhabitants, and me as recorder. It is a matter upon which I have a clear and strong opinion, and a matter which I ask you seriously and practically to consider.

1860 – WHAT IS DOING AT PORTSMOUTH?

Let us indulge in the supposition that the conductors of some spirited French journal were to despatch a special correspondent to a certain fortress Dockyard and naval station on the coast of Hampshire, immediately under the lee of the Isle of Wight – what would the foreign inquirer find in that important stronghold? How would he answer the question, "*Qu'est ce qu'on fait a Portsmouth?*" To make a clean breast of the matter, he would discover a place infinitely weaker, so far as mere granite fortifications go, than Cherbourg.

The Isle of Wight is the natural breakwater to Portsmouth, but it by no means "bristles with forts," and from the Nab to the Needles we should be puzzled to discern any great amount of preparation or even of common defence against warlike eventualities.

Then as to Portsmouth itself, there is certainly Henry VIII's old castle at Southsea; and there are two Russian trophy guns on the Clarence Parade, which would not, we think, be much more efficacious in warfare than Mon Meg at Edinburgh, or Queen Elizabeth's pocket pistol at Dover. There is the King's Bastion, and there is the Platform Battery. There is the famous Portsmouth "lines," with moats, drawbridges, ravelins, and counterscarps, according to the designs of the late Field-Marshal Vauban, but which are slightly, say a couple of centuries, behind the time.

There is the Blockhouse Fort at the throat of the harbour, a broadside from whose artillery would probably inflict considerable injury on the bathing rooms, and sink, if necessary, the floating bridge which plies between Gosport and "Point."

Southsea has its "lines" also, and its antiquated ramparts and gates. There are Cumberland Fort and Browndown; but the rich and populous suburbs of Landport and Southsea are entirely undefended. There are between three and four thousand men in garrison. The officers of the Regulars sneer at the officers of the Militia, and both concur in giving the cold shoulder to the admirable Volunteer companies of rifles and artillery which have been raised by the patriotism of the town. The band plays on the Governor's Green, and the troops have a field day occasionally, under the auspices of Lord William Paulet who so distinguished himself at Constantinople five years ago.

Beyond this the soldiers have little to do beyond getting drunk, and ravaging the peculiarly infamous back streets of Portsmouth and Portsea; and the officers of the line divide their time between innocent flirtations and disgraceful midnight broils with watermen and prostitutes on the Common Hard. Were this all that the traveller would see in Portsmouth, the nation would have cause to hang its head in shame; but near the entrance to the harbour there is a certain three decker called the *Britannia*, in which hundreds of stalwart lads, cadets and powder-monkeys as well, are being admirably trained for the naval service. On board the *Victory*, mere boys receive instruction from old and experienced seamen; and higher up the harbour is the *Excellent*, whose gunnery practice, still diligently carried on, is famous throughout the world.

The Dockyard is in "full blast," and nearly five thousand men are employed in its stupendous works. There are barracks full of those capital soldiers, the Royal Marines and Artillerymen, who are kept in constant practice at great guns. Finally, a few of the thousands recently voted for the defence of the realm are to be spent at Portsmouth, notably in the defence of Portsdown Hill and when we consider that a squadron yet rides at Spithead, that there are plenty of steamers in the dock basins, and that Portsmouth, after all, is not our only trump card, but that we possess Plymouth, Pembroke, Milford Haven, Cork, Sheerness, Chatham, Woolwich, and Deptford, we don't think that we need be thrown into any very great agitation expecting "what is being done at Cherbourg."

1861 – A NEW TRANSPORT CARRIAGE.

A new transport carriage for the removal of heavy guns has been forwarded to Portsmouth for the purpose of testing its powers in the removal of large class ordnance to and from different parts of the works, and has been found to answer admirably, contrasting very favourably when compared with the old sling wagon. The new carriage is very simple in character, and consists of four parts. A pole and axle, with two wheels, with projecting fork and upright pin over the axle; in fact, a "roller handspike" mounted on wheels. The pin, on the pole being raised, fits in a plate in the rear and under part of the slide of an eight-inch gun carriage, and by pulling down the pole, precisely as the handspike is used, the weight of the slide, carriage, and gun is taken off the ground and thrown on the fore axle of the transporting carriage. At the fore and under part of the slide, in line with the fore chase of the gun, are fittings to receive an iron axle, which is clamped into its place and then fitted with its two wheels. On ordinary roads the heaviest ordnance mounted on their carriage and traversing slides may thus be transported to any distance.

1861 – GREAT FIRE AT PORTSMOUTH

The fire broke out shortly after midnight on Thursday week in the stabling adjoining the equestrian establishment recently erected by Messrs. Cooke, at the back of Commercial Road, Landport. The circus was entirely burnt down, and an elephant, a camel, and eight of the most valuable horses of the stud were destroyed, including the famed "trick" horse Raven. The whole of Messrs. Cooke's wardrobe, properties, and equestrian paraphernalia also were entirely consumed. Thirty-seven horses and ponies were saved through great exertion. The houses in Buckingham Street, adjoining the circus, caught fire, and six of them were burnt through, and eight others were much damaged; one was partially pulled down to stop the course of the flames. The borough police, Dockyard police, 1st battalion 11th Regiment, 2nd battalion 19th Regiment, and Royal Engineers, with their engines, were speedily on the spot, and the flames were subdued at about three o'clock.

The ruins have been visited by at least 30,000 persons since the fire, and the spectacle presented is most lamentable. Nearly half a street of houses is completely gutted, and a space of about 100 square feet contains nothing but the debris of the once elegant circus.

On Friday evening there was a large meeting at Lion Gate Road, presided over by Alderman Scale, convened for the purpose of devising some scheme to benefit those families who have been deprived of a home by the melancholy occurrence. A series of resolutions were passed, and a committee to obtain

Fire at Portsmouth

subscriptions to afford immediate relief to the sufferers was established. There were about 3,000 persons present at the meeting, and nearly £200 was subscribed. A town council meeting was held on Saturday, when it was agreed that a committee of twelve should be appointed to act with the other committee in order to raise funds.

1861 - THE PARADE OF VICE.

It is not often that we have occasion to question the propriety or wisdom of the decisions of our Borough Magistrates, but it appears that, in their desire to check the immorality of the town, their zeal has rather overcome their prudence.

On Thursday last several informations were laid under the Towns' Police Clauses Act, incorporated with the local act, against publicans and beer house keepers in the town of Portsmouth for knowingly suffering prostitutes to assemble in their houses, contrary to the statute. In each case the offender was convicted, and the result has been that during the last two days public decency has been outraged by some dozens of prostitutes of the most degraded class promenading the public thoroughfares of the town, whether to elicit sympathy or for the mere sake of bravado, or to convert defeat into a triumph by a more shameful exhibition of vice, it is impossible to say.

Certain it is, however, that the spectacle has been one of the most disgusting it is possible to witness. Arm-in-arm patrolling the streets, were haggard old women and besotted girls, whose progress was heralded by the jubilant shouts of children, of both sexes, who appear to be receiving their first lessons of life in these filthy abodes of vice and infamy.

Now, it is very certain that vice cannot be transformed into virtue by the strong arm of the law. The experiment has been tried and has failed. Christian philanthropy must provide some other agent whose operations must be more gentle, but whose influence will be more powerful.

We do not inquire by whose authority these informations were laid, nor do we question the decision of the Justices so far as the mere interpretation of the Act is concerned. It may be that their judgment was a perfectly legal one, and that they lead no alternative but to convict; but, under any circumstances, it was unwise that the power of the law should have been tested. What has been gained, or, rather, what has been the sacrifice? Why, vice has been dragged from its courts of revelry, and public decency and virtue have been openly scandalised. The remedy has been worse than the disease. The agent employed to moderate the evil has aggravated it. The policy of the law, and of those who administer it, should be to mitigate the evil of what cannot be helped. If vice and immorality must exist, - and they will, despite the law, - at any rate let them revel in their obscurity, and apply the law only when they become a public nuisance, and when nothing else will suffice to mitigate or abolish them.

1861 – CHURCH EXTENSION IN THE PARISH OF PORTSEA.

About ten years ago many worthy people in this town and neighbourhood became suddenly imbued with a kind of enthusiasm in favour of church extension, and a scheme for building additional churches in Portsea was drawn up by the present Bishop of Rochester, then Archdeacon Wigram. The spiritual necessities of the large and increasing population were found to be very inadequately provided for. The Church was not fulfilling her mission. Acres of ground were being covered with inhabited dwellings, and hundreds were being added to the population year by year, but yet the Church remained stationary. Many a district was created without its tabernacle. The poor, the ignorant, and the irreligious were left in their poverty, ignorance, and irreligion, and no special effort until that time was made to help them. There was every reason why the effort should, if possible, have been carried out to a successful issue at the time, and a great responsibility rested upon those who had the pastoral supervision or the parish.

The sudden impulse, however, in favour of church extension, soon relapsed into apathy. The intention, it is true, was comprehensive, and three new churches were to be added without delay. But what is the result? Ten years have elapsed, and not one of the three is completed. The other two have scarcely been thought of; although the population of the borough numbers 20,000 more than it did ten years ago. It is impossible, perhaps, to point to any precise reason for this apathy on the part of the public, but the mere fact suggests considerations which are of deep importance, as affecting the moral and social wellbeing of this great community, equally with those which relate to its eternal welfare.

We are not aware how far the committee which was appointed to carry out Archdeacon Wigram's scheme may be held responsible for the delay which has been occasioned in the completion of St. Luke's Church. They had, no doubt, many difficulties to contend with, and much to discourage, even on the part of those from whom they might have expected to receive the most cordial sympathy and support. They had, however, to solicit the aid of a people who, according to the opinion of the Bishop of Winchester, "are not ordinarily unaccustomed to respond to pressing appeals," and who were, without doubt, deeply interested in this particular appeal. But there are many collateral circumstances which ought to be taken into consideration with respect to the apathy of the public in this particular case. Mr. Gillman's explanation came pretty near the mark when he said that there were few communities that did more in proportion to their means than the inhabitants of Portsmouth, to alleviate distress. "There was," he added, "raised here annually, upwards of 30,000l. in compulsory poor rates, and this formed a charge upon our property of 6s. in the pound, whereas the average charge in the United Kingdom was only about 2s. in the pound." It is, perhaps, right to mention, that heavy as our taxation is for the maintenance of the poor, it is not so heavy as it appears to be, because the borough and police rates are paid out of the same fund. These demands fall heavily upon the people, and leave but little to be disposed of in the way of voluntary benevolence.

The population of Portsmouth is not an affluent population. It is not like a large manufacturing community; whose wealth is profuse and very widely distributed. The principal sources of employment here are, of course, the Government establishments, but the great bulk of the expenditure made on their account is for labour, the proceeds of which are, as a rule, the only wealth possessed by the operative classes. We do not, of course, mean to insinuate that more could not be accomplished in the way of charity and philanthropy than is accomplished even by the people of Portsmouth, but we do say that the want of power is more conspicuous than the want of will, and that it is therefore a fair representation of the public character to say that the people "are not ordinarily unaccustomed to respond to pressing appeals."

There are, nevertheless, other reasons which may be cited to account for the apparent indifference of the public to this matter of church extension, and undertakings of a kindred character. It is quite true that Portsmouth, considering its population and the nature of its employment, is not on a par with the majority of large towns, which possess noble institutions, designed to promote their moral, social, religious, and intellectual well-being. It is essentially conservative, and does not appear to have any great ambition to take a prominent place in the list of towns which are pre-eminent for their intellectual culture, moral and religious character, and everything which tends to help on the great work of civilisation. How is this? Is it because there is little or no community of interests, and no community of sympathies between the various classes which compose its population? That this is the fact there can be little doubt, and it is unfortunate that it should be so. It will be a happy day for this borough, if it ever should come, when the various towns shall sink their differences, and combine with one fixed unity of spirit and purpose, to promote each other's welfare, and thereby, their own.

It is not difficult, however, to understand why there should be so little of what is commonly known as public spirit and united action. The population is to a very considerable extent a fluctuating population. It is scarcely reasonable to suppose that the more affluent of casual residents, who are here today and gone tomorrow, can feel any special interest in the permanent prosperity of the borough, and a large proportion of the operative classes, from the same reason, are not particularly concerned with anything that does not touch their immediate wants and necessities. These are amongst the chief difficulties, we think, with which the committee have had to contend, and it is owing to this and other collateral causes that the excellent scheme of the Bishop of Rochester is so far from being accomplished.

The result is, of course, to be deplored. It is a startling fact that fully one third of our population altogether disregard every form of divine worship, and that their numbers are increasing at the rate of 1,000 a year. It is a fact equally to be deplored that, although the accommodation which is provided is far from being commensurate with the population, yet, such as there is, it is to a very considerable extent neglected. The Bishop of Winchester's experience as may be very different from that of very many clergymen and ministers of various denominations in this district. The Right Reverend Prelate says, "You build your church and that will soon be filled when the doctrines of the Gospel are faithfully preached there. Build your church, and your accommodation is soon found inadequate to the pressing necessities of the people; enlarge your church, and the vacuum is soon filled, and there is no difficulty in finding occupants for every additional seat; enlarge it again, increase its accommodation, and still you find a pressure for places which shows that there is no indisposition to hear when something is delivered worth hearing, and that the people will come when the bell of that church invites them to hear the sounds of Divine love."

When something is delivered worth hearing! A good deal is, no doubt, implied in this observation but we venture to think that it is capable even of a wider interpretation than was intended by the Right. Rev. Prelate. Much depends upon the manner as well as the subject matter of a discourse. A dry dogmatic theology must have some charm infused into it to elicit the attention of a congregation Sabbath after Sabbath, and the dull platitudes which some congregations are condemned to listen to, may often be held responsible for a beggarly account of empty pews and benches. We know that the great truths of Christianity are the same from eternity to eternity, but every discovery of science furnishes them with a new exemplification, and a man who has a just appreciation of the important functions of his ministerial office, and has the capacity withal, may turn these to good account, and present religion in the light not merely of an exacting duty, but of a pleasure. Give something worth hearing, says the good Bishop, and your churches will be filled. There can no doubt that his dictum is correct, for experience his proved it over and over again.

It is right to observe, however, that the mere fact of our churches and chapels not being filled after they are built does not absolve professing Christians of any denomination from the responsibility of meeting the full requirements of a community. They are in duty bound to proceed on the assumption that congregations there are if provision be only made for them.

It is not, of course, the sole duty of the Church of England, although a special obligation rests upon it, and we do not sympathise with those who, in speaking of spiritual destitution, repudiate every non-conformist effort and ignore the fact that a remedy is provided in a district simply because there does not happen to be in it a branch of the church as by law established.

There is, however, abundant evidence to prove the necessity for increased church accommodation in the parish of Portsea, and in no locality was it more urgently needed than in the district of Marylebone. The church there is in the midst of a dense population, spiritually, and in numerous instances, temporally, destitute. The clergyman of the district, the Rev. B.D. Aldwell, is, we believe, just the man for this important missionary work, a man who efficiently discharges the duties of his ministerial office, and who is indefatigable in his pastoral visitation. We sincerely hope that the effort which is now being made will be crowned with success and that St. Luke's Church will no longer remain in a condition which implies an unpleasant reflection upon the public of Portsmouth in general and churchmen in particular.

1861 – BLONDIN AT PORTCHESTER.

Of course, everybody went to Portchester on Wednesday, for "all the world and his wife" was to be there to see Blondin on the rope, and so it turned out, for I should say there had not been such a gathering of sightseers within the walls of the Old Ruin for many a long year. Of course, your rambling correspondent was not to be outdone, nor to be behind time, so to prevent the crush at the station, by rail, took the road, not as a pedestrian, but as a humble guest of old Particular, who kindly gave me a seat in his dog cart, and away we rattled behind a nice piece of horseflesh to the scene of action.

Arriving at Portchester, the line of road to the Castle was one continuous stream of human beings, pouring their way from the Railway Station and other parts. At the Castle gate, we tendered our coin for admission, and after a great deal of the usual *et ceteras*, such as squeezing, pushing and apologising, we got fairly on the ground at about half-past four, and the ascent on the rope was to be about seven, so we calculated on plenty of time for reflection and seeing other things the bill of fare teemed with.

Right across the space of the enclosure was erected what seemed to be a Brobdingnag tight rope, stretching some 300ft., and about 70ft. high, tightly held by strong guys; heavy weights and sandbags were suspended at short distances, hanging from the rope to steady it. After a little conversation with an eccentric individual, with an extraordinary French accent and ditto appearance, he turned out to be M. Blondin's particular, and was giving some minute directions to some workmen relative to the rope at this end, he assuring us that it was part of the identical one that M. Blondin crossed the Niagara on, and he was the identical that was carried pick-a-back "o'er the roar of waters."

Being rather inquisitory on this specific occasion relative to the speculation, and going into pounds, shillings, and pence, he finally added that the railway has "a finger in the pie," M. Blondin taking "a good slice," and the rest—someone whispered to me that Manager Rutley of the Theatre Royal, was "in for a dig." Bon jour! and crossed to the other end of the rope, against the wall was erected a rickety abortion of a stage, where two gents begrimed as sooty minstrels, accompanied a lady, who presided at the harp, warbling "Beautiful Star." Not being in the vein for anything then, so sentimental, I wandered to the booth of creature comforts, and slaked my thirst in a draught of Bass's Pale—when a bell announced a fresh arrival on this done up-in-a hurry platform, and as genial as in my boyhood days, stood before me my old favourite the not-to-be-forgotten Charley Sloman the greatest and only English Improvisator of the day. How I have laughed at his jokes, his puns, and wit, many, many a time, and I was to laugh again, for you can always smile at what Charley says, for when he does open his mouth, a pearl of choicest wit is sure to drop from it.

Of course, in his song he made some capital hits on the present occasion and the company about him, everybody was pleased, and a repetition was the result. This over something else was on the move, new to Portsmouthtonians, that funny fellow Stead, the droll of Mr. Weston's Music Hall, in Holborn, came on in his stripy pants and long tail, and gave us a queer version of "As happy as a King," then "Presto! Change!" Hoora! The Cure! The Cure! and here we have him— the original, with his extraordinary St. Vitus dance, song and all into the bargain. He certainly did his best under peculiar disadvantages - horrid accompaniment and shaky *terra firma*.

A very clever contortionist wound up that performance, and it was now 6 o'clock, and another hour before the "great lion of the day" would show us some of his "airy somethings." What with reconnoitring one friend and the other, for everybody seemed to know everybody, a sort of family party on an extensive scale; and occasional strains from an over harsh brass band, the time soon slid by.

When the hour of seven arrived, every eye was turned towards the rope, which my friend remarked was not unlike an Equinoctial Line. All at once the band strikes up, "See the Conquering Hero Comes," and amid the moving mass from the gate, mingling with the crowd afoot, walked the Great, little Blondin, dressed as an Indian, feathers and all, with his blushing honours thick about him, arriving at the right end of the rope by the side of the mast, he was immediately drawn up to a small platform on a line with the rope, when unloosing his balance pole, which was fastened to prevent its falling, being weighty and long, the music playing a lively air, and away goes the Franco-American rope dancer, high in the air on his "little tour," now running, now performing all sorts of gyrations, laying on his back, standing on his head,

Blondin and his Tightrope at the Crystal Palace

turning a summersault, &c. &c., in fact, everything was done with that mechanical precision, that a failure would be impossible.

By this time
"The sky with clouds was overcast
And rain began to fall"

But it did in no way mar his performance, for arriving back to his starting point, he bandages his eyes, and envelopes his upper man in a sack, he then commences his journey number two, which is done with the same nonchalance, and in returning actually carries a man strapped to his back—the Frenchified individual whom I accosted in the early part of the afternoon. He was a taller man than Blondin and should say about 11 stone weight. Every anxious eye was now upturned, many a beating heart, for these were trying moments for man and man. On "he plods his weary way" with his big burden on his back, every step bending the rope, still with that firm assurance depicted on his countenance, all will be safe.

Arriving at the incline, a short distance from his original starting point, he finds it rather "uphill game with him," three seconds more and he will be himself again, 'tis done. Blondin has finished his work, and divests himself of his burden, amidst thousands of hearty cheers. The band plays, "God save the Queen," all is over, and M. Blondin has achieved another triumph.

So great was the excitement, that he was literally shouldered by the mob and carried out of the grounds, everyone trying to shake him by the hand. I followed the crowd, and soon reached the castle gate, where the confusion and bustle was now tenfold, so hastily taking my seat by the side of my old Particular, we trotted back again to Portsmouth, with the full conviction, of our highest gratification of M. Blondin, hoping he will ever be so successful as on that day, and with fine weather in the prospective, I guess he will reap a pretty good harvest, so for the present goodbye, making this sight an Epoch in my life, not easily to be forgotten.

1861 – LAST PORTSDOWN FAIR.

The annual fair at Portsdown commenced yesterday, and will terminate on Monday, after which Portsdown Fair will cease to be a yearly event. From the little interest evinced it would appear that if the fair had not been abolished by the means it will be, that it would have gradually died out for want of patronage as, for several years past, it has gradually declined in every respect. Special trains ran yesterday to Cosham, at intervals, but the passengers were not nearly so numerous as on former occasions. Conveyances of every description also thronged the Commercial Road, for the purpose of conveying parties to Portsdown Hill.

1861 – DANGEROUS NUISANCE IN EAST STREET.

Innumerable complaints have been made on account of the abominable nuisance arising from the stench in that closely packed and densely populated locality, East Street, Point, created by the Commissariat slaughter house, and from other slaughter houses and closets. The air around the locality to which we advert is impregnated with a foul effluvium, emanating from a stagnant pool at Broad Street side of the Camber, near the old Customs House, where the animal and vegetable manure from the slaughter houses run and remain, fouling the atmosphere of the whole neighbourhood. The nuisance has come before the Commissioners on various occasions, and only last Monday Mr. Raper and Mr. Garrington reported to that body the dangerous condition in which the inhabitants were placed by the disgusting and nauseous effluvia they were continually breathing.

The Commissariat slaughter house, although kept as clean as possible, must of necessity be a nuisance in such a populous neighbourhood. A proportionate number of beasts are being continually slaughtered, much to the annoyance of the inhabitants. We are informed that in Christmas week alone 100 head of cattle and from 150 to 200 sheep were killed, and a similar number is killed every week. The mud upon which the refuse deposits itself is exposed to the sun in warm weather, and of course the nuisance is infinitely greater than at the present time, bad as it is. Another nuisance is created by the driving of a large number of cattle through the narrow streets of the town during the day. The Government possess ground suitable for the purpose in the outskirts of the borough, and we hope that it will be appropriated.

The report of Dr. Raper and Mr. Garrington will be placed before the Finance Committee of the Council, and we hope that steps will be immediately taken to rid the locality of such a serious cause of complaint.

1861 – LAUNCH OF H.M.S. GLASGOW.

On Thursday last, at a few minutes before twelve o'clock, the *Glasgow*, screw frigate, 51 guns, and of 600 horsepower, which has been built on the same slip as the *Bacchante* was built on about 18 months since, was successfully launched.

Circumstances in every respect, favoured the event, the sun shone brightly, and the day was essentially a spring one. Long before the hour for launching, the Dockyard gates were thronged with persons anxious to gain admission, and when, at length, the gates were opened, some thousands made their way towards No. 1 slip, where the frigate rested. The company occupied the vacant spaces alongside the vessel and included the chief naval and military officers of the port and garrison. The bands of the Dockyard and 3rd Hants Artillery Corps were present and added to the gaiety of this scene by their lively strains.

At about six minutes to twelve o'clock, the dog shores were knocked away, and the fine frigate quietly glided into the harbour amidst the long and hearty shouts of the assemblage. There was no mishap, and the launch was one of the most successful that ever took place in this yard. The ceremony of christening the vessel was performed by Mrs. Alexander, daughter of Admiral Bruce, Naval-Commander-in-Chief at this port, The *Glasgow* was laid down the same month the *Bacchante* was launched, and on the same slipway.

Immediately after the launch, the *Glasgow* was towed into the steam basin, to be docked coppered, then fitted with her machinery. Her armament will consist, on the main deck, of 30 guns, 8-inch, 65 cwt., 9 feet 6 inch in length. She will also carry two of Armstrong's 100lb. pivot guns on her upper deck. We are informed it is not expected there will be another launch for twelve months, as no orders have been received with respect to launching any vessel at present building.

1861 – DEATH OF THE PRINCE CONSORT.

The news of the death of the Prince Consort caused quite a consternation here among the army, navy, and general public, as it was most unexpected. All classes grieve for her Majesty as much as they do at the Prince's death. The squadron struck their colours, and on board the *Victory* the Royal ensign of England and that of the late Prince were hoisted half-mast high.

The Royal standard also floated half-mast high above the town gates, the dock gate, the Gunwharf, Southsea Castle, Blockhouse, the fort, the ramparts, and all Government departments, as well as above the Sailors' Home and several private establishments.

Most of the principal shops and many private houses have since remained partially closed. A special meeting of the Town Council was convened on Thursday afternoon, for the purpose of taking steps to communicate to her Majesty the very deep feelings of condolence entertained for her in her bereavement by the inhabitants of Portsmouth. The Mayor (Mr. Ald. Humby), occupied the chair, and made some very appropriate remarks upon the melancholy event which had called them together. On the motion of Mr. C.B. Hellard the ex-Mayor, seconded by Mr. E. Galt, it was resolved that an address of condolence should be presented to her Majesty.

The Mayor, the mover and seconder, Mr. Ald. Stigant (who supported the resolution), and the Town Clerk then retired and prepared a suitable address. On the motion of Mr. Alderman Sheppard seconded by Mr. Vandenberg, it was resolved that the address should be adopted by the Council, and presented in the usual way. Some conversation ensued in reference to a suggestion which was made by Mr. Emanuel that business should be partially suspended on next Monday the day fixed for the funeral of the lamented Prince; and it was ultimately resolved, on the motion of Mr. Emanuel seconded by Mr. Alderman White, that his Worship the Mayor should be requested to recommend that all business establishments be closed, as far as may be practicable from 12 to 2 o'clock on that day. It was stated by some of the members that they intended to close their establishments during the whole day.

1861 – IMPROVEMENTS TO LUMPS FORT.

Within the last twelve months, the Government has materially added to the fortifications round Portsmouth, and perhaps at no part more than on the south beach at Lumps, where the fort has been raised of considerable power to protect the sea front and communicate with the fire of Southsea Castle. But since its completion the sea has made some awkward approaches upon the land in its vicinity, and doubts have been raised as to the permanency of the fort. It should be mentioned that the present Lumps Fort is built at the rear of an old fort, which has been entirely swept away by the sea.

We alluded to these encroachments in this journal at the commencement of the new fort, and predicted the probable result, unless proper precautions were taken. We recommended groins being run out into the sea to lock the shingle in their dead angles; and now that these groins are being constructed, doubts have been expressed as to their utility. But it should be borne in mind that the encroachments that have taken place at this spot during the recent severe gales have taken place not in defiance of the groins, but really because they were not sufficiently complete to act. They are not even half finished at the present moment. That groins are effectual remedies in almost all instances where they have been constructed and adapted to the law of the coast, is evidenced by all writers and engineers who have studied the "shingle movement." The law that governs the motions of these erratic pebbles is very easy to understand. Thus, continuous flow of beach stones and sea-drift, composed of the debris of rocks of all denominations, is going on from west to east the whole length of our Channel. This phenomenon is observable not only on the English but on the French coast, as noticed by M. Larablardie in his "Memoire sur les Cotes de la haute Normandie."

The theory is that the movement of the shingle is owing to the formation of the English Channel, which expands to the westward, and contracts to the eastward. A more violent sea consequently comes from the south western than from the south eastern quarter. And although in heavy south eastern gales the shingle may in some degree and in some localities be moved westward, yet as the prevalent winds are in the contrary direction, the general motion is from west to east. Again, on the east coast of England the movement of the shingle and sea-drift is also due to the preponderating sea-stroke, which is there from north to south; and the movement of the beach being determined by the sea-stroke, the travelling of the shingle is from north to south, because the heaviest gales and the heaviest seas come from the north east quarter.

These are facts so well known as scarcely to need repeating, and the result is, that whenever piers or groins have been run out into the sea, they obstruct the coast drift, and form new land by the heaping up power of the waves. That such will be the case at the new fort at Lumps we have no doubt, for the piles that are already driven show that the engineer knows the character of the beach he has to deal with, and is treating it upon its own merits.

1861 – THE ARRIVAL OF THE WARRIOR.

The iron plated steam frigate, *Warrior*, Captain Cochrane, arrived in safety at Spithead on the 20th, from Greenhithe. She saluted the flagship, *Victory*, bearing the flag of Sir H.W. Bruce, Port Admiral, whose salute was returned from the flagship. A vast amount of excitement was created in the port on the arrival of the frigate, and from the hour of arrival until she came into harbour, the beach at Southsea ramparts at Portsmouth, and the two piers at each place, were crowded by people desirous of seeing this queen of the ocean. The *Warrior* lay at Spithead alongside the *Emerald*, frigate of the modem class; but the difference in length of the two ships was so great that the *Emerald*, although a splendid frigate, appeared quite insignificant by the side of the iron plated frigate.

It was announced that the *Warrior* would come into harbour at about noon, and several hundred persons awaited her coming. She steamed from Spithead about one o'clock, and made a magnificent entrance into the harbour's mouth. The sight when she passed the bar and entered the harbour's mouth was a splendid one, and called forth a hearty cheer from the many spectators.

The *Warrior* brought up and berthed alongside the sheer jetty in the Dockyard, where she commenced taking her powder out. She was to be taken into dock on Saturday, and will be painted with Mr. Hay's composition. This frigate left Greenhithe at eleven o'clock, a.m., on Thursday, and proceeding from the Nore, passed Sheerness, where she saluted the flag of the Port Admiral at that port. We learn from the little information we have been enabled to glean (as while the powder being taken out no person is permitted on board) that she made between eleven and twelve knots per hour, that she answered her helm well, and that the trip was in every way a successful one. She will as soon as possible make a trial of her speed at the measured mile in Stokes Bay.

1861 – NAVAL AND MILITARY PREPARATIONS.

The following notice has been posted at the gates of the Dockyard at Portsmouth by the Admiralty: "All men who have been absent one month are required to return to their respective ships immediately."

The *Warrior* is taking 760 tons of coal alongside Portsmouth Dockyard preparatory to service on the North American coast, should she be required. The following troops at Aldershot are ordered to be in readiness to proceed to Canada: — Leslie's 6th Battery Artillery; 2nd battalion 20th Regiment; 16th and 45th Regiments; and a detachment of 16th Lancers. The battery served in the Crimea and is furnished with Armstrongs.

Colonel Gordon, R.E. is ordered to be in readiness to proceed to Canada in the *Melbourne*. It is stated that a large force of Engineers will be sent to Canada. 100 pounder Armstrong guns are now being rapidly distributed among the ships preparing for sea. The *Defence*, an iron plated frigate, is to have a crew of 450. She will be manned without the least difficulty.

1861 – NEW DRINKING FOUNTAIN ON SOUTHSEA COMMON.

A very picturesque fountain has been recently erected on Southsea Common, Portsmouth, near the foot of the Glacis, and close to Hollingsworth's bathing rooms. It is the farewell gift of Major-General Sir James Yorke Scarlett, C.B., to the inhabitants and garrison of that town, of which he was the late respected Lieutenant-Governor.

The structure is an obelisk in form, standing about twenty feet high, and is composed of the best Portland stone. At each angle there are four bold projecting pedestals, upon the faces of which are alternately sculptured the arms of Sir James Yorke Scarlett and those of the borough of Portsmouth. Upon the cap of each pedestal a bronzed iron vase is placed to receive a jet of running water flowing from a dolphin made of similar material, four of which adorn the fountain. In the hollow panels of the enriched cap there are four emblematical shells, from each of which also issues a jet of water, so that there are eight issues of the sparkling element constantly running, which gives the fountain a very animated and brilliant appearance. The bronzed iron figures of the dolphins, vases, and shells stand out in bold relief, and their dark forms present a pleasing contrast with the light shades of the Portland stone.

There are also four drinking cups of the same bronze material placed round the fountain. The water is supplied from the town water works in patent bituminised pipes, which are cheaper and more durable, it is said, than iron.

The summit of this very elegant structure is crowned with a handsome glass globe for the purpose of gas illumination, which at night lights up the gushing waters and adds to it additional novelty and brilliancy. The design reflects great credit upon the sculptor, Mr. Baker, of Southsea.

New Drinking Fountain at Southsea

1861 – SOUTHSEA PIER AND THE CABMEN.

We understand that the War Department has, with the approval of the Lieutenant-Governor, sanctioned the establishment of a cab stand adjoining the Esplanade, on payment of an annual nominal sum in recognition of the rights of the Department, and for subject to its removal at any time. Reference is made to the annoyance that the public have suffered from the want of regulations regarding omnibuses and cabs, and reminding the Committee of the Esplanade that the Government had permitted its construction for the recreation of inhabitants and visitors, and that it must be therefore understood that the permission for a cab stand is intended for the convenience of the public, and not for the benefit of the Pier Company.

A condition is made to the assent that cabs or other vehicles shall remain on the stand until called up, and not in the roadway opposite the Pier; that here must be no monopoly, but the traffic open to all duly appointed cabs.

1861 – VISITS TO THE WARRIOR.

We may state for the information of intending visitors to the Dockyard that on Monday the *Warrior*, iron cased frigate, will commence painting; and the public will therefore be excluded from going on board. Lord Palmerston visited the noble ship on Wednesday, and the Lord Bishop of Winchester on the previous day. The Grand Duke Constantine has not yet gone over the ship, but is expected to do so next week. During the past few days, hundreds of people have been on board. The ship will not, according to former arrangements, be un-docked today (Saturday), and her official trial has been postponed some days beyond the time originally intended.

1862 – MURDEROUS ATTACK ON A CONVICT WARDER AT PORTSMOUTH DOCKYARD.

Another diabolical attempt to murder a convict keeper was perpetrated on Friday at Portsmouth Dockyard, under the following; circumstances:- While a party of convicts were employed in the old rope store, under a keeper named Deane, who had incurred the animosity of a convict named Frazer, the latter seized an opportunity to make a murderous assault on the keeper, by striking him on the forehead with a piece of teak wood about three feet in length by five inches in circumference, which formed one of the steps of what is termed "Jacob's ladder." Other prisoners are said to be concerned by the outrage. This is the second case during the past week of a similar nature, and only last week a convict belonging to the same prison was sentenced to fifteen years' penal servitude for assaulting a keeper named Martin Gibbs.

1862 – THE NEW DEFENCES OF PORTSMOUTH.

In addition to the circumstance of their recent inspection by the Commander-in-Chief, few subjects are invested with livelier interest to the public mind than that of the feasibility of the gigantic works now in course of construction for the defence of our great naval station with all its costly treasures, and the vital importance of its security to the wellbeing and even existence of our nation. At the same time, notwithstanding the elaborate reports of the commission, the protracted discussions of the two Houses, and the many interesting remarks on them which have appeared in the public prints, there is general indistinctness of apprehension as to the character and arrangement of the works themselves amongst readers not versed in military matters. There are, besides, many constructions details of vast importance to the practical use of fortifications, should the necessity of their being tested arise, and a great degree of imperfection and a want of decision to which of various modes should be finally adopted, resulting, of course, in occasional alterations of structures just finished which might have been prevented by plans more matured before the execution of the works. It is, however, only just to say that these defects are perhaps mainly attributable to the urgent necessity laid on the departments to forward the defences, so that the main lines should be executed whilst their details were being matured, and the nation be thus in some sort prepared in the emergency of war.

We therefore resolved personally to examine all the works, and give a fair resume of their arrangements, character, and progress.

Our feeling was that, to make the thing clear to the unprofessional reader the description should commence from the centre and thence conduct him from one exterior circle of defence to another. But, as the Government and professional writers have adopted the term first line of defence for the fleet on the seaboard and the moving army landward, second line of defences for the very outermost series of static instructions built so far from the place to be defended, that cannon of the modern construction, with rifle bore, and having a range of from five to seven miles, would be utterly unable to throw anything into it; third line of defence for that which, at an average distance of three miles, would protect the enceinte from the guns and mortars of dates anterior to the middle of this country; and fourth line of defence, to the immediate enceinte and its associated outworks, we shall be compelled to regard this order.

Fort Nelson on Portsdown Hill

Fort Wallington

We presume all our readers are well acquainted with the positions of the above places, or, if not will refer to a map. Suffice it to say that three extensive estuaries, Portsmouth, Langstone and Chichester harbours, with very narrow openings, cut into the main land opposite the east end of the Isle of Wight, and are united by tidal channels to the north, leaving two large islands, Portsea (west) and Hayling (east), with several smaller ones in their midst. The western estuary, Portsmouth Harbour, is entered from the great anchorage of Spithead, and directly on getting inside the two projecting tongues of Blockhouse (west) and Point (east), where the harbour is still contracted to little more than a wide channel, the town of Gosport, with Weevil Biscuit Factory and Priddy's Hard powder magazine, is on the mainland west; and east, upon the shores of Portsea Island, is Portsmouth; and higher north, but adjoining it, is the town of Portsea, the Arsenal (locally called the Gun Wharf), and the Dockyard. All these places are surrounded on the landsides with ramparts, ditches, and outworks, forming the fourth or inner line of defence, and their unprotected faces respectively about on opposite shores, the enceinte is completed by Blockhouse and Point Forts and the ancient chain boom at the mouth of the harbour and to the northward by the extensive and impassable low tide mud banks of the estuary where it expands to its full width above the towns.

The three towns and the government establishments are thus united into one body and although the fortifications of Portsmouth and Portsea were separately built, and on distinct plans, the little separation which exists is to be swept away, and the two formed into a continuous range. This fourth or inner line of defence has rather more an average radius reckoned from the south point of the Dockyard, rather Gunwharf, to the glacis. The third line of defence, that which places the Dockyard beyond the range of artillery, dating from 1850 averages a distance of nearly three miles from the common centre. It is necessarily very irregular, and partly composed of old, partly of recent, and partly of progressing and proposed works. To the south its circle would have to be completed by floating batteries or other shipping at the mouth of the harbour, or one or two forts on the nearer shoals to the south east, on the east coast of Portsea Island, by Southsea, Lumps, Eastney and Cumberland Forts; to the east, by the shore of the island and the mudlands of Langstone Harbour; to the north-east, the shore on the creek separating from the mainland and connecting Portsmouth and Langstone harbours, called Hilsea, where powerful batteries and other works are being constructed; to the north-west by the unoccupied lands of Horsea Inland and the mud tints of Portchester and Fareham, in the north of Portsmouth Harbour.

To the west, a magnificent range of forts with connecting works will isolate, not insulate, the peninsula in which Gosport stands. Passing southward there are (in this line) Elson, Brockhurst, Rowner, Grange, and Gomer Forts. The latter place is now the point where Browndown and Stokes Bay batteries form the south-west lines on the coast and effect a junction with Quicksilver and Monckton forts and outworks, which occupy the southernmost point of the mainland, corresponding to the portion of Southsea Castle at the opposite side of the harbour mouth, on the projecting point of Portsea Island.

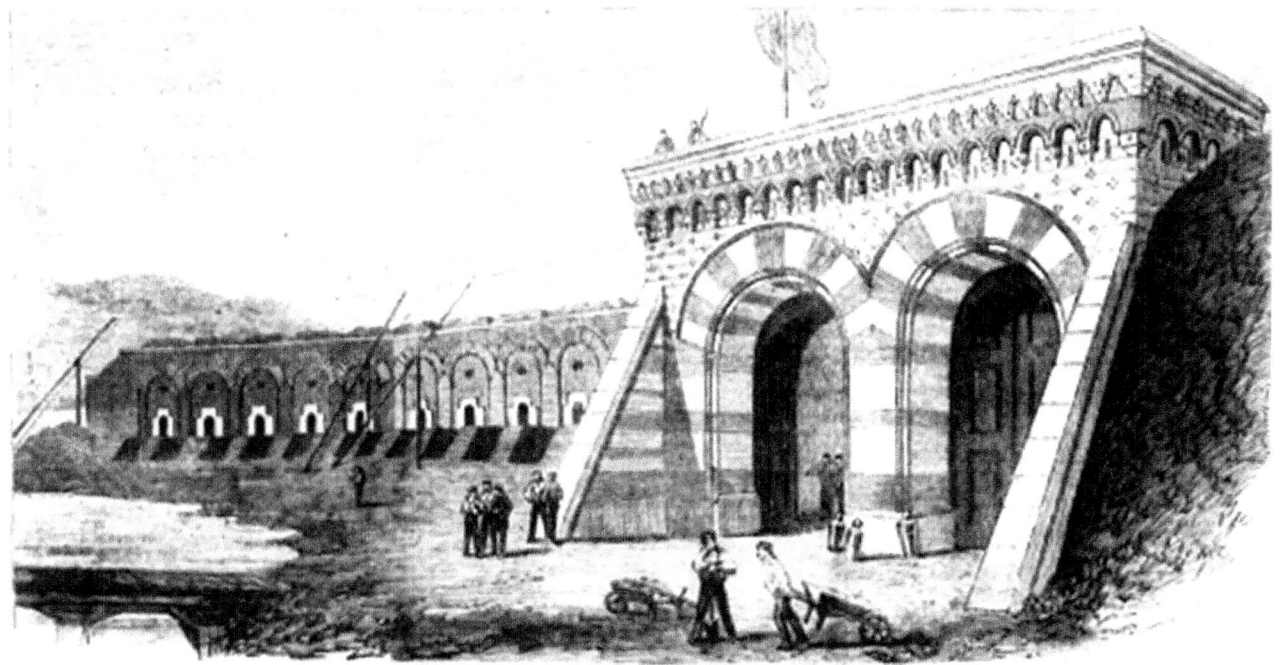

Fort Hilsea Showing the New Gateway for the Diverted London Road

The second or outermost line of static defences has a direct average radius from the Dockyard of five miles, and a command of not less than seven - in other words it would be impossible to occupy ground for any inimical purpose, and certainly for a battery, when these works are completed, within seven miles of that point; and further, from the form of the land, and the elevations being occupied by this line of defence, even supposing it possible that artillery improvements will give projectiles a greater range than that, it would be of no service to an invading army because there are so few points from which the great object of attack, the Dockyard, would be visible. This line is mainly contrived on the advantage given by the existence of Portsdown hill, which at about one to two miles from the north shores of Hilsea Channel, Langstone and Portsmouth harbours rises into a vast natural rampart seven miles long and about 500ft high, only requiring its crest to be scarped into proper form to become an impregnable fortress from end to end.

This, then, determines the form of the great polygon, which is an irregular five-sided figure, with its base north on the ridge of Portsdown hill and its apex south in the sea on No Man's Land at the works now constructed there. The base, or north side stretches nearly seven miles, and comprehends many prodigious works wrought out of the solid chalk from Fort Farlington in the east, to Fort Wallington in the west, commanding the town of Fareham and its creek, which is the north-west part of Portsmouth harbour, the north-west side extends nearly five miles, and comprehends the great works of Fareham, Roome, and Lee Farm, where it meets the shore. The south-west side stretches nearly seven miles obliquely across the Solent Sea. It intersects and amalgamates with the interior hue at Browndown and Fort Gomer, and comprehends the Sturbridge and No Man's Land Forts on the shallow upon the Isle of Wight side of the main channel to Spithead. The south-east side extends for five miles from the last fort, including the Horse and intermediate forts on the Horse Land to Cumberland Fort, where the second and third lines of defence again amalgamate, being nearly identical on the east side, which is also nearly five miles from the last fort to that of Farlington on Portsdown hill. In fact, the proposed works at Forts Farlington and Nelson another intermediate line of defence is secured; so that, supposing if all of the forts on the three southern and western sides of the great pentagon were destroyed, there would still remain a complete quadrangle of about five miles and a half each side, consisting of six forts on Portsdown hill and to the west, south, and east of the lines of the third or inner defences.

It is not only in the magnitude, the ingenuity, and the completeness of these arrangements that the public will find matter of interest; but there is too much that is at the present time novel in the plans and details of

Lumps Fort at Southsea

the different works which form items of this whole that their consideration will probably interest even the most unscientific. Everyone is of course well aware that all that characterises the "castle" of medieval times has passed away with the introduction of cannon. The old systems of fortifying, as usually happens in such changes, were superseded by those which carried the new principles to their extreme application almost to the *reductum ad absurdum*. Hence the French military engineering, culminating in Vandun and Cormontaigne introduced the bastion system, in which a place was defended by dividing its whole circumference into sides having the length of the range of musket shot; and on the meeting of each pair of sides projecting a bastion from the wall, with two flanks, and then two faces meeting in a sharp angle pointing outwards. The guns of each of the flanks, fired point blank, swept over the whole of the intervening wall, called the "curtain," and the faces of the opposite bastion; and the guns of the curtain swept over the flanks and all the country before the fortress. Or, in small forts, the whole wall was formed into triangular projections, the fire from each face point blank sweeping the adjoining face.

Then again, when considered not strong enough, there were outworks, such as the ravelin, which was a triangular work before the curtain, low enough to be fired over, and its two faces in their turn swept by the fire of the two bastion faces. Gateways and entrances were generally made through these, so as to give a winding road cover from shot. But the bastions were often found weak and the very points which could be easily breached, and this is the great objection to the system. Whilst, therefore, some of the new works on the Portsmouth lines are necessarily planned on the bastion principle unqualified, others present a very considerable modification of it, and others, again, may perhaps be unsatisfactory from too strict an adherence to it.

The general plans adopted, however, are these. Firstly, as the lines are so extended, their defence will be chiefly dependent on the crossing fire, and so rendering the intervals between main works difficult to be passed or forced, and as the present rifle range is so long, a comparatively small body of troops may maintain a position of very wide command. The arrangement adopted, then, has been to plant forts of a very simple plan, but, military parlance, strong trace, and, in plain English, of prodigious strength, at intervals of about a mile or so apart; and to let the base lines of their figures abut on a common base line, which in the outset will be only a military road, but, when required, will be covered with breastwork, and, where desirable, will be converted into a rampart and parapet, with a wet or dry moat joining those of the forts.

The figure most frequently adopted is that of a pentagon, corresponding to the general form of bastion, only that its salient points are far less acute, the apex, of course, pointing outwards, and its opposite

Eastney Fort with Fort Cumberland in the Distance

side, or base, to the road. The base line of these forts will be partially open to the military way; but the most striking feature is that this partially-opened side, or gorge, as it is termed, will almost wholly be occupied with the works of a very powerful casemated keep tower, with its separate moats and drawbridges, so that if an enemy gained the main work, the covered fire from the keep—to which the garrison would in that case retire sweeping the whole space, ramparts, and works before it, would render the attack untenable, whilst a long time must elapse before any guns could be brought to bear on it.

As to the *enceinte* it will be observed that although some of these forts cover a very great area and have sides of considerable length, there are no bastions, except we look on the whole work as one extensive bastion, with the military road as the face of the internal polygon, the keep tower as an enormous cavalier. This is, however, *outre*; and as they are obviously, notwithstanding the road in their rear, independent fortresses, the question is, how are the faces flanked, covered and swept in case of the enemy gaining the glacis and ditch? This is accomplished by constructing at the angles of the scarp (i.e., the face of the wall), in the ditch, a cassionaire which is a bombproof covered passage, with loopholes for musketry cannon. Both these cassionaires are wholly in the ditch which they flank, and below the level of the glacis, and they are bombproof. They could remain uninjured even if the enemy breached the wall above. The most important objects are thus long faces, which can direct a point-blank concentrated fire to any jaunt of the surrounding country; angles, that, being exceedingly obtuse, will be difficult to breach; together giving powerful command to an extent which a bastion face could not have given. Added to this, each of the salient angles will generally be surmounted by a sort of cavalier (or rider), a mass of wall and parapet raised the main work to a certain height above it. This will carry a large gun on traversing a platform to be trained to any angle, so to be directed across the country, or to cooperate with the cassionaires in resisting a coup de-main is probable, too, carrying out the connecting lines, that small batteries placed on the military road will be employed to flank the front faces of the forts.

The exact configuration of each fortress, the proportions and positions of its faces and other details, are, however, determined more as the contour of the site and the steps necessary to secure a perfect command of the country than any prescribed form. As to the materials of construction, experience has proved that a well-constructed earthen rampart, with slope of depth, is the very best contrivance for the resistance of cannonade, and the heavier the shot the more this rule applies. For this reason, all the works are being arranged so that, as far as possible, nothing can be presented to an enemy but enormous earth banks or mounds, and all the vertical faces of masonry are, to the utmost practicable extent, either concealed by the deep and wide moats by elevated glacis or else covered by an outer turf wall, as with the casemates of the new works on the lines.

The order in which these works are being executed is this:—The work of excavating ditches, throwing the ramparts and parapets, the construction of bombproof casemates, and other essential parts of the *encientes*, are given out to contract, and are being vigorously pushed forward. The revetments—that is, the facings of the two sides, the ditch in brickwork or masonry—the formation of military roads, connecting lines, advanced and detached works, such as separate batteries, redans, and forth, will be postponed till the forts are completed or necessity calls for them. The reader will now turn to the sketch of Fort Nelson, which gives an idea of that work when complete, the general form, the character and position of the caissonnaires, and of the great keep tower, will be clearly apparent. The inspection of the fortifications by the Commander-in-Chief commenced with those nearest Portsmouth and passing by Hilsea lines to the eastern end of Portsdown hill. His Grace and Staff proceeded westerly to advanced works beyond Gosport, and shall follow the same order, commencing with the Hill Forts of Portsdown.

The commissioners describe the material of this lofty ridge as hard chalk; it is not, however, what geologists recognise under that designation, a distinction to observe, as some of the Isle of Wight works are on rocks of that character This is nevertheless, unusually firm and compact, and eminently adapted for military constructions. The ditches are on a general scale of 50ft and upwards in width and about 10ft deep, cut down vertically in the solid chalk rock, and rendered practically deeper by the application of the material excavated to the raising of a steep glacis externally, giving ample space for covered ways, and internally by the construction of a lofty rampart and parapet, which will thus average from 50ft to 80ft in height, reckoned from the bottom of the ditch. Each angle of the excavation will be extended into a circular bay, better form to give effect to the cavalier guns above and giving space for the construction of the caissonnaires in the fosse below. In some cases, as shown in the Engraving of Fort Nelson, these will be double; but the majority are contrived so that, each being projected in the line of one face, the ditch, its rear swept by the one projecting at the other end, and its front, in turn, sweeps the ditch around it. This they will do effectively, their base will consist of casemates with heavy guns, and above will be more floors with loopholes for riflemen. The base, or partially open sides of the forts, with the keep towers and the military line of communication, will all be on the south or interior side; and we need scarcely remark that the old roads, with the exception of the London road, are all broken up and diverted by the vast piles of snowy rubble and deep yawning chasms which the summits are either gashed through and through or raised to yet loftier ridges.

The eastern termination of the hill is fortified with peculiar care, having the fort or redoubt of Farlington on the descending spur to the south-east; then proceeding westerly to that of Crookhorn, a little to the north another of the slopes, to guard against the positions which the lowlands give on that side; and on the extremity of the ridge summit above the Fort Purbrook, the whole presenting one group—the two former being regarded as outworks of the latter. From the first of them a line of rampart and fosse is to be carried south to the shore of Langstone Harbour, completing the common side of the second and third line of defences which terminates in Fort Cumberland. At the same point is an interesting relic of the machinery of our last Gallic wars in the dismantled telegraph station, standing on the gentle turf slopes, and giving, *pro tempore*, habitation to some of the clerks of the works now engaged.

At Crookhorn, the excavations reach the tertiary beds, and these furnish material for some of the vast quantities of bricks required in the undertakings. Purbrook, in its present state, gives the best idea of the magnificent scale of these works. The six clumps of fir trees, long known as mariners' marks, are rapidly disappearing. Though few are still left on the summit knoll enclosed within the ditch, which is in great part completed; and huge piles of bricks and timber; the storing flints for revetments and other walling; and the accumulation of materials and construction of diverted roads and other works, with a forest of contour staves to show the heights to which rampart and glacis are to be elevated, all exhibit the earnestness with which the whole being is carried forward.

Crossing the London road, Fort Widley occupies a very elevated and narrow part of the ridge; an old windmill, ruinous and dismantled and a hamlet

Fort Widley Western Entrance

which must soon give way to the growing slopes, for a while impart interest to the scene. Here the narrow width and steep slopes of the hill north and south cause a great deal of additional labour in the formation of the embankments, which we were pleased to see, were carefully built up out of the rubble, although hard and dry, instead of being simply thrown down at random.

Southwick, the next work, is being carried out with the same care as that of Widley, and is in about the same stage of progress. The next immediately beyond the lofty obelisk - formed monument to Lord Nelson, occupying the westernmost point of the ridge, and is called Fort Nelson.

We have shown this as if completed, and the Engraving indicates the low-lying lands, the harbour, Dockyard, and buildings of Portsmouth, and the Isle of Wight in the distance; and it will be obvious that the command of this lofty and singular ridge of the country both sides of it will be as complete as the prospects it affords are beautiful. Below this, on the descending slopes, a little to the northward, is Fort Wallington, not only commanding the country and to the north of it, but completely overlooking the town of Fareham and its creek, with the railway, and crossing fire with Fort Fareham, on the other side of the town. Here the excavations trench on the tertiary strata, and afford many interesting illustrations of geology incident to its situation. In addition to the other works, it is to have at its north-east side a heavy mortar battery at an elevation below that of the rampart. It is from this fort also that, in addition to its forming a line with the rest of the exterior forts, a work carried down to Fareham creek in a line with Fort Nelson, combines it, as previously explained, with the interior plan of defence. It is the last of the Hill Forts, as all the others are either on low beach levels, or at least on very gentle elevations.

1862 – THE TUSCARORA.

On Thursday an American man-of-war, flying the Federal flag was observed from Portsmouth passing through Spithead, and intelligence was very shortly conveyed to the Port Admiral that the stranger had anchored off Osborne This could not be endured, so Sir Henry Bruce despatched the *Pigmy*, his steam tender, with civil instructions that the interloper should either proceed to Cowes or return to the usual anchorage at Spithead. The hint was taken, as a matter of course and our friend the *Tuscarora*, for she it was, made her way up again to her old position off the decks.

1862 – EAST HANTS CRICKET GROUND.

With the view of meeting a requirement which has long been needed, Mr. Baker, the proprietor of the above ground at Southsea, has formed a racecourse in his grounds, which is likely to be a source of great attraction. We perceive that races for silver cups will come off on Monday next, when it is expected that there will be a large attendance of the lovers of the sport. For the accommodation of his patrons, Mr. Baker has also established a hunting and exercising ground, so that ladies and gentlemen have now an opportunity, at a small cost, of perfecting themselves in a most noble and healthy exercise.

1862 – SOLDIERS' INSTITUTES.

The following is an extract from the report by Captain Pilkington Jackson, R.A., to the Secretary of State for War on Soldiers' Institutes.

"The temptations leading to intoxication and lust are very great at Portsmouth. To the large military force which is permanently established there is added a large naval force; combined the number of men stationed there at all times is larger than at most garrison towns, and in the same proportion is the number of brothels and public houses.

A glance at the plan (not printed) will show how thickly certain parts of the town are studded with these centres of disease and crime; within a circle having a radius of 1,100 feet, there are more than 100 public houses, many of which are known to be brothels in disguise. As an example of the bold and defiant spirit of the prostitutes in Portsmouth, I would refer to a display they made only a few months since, when a legal attempt was made to expel them from the houses, they occupied or frequented; on this occasion they mustered in strong force, trooped through the main streets, and made a public exhibition of their infamous calling. The Magistrates, from prudential motives, I suppose, did not persevere in carrying their determination into effect.

Those parts of the town in which these places of resort are principally situated, are about the worst in the country. Vice in its most offensive forms revels and thrives there. The utmost that can be done by the military and civil police to preserve the appearance of decency in the principal thoroughfare, is to try to keep the prostitutes and their companions within certain boundaries. It may be readily imagined that under such a state of things offences of various kinds, both military and civil, are numerous. Experience has proved that the efforts of Commanding Officers, chaplains, and surgeons, generally produce only transient effects, unless the appetites and passions are held in abeyance, and under self-control, by a training of the mental faculties. That strength of mind to resist temptation may be cultivated and we have ample proof in other classes of society; in these we find it acts as a corrective to the grosser tendencies of our nature, and although it may be impossible to entirely eradicate these tendencies, the evils connected therewith may be mitigated and reduced to a minimum.

It has been proved that this can best be done in the case of soldiers by supplying them with healthy and pleasant occupation when off duty and most liable to temptations. This is the critical period when they most require a friendly hand to guide them, and by judicious treatment they may as easily be led into an Institute, where they will gradually acquire a taste for harmless and improving recreations, as they are now led into the wretched haunts of sensuality, disease, and crime.

The reading rooms in barracks are not a sufficient check to the strong desire most of the men have for a change of scene; they like to go out for a walk to see the shops by day, and the streets lighted up by night, and to escape from an atmosphere of force and restraint, to one of greater freedom; and in seeking for some kind of amusement, they fall naturally into bad company, and involuntarily acquire bad habits. If the reading rooms in barracks were improved, a greater number of men would occasionally remain in them than at present; but it would scarcely be possible to furnish amusements in the shape of reading and recreation rooms for all of them in barracks; the want of space would prevent it; but if this difficulty could be overcome, and great expense incurred in so doing, it would still be unsatisfactory, on account of the great variety of tastes and dispositions to be dealt with.

If an Institute in the town were well situated, well organized, and well managed, and under the special patronage of Government, offering counter attractions in the shape of well lighted, comfortable, and cheerful rooms, with good and cheap refreshments, and plenty of amusements, most of the men who had left the barracks would unquestionably avail themselves of it, in preference to frequenting, as they now do, the vile haunts which entail upon them disgrace and disease, and render them discontented with their lot.

The primary object of the barrack reading rooms, town institutes, and garrison library, is identically the same, viz., to improve the habits of the men, not viewing them simply as inhabitants of a barrack, but units of the human family. The Institute should, therefore, be independent of, but related to, the barrack reading room, and to the garrison library.

In proposing the establishment of such an Institute, I would respectfully submit, that in a large garrison town, like Portsmouth, it ought to be wholly military, essentially secular, and equally independent of civil aid, and of pecuniary assistance from regimental officers; and further, that it should be established by Government, and afterwards be supported by the recipients its benefits. The efficiency of the Army is materially involved in the good conduct of the men who compose it, and the sole object of the Institute or "Home" should be to produce this effect. In this respect it would take a middle position, between military discipline, on the one hand, and sanitary arrangements on the other; it would be found, if properly conducted, to be a most useful auxiliary to both; for in proportion the general conduct of the men improved, they would become more amenable to discipline, less liable to offences, and comparative strangers to the hospital and prison. For these reasons, if for no other, the Institute should be established by Government.

I have said that a Soldiers' Institute or Home should be independent of civil aid. In this I am taking a purely military view of what its character ought to be; but as many benevolent civilians take a deep interest in the soldier's welfare, and are desirous of promoting it, and there are others who would view the Institute as being of decided advantage to the town, in rendering it more quiet and orderly, there can be no reason for declining such voluntary contributions as may from time to time be made, and approved of by the board of management.

Since the attendance at an Institute is optional to the men, and its establishment useless unless it be frequented by them, it is necessary not only that its situation be well selected, and that its appearance homelike, comfortable, and attractive, but that its management should be placed upon such a basis as will afford a fair prospect of giving general satisfaction.

1862 – REDUCTION OF THE FLEET.

An order has been received at Portsmouth to reduce the number of guns and men of ships in commission. As the order is read at present this measure will reduce a 50-gun frigate to 36 guns, and take from her crew 50 of her petty officers and seamen, increasing the complement of boys. The naval correspondent of the *Times* adds that motives of economy may have dictated this new policy, but there can be no true economy in maintaining, for this country at least, an under-manned fleet.

1862 – THE PORTSMOUTH FORTIFICATIONS.

A more difficult question than that which has come so frequently before Parliament as to the best mode of defending our Dockyards and arsenals can scarcely be conceived. The problem comes to this – to construct a comprehensive scheme which shall adapt itself equally to the present and the future. It matters not what the plan is, it is certain to be open to attacks of those who insist upon having conclusive proof where nothing but more or less reasonable conjecture is possible.

The discussions in the two Houses of Parliament show some indications of a temper of mind which almost always supervenes upon the consideration of an important and uncertain question. Not knowing how to decide, bewildered by conflicting doubts, seeing the possibility, almost the probability, of going more or less astray whatever direction may be taken, it is as natural as it is hopeless to take refuge in a determination not to decide at all. But it is forgotten that to postpone decision indefinitely is in fact to decide, and perhaps to decide in the way which may turn out to be the worst of all the contradictory proposals.

There is a section of the House of Commons which has arrived at the definite conclusion that fixed fortifications, whether formed upon land or built in the sea, are of little use against modern weapons of attack, and are destined to become less serviceable with every improvement in military science. There is another small body of enthusiasts for forts, who discern in the future the inventions which are to increase indefinitely the range of protection which a first-class battery can command, while they are blind to the possibility that the resources of engineering may increase the existing powers of a ship as rapidly as the destructive force of artillery. Both of these positions are intelligible, and both are probably wrong.

Below is an engraving of a monster gun, cast in Liverpool, and which has stood the severest tests. Our own opinion is that such guns as this manned by Englishmen, will suffice to protect our Dockyards from molestation.

1863 – BALL AT THE PORTLAND HALL.

The officers of the Royal Artillery and Royal Engineers gave a ball at the Portland Hall, Southsea, on Tuesday, the 28th ult., which was pronounced by all present to be one of the very best that has been given in the

Gun at Portsmouth

neighbourhood for years past. Between 400 and 500 were present, more than half the gentlemen being in uniform. The scarlet, blue, and gold blended so beautifully with the elegant and superb dresses of the ladies, that the effect was truly enchanting. The great feature of the ball was that the matchless band of the Royal Artillery were brought from Woolwich for the occasion. 25 of the above band were selected, and led by the distinguished master, Mr. Smyth. Of this orchestra, it may with much truth, be said that none but itself can be its parallel; never was dance music played to greater perfection, and in those tunes when the voices are introduced, the effect was exceedingly good. The handsome uniforms of these 25 artistes, judiciously arranged as they were on a raised dais, produced a grand effect.

As the Portland Assembly Rooms were on their trial as to their capabilities for a large ball, it should be stated that though from 400 to 500 persons were in the Hall at once, at no time was it found to be inconveniently crowded. In addition to the Hall, the lobby and reading room were used for dancing, the non-dancers finding ample accommodation on the platform, and on seats arranged along the sides of room, numbers using the balcony, which was tastefully decorated and lighted for the occasion. The suite of rooms is painted and ornamented by the introduction of colours on the ceiling, and wherever it could be put with effect, thereby precluding the necessity of extra ornament, but some very handsome flags were arranged with great taste in various parts of the room.

As a contrast to the brilliantly lighted hall, &c., the very elegant conservatory leading to the hotel was lit with Chinese lanterns, and the effect was really charming and the theme of general admiration. Refreshments were served on a very liberal scale in several parts of the room, and at 12 o'clock the coffee room of the hotel was thrown open, where a sumptuous supper of the most recherché character was served, with an unlimited supply of champagne and other choice wines. It needs scarcely be said that dancing was kept up with great spirit till daylight was far advanced.

1863 – INSPECTION OF THE GARRISON OF PORTSMOUTH BY THE DUKE OF CAMBRIDGE.

The troops stationed in the town and outlying fortifications of Portsmouth were inspected by his Royal Highness the Commander-in-Chief on the 9th inst., on Southsea Common. A little before eleven the following force was drawn up at quarter-distance column, the Royal and Marine Artillery being respectively on the right and left of the line of infantry, and a battery of field artillery being on either flank; I and K batteries of field artillery, under Colonel Anderson, C.B., 182 officers and men, 184 horses, 10 12-pounder Armstrong guns, and 19 carriages; 6th Brigade Royal Artillery, under Colonel Warbeck, 385 officers and men, the whole of the artillery being under the command of Colonel Warde, C.B.; 2nd battalion 20th Regiment, under Colonel Radcliffe, 566 officers and men; 53rd Regiment, under Colonel English, C.B., 301 officers and men; 18th Regiment, under Colonel Hume, 537 officers and men; 2nd battalion 60th Rifles, under Colonel Palmer, C.B., 543 officers and men; Royal Marine Artillery, under Colonel Tate, officers and men; total, 3,045 officers and men, 184 horses, 10 guns, and 19 carriages.

The whole formed an imposing little army of infantry and artillery, but was necessarily destitute of cavalry. At eleven o'clock precisely the Duke of Cambridge arrived on the ground, accompanied by Quartermaster-General Sir Richard Airey, K.C.B.; Colonel Bingham, Deputy Adjutant-General Royal Artillery; Colonel Clifton, A.D.C., and other officers, and was received by Major-General Lord W. Paulet, C.B., attended by his Staff, in the centre and front of the line, the troops presenting a general salute, with colours lowered. After riding slowly along the front of the line, the Duke took up a position with his Staff at the saluting point, and the force prepared for marching past in review order.

Each regiment seemed put upon their metal to do their best, and the result was such a display of marching past, especially in grand divisions, as is seldom witnessed on Southsea Common. The field batteries going by in mathematical order at a smart trot finished the ceremony of marching past, and preparations were immediately made for the more important movements of the day, by re-forming a column on the original alignment with field batteries on each flank. The first move was made with the right in front into echelon line of columns, the field batteries galloping to the front and left, and unlimbering and opening rapid fire considerably in advance of the force. The 60th Rifles at the same time moved out advance, and threw out a strong line of skirmishers across the common, the main body having changed their echelon formation into two lines of contiguous columns. The batteries now retired behind the line of skirmishers and re-formed on the right and left of the advanced line, composed of the garrison artillery, 20th and 55th Regiments; and, the 60th Rifles by this time having completed the discomfiture of the enemy, already partially accomplished by the artillery previous their giving place to the 60th, a general advance was ordered, the rifles feeling the way.

In this manner the further end of the common was nearly reached. There the rifles received a check. They had apparently come upon the enemy in superior numbers, for they were speedily driven in, and the main body, which had been moving up in two long lines, commenced a retrograde echelon movement, left in front, the ten 12-pounder guns covering the retreat unlimbering on every commanding position of the ground they were retiring over, and blazing away fiercely in the direction of the supposed, enemy. Foiled in this quarter, the enemy made a feint in another direction; and Lord Paulet, changing his front to the right, again sent out the 60th in skirmishing order. The latter, however, soon closed in to their supports and retired upon the main body; but the enemy must have been repulsed by some means or other, for Lord Paulet had ample leisure to re-form his force at quarter distance on their original alignment, a battery of field artillery being, as before, on each flank. This done, the line advanced, a general salute was given, colours were lowered to the ground, and the inspection was over. By direction of his Royal Highness commanding officers were now called to the front and addressed shortly by him in terms generally eulogistic of the manner in which the movements had been performed and the appearance of the men under their command.

1863 – MEMORIAL CROSS OF THE 8TH (KING'S) REGIMENT.

A very handsome cross has been erected on the Grand Parade, Portsmouth, in honour of the officers and men of the 8th Regiment of Foot who were slain or died from disease during the Indian mutiny. The form chosen for the monument is that of the old Irish cross, which exhibits beauty and simplicity of outline with breadth and massiveness, and is peculiarly adapted for illustrative bas-reliefs. Of these there are four, one, above the arms of the cross, a single figure, representing the Ascension of Christ, and on the shaft a series of three, which delineate the most characteristic incidents in the life of a soldier on the battlefield, the Encampment, the Combat, and the Death. In each of these the subject is simply and vigorously rendered by two or three effective figures, unencumbered by much detail. The treatment of the last, a dead soldier, borne by two of his comrades,

The 6th Brigade Royal Artillery March Past the Duke in Grand Divisions

is exceedingly impressive. The cross is composed of Sicilian marble, the plinth of red Mansfield stone, serpentine and green marbles, and the sub-plinth of granite.

When completed the plinth will bear the following inscription:

THIS CROSS
COMMEMORATES THE SERVICES
AND DEATH OF
243 OFFICERS, N.C. OFFICERS,
AND PRIVATE SOLDIERS,
LOST BY THE
8th, THE KING'S REGIMENT,
WHILE ENGAGED IN SUPPRESSING
THE SEPOY MUTINY
OF 1857-1858.
SOME DIED IN BATTLE, SOME OF
WOUNDS, SOME OF DISEASE,
ALL IN DEVOTED PERFORMANCE OF DUTY.

The names of the officers and men will be engraved on the shaft. The measurements of the monument are as follows:- height, 21 feet; width of arm across, 6 feet; width of shaft, 28 inches; lower base, 6 feet; outside measurement, 8 feet 4 inches. A dwarf Gothic railing will enclose the cross. The work is from the studio of Mr. H.S. Leifehild, 111, Stanhope Street, Regent's Park, London; and the contractor is Mr. J. Underwood, of High Street, Camden Town.

The monument is chaste and appropriate in design and highly creditable to the skill which executed it; but, in our judgment, its effect is considerably diminished by the peculiar position in which it is placed. It is erected at the foot of the slope leading to the ramparts, and looks as if it has been deposited there to await an opportunity for its removal to a more suitable place. Of course, this is not the fault of the architect, who has, no doubt, selected the best position that was offered him; but it is to be regretted that so handsome a monument, which is creditable alike to the feeling which prompted its erection and the object for which it was designed, should not have been raised on a more appropriate site.

1863 – RURAL FETE AT EAST COSHAM.

A rustic gala on a liberal scale took place at East Cosham on Wednesday last, under the auspices of Admiral Sir Lucius Curtis, Bart., K.C.B. who successfully carried out his entertainment to the children belonging to the school bearing his name, together with their parents and relatives. Early in the afternoon, a number of the children were conveyed in waggons kindly lent by J. Burrill, Esq., to the schoolroom at Cosham, where they were joined by their school fellows who resided in the immediate neighbourhood of the school, and proceeded to a large meadow at East Cosham, placed at their disposal by the Rev. E.S. Phelps, whose residence overlooks the field. The spot selected for the fete was admirably adapted for a gala ground, the meadow being very spacious, and conveniently shaded by large trees, the open glades being sufficiently spacious for the villagers to carry on the games. The excellent band of the Dockyard (Metropolitan) Police was present, by permission, and during the afternoon and evening performed a variety of music, under the able direction of Mr. Jones.

Admission to the fete was strictly confined to those who resided in the parish, and to those who were personally interested in Sir Lucius Curtis' School, so that by these means it was rendered essentially a merry-making for the villagers, and certainly nothing

Memorial Cross of the 8th (Kings) Regiment

appeared to have been forgotten by the promoters of the treat that was at all likely to increase the pleasure and happiness of the parishioners and their children. Young and old had been considered and their tastes studied, for on the ground was erected "Rollen's grand panorama," which was exhibited gratis every few minutes, a capital merry-go-round, a skittle alley, and a variety of other amusements, all of which were sources of considerable attractions to the country folks. The children were entertained shortly after their arrival on the ground, refreshments on a very liberal scale having been provided for them in a booth, where 125 of the scholars were regaled to their heart's content. Tea, cake, &c., were provided by Miss Curtis, who, with the energetic governess, Miss Matthias, worked zealously to entertain her young guests. A substantial repast was provided in another large booth in the centre of the field by Mr. Rogers, of Cosham, where upwards of 300 parishioners of both sexes sat down to a good dinner.

These booths were decorated with flags and the mottoes "God save the Queen," "God bless the Prince and Princess of Wales." Mr. Burrill, in order to cooperate with the promoters of the treat, generously gave his employees a holiday, and with waving banners, seated in large farm waggons, the villagers entered the ground, cheering heartily. Having partaken of the refreshment, the children betook themselves to the various attractions provided for them, and all appeared to thoroughly enjoy themselves. The adults also found ample amusement, and a variety of sports occupied their attention until nightfall, when the largest booth was illuminated by means of five chandeliers, nitrous variegated lamps and Chinese lanterns, being lit on either side of the tent, presenting a very pretty effect.

In the meantime, a collation was provided in the booth vacated by the children to which several of the subscribers and friends of the school sat down. The collation was also provided with the same liberality which characterised the entire arrangements. A number of subscribers, friends and parishioners, who could not be accommodated in the tent, partook of a collation provided in the grounds attached to the residence of the Rev. Mr. Phelps, whose assiduous energy largely contributed to the success of the fete. The Rev. Gentleman has always evinced a warm interest in the rise and progress of this school, and has even lent his aid to promote the welfare of the scholars.

The number of parishioners admitted had, towards the evening, largely increased, and nearly 500 adults partook of Sir Lucius Curtis's hospitality, none but parishioners being admitted upon the green sward. During the evening, and after darkness had set in, dancing was kept up with considerable spirit, both in the booths and in the field. "Drop handkerchief," "Kiss in the Ring," and other round games continued till dark, the company being divided over the field. Those who preferred enjoyment of a more manly character played at cricket, skittles, &c.

During the evening, a number of the parents and friends of the children assembled around Sir Lucius, with the intention of thanking him for the treat. Their numbers became augmented, until a circle of upwards of 450 persons formed around their patron and cheered him heartily. The cheering continued for some minutes, and Sir Lucius made several fruitless attempts to obtain a hearing. At length he said he thanked them very much for their kind wishes. It gave him more pleasure than he could express to see so many of his neighbours around him on that pleasing occasion. Words failed to express the pleasure and delight it afforded him to see also so many of those young branches belonging to them assembled around, enjoying themselves and making themselves happy, as they all appeared to be. It not only afforded unbounded pleasure to him, but equally gratified his daughter, Miss Curtis, who not only took a deep interest in them, but a lively interest in their children. Looking around him and seeing so many happy faces, made him at that moment feel a sensation he could not express. It was his pleasure to contribute to their happiness, and he was sorry he could not give them that attention a younger person could. (Cheers, and "You're young yet, Sir Lucius," "Long may he live") He would only repeat that he was glad to see them there; he was delighted to see assembled around him those who were attached to our ancient church. While they stuck to that church, the old true English church, with none of their fandangles, they would, he was sure, be happy.

Having referred to the period when the Rev. Mr. Henville laboured amongst them, he again thanked them for their wishes that he might live long. He hoped that he might live another year or two amongst them and that he might continue to witness their health and happiness, and that of their children. (A voice: "We hope so," and cheers). Three cheers were proposed for Miss Curtis, and vociferously responded to again and again. Sir Lucius then advanced to the centre of the circle and said he must return thanks for his daughter, who, as they all knew, took as much interest in the welfare of the school as he did. He wished she was present to make a speech to them, for ladies, he thought, were best at that sort of thing. He would take good care, however, to convey to Miss Curtis their kind wishes for her health and happiness. They had an excellent governess to superintend the schools (three cheers were given for Miss Matthias.) Having spoken of the governess in the highest terms of praise, Sir Lucius said he would acquaint those ladies who belonged to the school of the way in which their services had been acknowledged.

The large party again betook themselves to such enjoyment as best pleased them, and after spending a very happy afternoon and evening the company dispersed at a late hour, both old and young being much gratified at the result of a treat which will be long remembered in that locality.

It may not be out of place to refer to the establishment of this school and the progress it has made since its foundation. It appears that in 1855 Miss Curtis and Miss Warren, knowing that a large number of small children were accustomed to run and play about the streets uncared for and uneducated, thought that something might be done to bring about a better state of things. Accordingly, an infant school was established, with the sanction of the late vicar. The scheme proved successful, and it soon became necessary that larger premises should be secured, and those where the school is now held were rented. On the 5th of February, 1860, owing to some misunderstanding, to which we need not further refer, the present vicar publicly declared the school closed. Sir Lucius Curtis, having obtained the sole lease of the school premises, called a meeting of the subscribers, who unanimously voted him the school furniture and the money in hand. The present school was reopened with 25 scholars, under the old committee, the same system being adopted as before. Since that time, the school has steadily increased, and now numbers 125 scholars, all of whom, with two exceptions, are parishioners who have voluntarily sought the advantages of the establishment, which, we are informed, is supported by about 80 subscribers, all being ratepayers, amongst them some of the chief landowners in the parish.

1863 – CELEBRATION OF THE PRINCE OF WALES MARRIAGE.

We are inclined to think that the borough of Portsmouth astonished itself on Tuesday last. A fortnight ago there was a prospect of the great historic and domestic event of the year being a very flat business indeed so far as this "ancient and loyal" borough was concerned, and some rather odious comparisons were very naturally made with towns that made less pretensions to importance, although they may not be less demonstrative in their loyalty to the person and office of our sovereign lady the Queen.

It is true that the Corporation as is duty bound, took the initiative in making the necessary preliminary arrangements, and, if modesty be a virtue, they exhibited it in a very remarkable degree. A committee was appointed, and, after much deliberation, it presented a series of recommendations to the Council which that body agreed to. Modest, however, as the programme was, it has not been very faithfully observed, for the simple reason that the townspeople were more hearty and enthusiastic and more determined than their rulers to make the day long to be remembered by living generations.

The Council did not recommend a general illumination, and they perhaps acted wisely in that respect; but the inhabitants of principal thoroughfares preferred to act upon their own judgement and those thoroughfares were consequently dressed in festal garments, and everything was done that could be done to delight the eye and mark the occasion.

The Council did resolve to honour the event after the manner peculiar to Englishmen, namely by dining together and asking the burgesses to join them, and also to make a public collection for feasting the children of the various schools, and these resolves, with the recommendation that Coventry rosettes should be worn, formed the gist of the original programme.

But the first proposal was so eminently selfish in its character, that the Council were not agreed upon it, and, as might have been expected, it met with very little sympathy and encouragement out of doors, and had eventually to be abandoned. It was not a day for rigid exclusiveness, to be tolerated, and ladies of Portsmouth did not appreciate any plan by which "their lords" proposed to honour the marriage of the Prince of Wales, and feast and glorify themselves, and in which the conventionalities of society would preclude the ladies from taking any part.

The other features of the programme were more generally approved, and the result will appear hereafter. On no previous occasion, perhaps, did the old borough put on a more holiday aspect. As the great day approached it thoroughly awoke from its sleepy apathy, and caught the contagion of enthusiasm which became, as it were, epidemic throughout the whole country. And we do not hesitate to say that a noble sentiment of loyalty pervaded the minds of the many thousands who took part in the demonstration. One could not fail to recognise the significance of these external symbols, and to connect them with the event for which they were designed to celebrate and to honour.

At an early hour in the morning, though not so early as mentioned in the programme, the bells of St. Thomas's Church began a merry peel, which was repeated at intervals throughout the day, interspersed, however with the tinkling of a solitary bell, which sounded very much like a funeral bell, although in a different key. The streets soon became thronged, and towards eleven o'clock there was at constant stream of people along all the main thoroughfares leading to Southsea Common.

The troops of the garrison assembled there shortly after eleven o'clock, and consisted of the J and K Batteries 4th Brigade of Royal Artillery, consisting of 9 officers, 12 sergeants, 170 rank and file, commanded by Lieutenant-Colonel Anderson, C.B.; 6th Brigade Royal Artillery, 24 officers, 30 sergeants, 498 rank and file, Colonel Warde, C.B.; 2nd Battalion 20th Regiment, 21 officers, 29 sergeants, 523 rank and file, as well as many others. To these must be added the 2nd and 3rd Administrative Battalions of the Hants Rifle Volunteers, under the Command of Colonel Conran and the 2nd and 3rd Hants Artillery, commanded by Major Sturdee, the local corps numbering in all about 800.

The troops formed three sides of a square, the volunteers on the left flank. Two mounted batteries

The Marriage of the Prince of Wales and Princess Alexandra

of artillery, each with six Armstrong guns, were drawn up in front of the line. Shortly before noon Major-General Lord William Paulet; commanding the South-Western District, attended by other officers, rode upon the ground, and, after his lordship had inspected the troops, the saluting battery of the garrison, at twelve o'clock, fired a Royal salute. The firing was taken up by the mounted brigades of artillery on the Common, and the troops of the line fired a *feu-de-joie* and afterwards gave three hearty cheers, which were led by the gallant Major-General.

The troops then marched past in review order, and went through a brief series of manoeuvres incidental to attack and defence, finally retreating into the garrison under cover of the guns commanding Southsea Common. A vast concourse of people assembled on the Common, and appeared to be delighted with the proceedings of the morning.

At one o'clock, the squadron at Spithead, under the command of Rear-Admiral Robert Smart, fired a royal salute. The ships of the squadron anchored at Spithead in the following order, beginning from the west: - *Racoon, Resistance, Defence, Revenge, Warrior, Emerald, Melpomone* and *Imperieuse*. They were each dressed in colours of the English and Danish flags at the main and garlands at the mastheads

THE CHILDREN'S TREAT.

By two 'clock this afternoon the Common was again the scene of gaiety and bustle. The pleasure seekers, having dined, thronged the approaches in every direction, anxious to see the children belonging to the various schools assemble around the landmark. Booths, stalls, "Aunt Sallys," rifle galleries and various amusements were on the ground, and there could not have been less than 30,000 people assembled. The house tops were crowded by spectators, and every window in and about Clarence Parade was occupied. The favour of Coventry ribbon was displayed by nearly all, and every person appeared bent on enjoyment.

At two o'clock the Mayor, W.G. Chambers, Esq., and Corporation assembled at the Queen's Hotel, where a *dejeuner* was served in a manner reflecting credit upon Mr. Kemp, the host. About 30 Aldermen and Councillors sat down, together with the Vicar of Portsmouth, the Rev. J.P. McGhie, and the Town Clerk, (John Howard, Esq.) At the conclusion of the refreshment His Worship proposed the health of the Queen in appropriate terms, the toast being loyally responded to by those present. The toast of the day followed, being also proposed by the Mayor, who, in brief but expressive language, proposed health, long life, and happiness to the bride and bridegroom. This toast was drank with enthusiasm. Mr. Alderman Stigant then proposed the health of the Mayor, and Mr. Chambers responded.

At three o'clock the Corporation, headed by the Mayor, Vicar, and Town Clerk, walked to the Common, accompanied by a body of police, headed by Mr. Barber, the superintendent. The Mayor and Corporation having taken possession of the platform erected near the landmark, around which an innumerable crowd had assembled, three hearty cheers were given for His Worship, in which the children joined. The band of the 60th Rifles were present by kind permission of the officers, and played several favourite selections of popular music.

The children poured onto the Common in streams from the various districts and made their way to the landmark, around which they formed an oblong square, about 50 yards by 70, divided by four sub-squares, and each column of children entered into the square allotted to it. Considering all things, the arrangements were managed admirably, and there appeared to be very little confusion.

The children from Portsmouth and Portsea came through King William Gate. The children of Landport district were composed of two columns, one of which entered the Common via King's terrace, and the other via the Cricketer's tavern. Southsea Schools entered by Castle Road, the whole of the schools making for one centre in orderly precision.

The following was the return: - Green Row School, 182; Daniel Street, 200; Arundel Street, 850; Little Southsea Street, 109; Highland Road, 80, Cumberland Fort, 142; Beneficial Society's Hall, 350; Zion Chapel, 204; Allen's Fields, 130; Bonfire Corner, 177; St. Jude's, 300; Grosvenor Street, 212; St. Luke's, 310; Middle Street, 100; White's Row, 80; Clarence Street, 300; Orange Street, 380; Milton, 30; Rudmore, 205; Green Row National 312; Ebenezer, 206; Buckland, 440; Bath Square, 120; Marine Orphans, 122; St. Paul's Square, 270; Kent Street, 230; Lancastrian, 390; St. Paul's National, 353 ; All Saints ditto, 638; Kingston ditto, 102; Oxford Street Ragged, 150; Marylebone Day School, 120; Lake Road, 300; Catholic, 102; Commissioners' Hall; 90; Circus, 442; Oyster Street, 330; Highbury, 160; Clarendon Place, 190; Elm Lane Industrial, 100; Scotch (Iron) Church, 103; St. John's, 230; Somers Road, 150; Stamford Street, 183; Fratton Street, 68; Broad Street, 55; Marylebone Street Ragged school, 90; Unitarian, 75; Victoria Street, 180; St. Mary's Infant, 88; Milton National, 120; Orange Street Day, 70; ditto Sunday, 250; Union children, 400; showing a total of about 10,000.

The children having taken their places, silence was restored, when His Worship addressed them in the following terms: "My, dear young friends. We are assembled this day to manifest our rejoicing on the marriage of our noble young Prince, to add our prayers to those of our fellow countrymen, that every happiness may attend the youthful pair, and it may please our Almighty Father, the God and Protector of us all, to grant them his blessing. The homage of loyalty and affection for our beloved Queen, we desire to show on this day has never been equalled in the whole world, it far exceeds the glory of a conqueror because it springs from the heart of each individual in this vast empire. It is an homage that no wealth could purchase, and no conqueror, however powerful, could obtain. This day will never be forgotten by any one of us, and when you think of it in after life, recollect that the Prince of Wales, although so exalted in station, had duties to perform as well as each of you, and that he has shown you such example of affection and obedience to his parents, such respect and attention to his tutors; such a desire to improve his talents, and acquire the knowledge necessary to fit him for his high station, as to command the love and respect of many millions of his fellow subjects. A path of duty is also before each of you. Follow it, resist every temptation to do wrong, and be assured a life of virtue is equally pleasing to our Heavenly Father, whether it shines from the Royal palace or the poorest corner of Her Majesty's dominions. The inhabitants of this neighbourhood have endeavoured to help you enjoy today. I hope that you do so as the kindness of your parents and friends immediately connected with your schools has greatly assisted. I trust their efforts will be crowned with success, and that it will prove to be a day of pleasure and satisfaction to us all, which will never he effaced from our memory. We shall all join heart and voice in the National Anthem you are about to sing, trusting that it may please God to hear our Prayers and bless our Queen, by granting health and happiness to all her family; and especially to bless the marriage of their R.H. the Prince and Princess of Wales, which has this day been solemnized."

The juvenile assemblage then sang their different hymns and afterwards the "National Anthem" led by the Rifle band. The voices of 10,000 children, with half as many adults, had a thrilling effect which would have been increased had better arrangement been made to secure unison in the enunciation of the words. "Rule Britannia" was then sung, and three cheers for the Mayor and Corporation brought the proceedings to a close. The different schools, we should mention, displayed a number of handsome banners, and nearly all the children wore white favours. In the most orderly manner, the scholars departed and reached the respective schools, where a treat was provided for them according to the arrangement entered into by the superintendents. Tickets were given to each child, representing the value of 4d. and 5d. The former sum was given to the Sunday scholars, and the larger amount to the charity children.

The Corporation then retired to the hotel.

ILLUMINATION OF THE FLEET.

The illumination of the squadron at Spithead, under the command of Rear-Admiral Smart, was eagerly expected by tens of thousands on both sides of the water, and the display from the fleet was regarded not only as a local but as a national expression of joy. It was unquestionably the chief attraction in this and surrounding neighbourhoods and hundreds of visitors came to Portsmouth to witness this grand and imposing spectacle. The afternoon's festivities closed merrily, and darkness set in, with a prospect of a favourable evening, but unfortunately about seven o'clock the rain poured down, and disappointment was everywhere expressed. Despite the rain (which, however, was only intermittent, and did not continue long), one continuous stream of pleasure-seekers poured towards the Common, and hundreds of cabs crowded the thoroughfares, the lights from which formed, in themselves, a line of illumination along the Esplanade.

From the iron railings to the water's edge the people thronged, anxious for the signal to illuminate. The atmosphere was bitterly cold and damp, but in other respects the night was very favourable for the pyrotechnic display. The houses and villa residences facing the sea where thronged with people, and almost every house top was crowded. It is impossible to form any correct estimate of the number of people on the Common, but there were, certainly, tens of thousands.

At eight o'clock the first gun of the Royal salute boomed forth from the *Revenge*, and the firing was immediately taken up by the other seven vessels, all heavily armed, and as if by magic the whole squadron was brilliantly illuminated at every yard-arm, presenting a spectacle which it would be difficult either to imagine or describe. At the same moment there was a lurid display of coloured fire from the salient points of the tower and the upper part of the dome of St. Thomas's Church, which shared the honours of admiration with the fleet.

The last gun of the salute having been fired, there was a brilliant discharge of rockets *en mass* from some of the ships. Shell firing then commenced from the west, the first round being fired in succession down the line of ships, with an interval of half-a-minute between each. 5-inch shells were fired first, then the 8-inch, and lastly the bright 10-inch. The effect was brilliant, the smaller shells showering stars of blue, yellow, red, and green; green, blue, and yellow flames. The 8-inch shells were, perhaps, the most effective, rising gracefully to a great altitude, as the burning fuses indicated, and shedding a mass of gold-coloured fire, tailing beautifully when about half way down.

The 10-inch shells, of which there were twenty, consisted of a number of brilliant stars, which as they descended, illuminated the surrounding shipping, which by this time was enveloped again in darkness, the last illuminating blue light having gradually expired. The shell firing was interspersed with the firing of brilliant rockets, and when they were fired in volleys the effect was magnificent, the brilliant parti-coloured lights from innumerable particles of flame lighting up the whole sheet of water stretching from the shore to Spithead. Again and again, during the display the eye turned from the fleet to the brilliant tower of St. Thomas's. The fireworks continued for half an hour, and by this time the sky was one lurid mass on all sides, the clouds reflecting the flames emanating from bonfires lighted on the most prominent downs in South Hants, Sussex, and the Isle of Wight, so that the Island of Portsea was literally encircled in flame.

In the neighbourhood of Osborne and Ryde the glare was particularly bright, and no better view in perspective could be obtained of the fleet and of the downs stretching far down the Solent to the west, and along the shore of Sussex to the east, than from the turrets at Osborne.

Some idea of the liberal manner with which the Government provided the display of fireworks may be arrived at when it becomes known that each vessel was provided with 20 long lights, 26 shells, 32 firework mortars, 20 golden rain shells, 20 tall shells, 20 crackers, 20 squib shells, 20 shells of various sorts, 160 rockets, in all 300 pieces of fireworks to each ship. The fleet threw off, altogether, about, 2,400 fireworks. We hear that there were illuminated devices, appropriate to the happy event, on board some of the ships, but these, as a matter of course, could not be seen from Southsea. We should here mention that the lights burnt on the Church tower were provided by the Mayor, W.G. Chambers, Esq.

The display of the fleet being concluded the fireworks provided by the Corporation commenced. They were varied in description, and, considering the sum appropriated for this purpose, we are inclined to think that the pyrotechnics gave us our money's worth. The rockets, as a matter of course, suffered by comparison with those supplied by the government, but the composite works were very pretty, and appeared to give great pleasure to the sightseers. This being the case the intentions of the authorities were fully carried out. A number of superior rockets were fired from the ground fronting the Clarence Parade, amidst loud cheers of the bystanders. We should not forget to mention that during the evening a number of blue lights were lit on the Victoria Pier, which was crowded by spectators.

The grand tableau of the evening being concluded the immense crowd moved toward the eastward, where a large bonfire had been built, under the superintendence of Mr. G. Rake, and the material for the most part was purchased by private subscription. This mass, when ignited, burnt with amazing swiftness, and the glare could be seen for many miles. The crowd assembled around this blaze must have numbered some twenty thousand, and the reflection upon the upturned faces of this multitude produced a very singular effect. The Tattoo having been postponed until ten o'clock, hundreds of soldiers were attracted to the bonfire which was a complete success,

After the bonfire had been well lit a number of tar barrels placed on poles along the Esplanade were ignited, and materially contributed to the scenic effect, although the flames from them were by no means brilliant.

ILLUMINATION IN THE HARBOUR.
Thousands of persons thronged the Hard, Portsea, after the display on Southsea Common, to witness the harbour illuminations, and appeared to be gratified at the sight presented to them, many observing that the appearances of the *Victory*, Captain F. Scott, and the *St. Vincent*, Commander Marcus Lowther, eclipsed the illumination of the squadron for effective grandeur. The sight was quietly imposing; there was no whiz of fireworks in the harbour, nor blaze of bonfire, but the thousand lights reflected in the calm water of the harbour was exceedingly pretty, not to say imposing. The old *Victory* was illuminated once more, as she had often been before, but this illumination told no tale of carnage on the sea, but simply betokened the gladness of British sailors on an occasion never to be forgotten by them. The outline, hull, and rigging, was clearly depicted by the myriad of lights. Every porthole had its light and each yard-arm exhibited a row of lanterns which were also suspended on various parts of the rigging.

The *St. Vincent* had a light at each porthole and along the awning ridge ropes, across the yards and from the jib-boom end to the spanker-boom. There was also a long light at each yard-arm, and across the stern a row and festoon of lamps. Like the *Victory*, she was also decorated with flags and bunting. As it unfortunately happened that sickness had been in the ship for some days the boys were not allowed to go on shore to enjoy themselves as was contemplated, but abundant provision for their entertainment on board, consisting of plum pudding, meat, roast, baked, and boiled, with vegetables. There were also 81 gallons of ale, and for dessert four bushels of nuts and 1,200 oranges. The lower deck was tastefully decorated with miniature English and Danish flags crossed, presented by Mrs. Lowther, the junction of the flag staves forming the Prince of Wales's emblem.

When grace was said by the Rev. W. Whitmarsh, M.A, at 12.20, the Captain and officers went on the lower deck, and the Captain proposed the "health of the Royal pair," which was loyally and loudly responded to by the boys. When the Royal salute was fired at one p.m. about 500 voices struck up the National Anthem with very good effect. The boys then enjoyed themselves all day in their own way, perambulating the decks, beating drums, cheering their officers, and, in fact, highly delighted with themselves and everyone else; and, no doubt, it was a day that they will remember as long as they live. Other ships in the harbour were also illuminated, but all that could be conspicuously discerned from the Hard were those specially mentioned, excepting the water police ship, which exhibited a different coloured light from each porthole.

THE DECORATIONS AND ILLUMINATIONS.
The inhabitants manifested their attachment to Royalty by decorating the streets and houses in the most profuse manner. Such a general decoration was certainly not anticipated. Neighbouring towns were making preparations for weeks before the event, but the people of this place decorated the borough simultaneously, and, like Aladdin's palace, they were reared in a night. The majority of the flags displayed were real bunting of large dimensions, and government departments furnished them to a large extent. The High Street presented a gay, pleasing appearance and we might say truly that there was scarcely one second-rate flag hanging in the street. From house top to house top in this street strings of flags hung, intermixed with laurels and Chinese lanterns. The decorations were profuse, and arranged with tasteful nicety.

Passing from Broad Street, there were similar manifestations of loyalty. The customs house was, as a matter of course, decorated, as were also the government offices leading to the Gunwharf. Across the roads from Ordnance Row to the commencement of the Hard, hundreds of flags of all nations were hung, the Portsea police station being the chief point for display. The Albert Pier and the Common Hard were hung with hundreds of large flags and evergreens. A splendid standard waved from the high staff at the Dockyard Gates and also from the Semaphore. A triumphal arch composed of laurels, evergreens and flags was erected in Half Moon Street from between Messrs. Lancaster, Antill, and Norman's residences. This arch was very effective in appearance. Clock Street and Camden Alley also displayed fitting emblems of attachment to the Queen and to the happy pair.

Queen Street was literally covered with flags and devices, and presented a splendid sight. The vast amount of trouble in arranging these decorations was amply repaid by the gay and beautiful effect produced. Kent Street, St. James's Street, and the various connecting thoroughfares followed in the general wake, and almost every bye-street displayed an ensign. From thence we pass into Lion Gate Road, through the archway, which, had it been decorated, would have been a principal feature of the display of this locality, but from that part of the town to the east end of the road, very little had been done. In Commercial Road the display was unsurpassed in many parts of the metropolis. From Eden Brewery many flags were hung, and Charlotte Street was by no means backward in display. The various tributary thoroughfares leading to Portsea, Fratton, Buckland &c., were draped, and even ragged Oxford Street evinced a loyal emulation.

Lake Road, for a thoroughfare chiefly comprised of private houses, was scarcely inferior to any part of the Borough, and passing to Kingston Cross, and Crescent there were the same outward manifestations of loyalty. In one part of Landport an amateur artist seems to have had it all his own way, for the eye rests upon many banners painted and mottoed by the same hand. These banners were not exactly artistic in appearance or design, yet they proved that the inhabitants from whose houses they were suspended had the same aim. Russell Street formed an effective line in the decorations from Kingston to Southsea. There were strings of banners hung across the street into Brunswick Road, and the inhabitants residing in the intermediate streets between this locality and King Street exhibited their joy in like manner, as also did the residents in Hyde Park Corner and the streets running from the railway station to Somers Road and Fratton.

St. James's Road displayed a line of banners and evergreens. Passing into Upper and Lower King Street we perceive like decorations, and from thence into Norfolk Square, where banners and evergreens were also hung. Little Eldon Street was distinguished for the profusion of its decorations, while Wish Street was unsurpassed for tasteful array in this part of the outwards. The terraces were gaily decorated, and the streets at the rear of Kings Terrace and the neighbouring thoroughfares were profusely decorated.

The road to the Wheelbarrow Castle was gaily dressed, and the last-named tavern displayed evergreens, flags, and devices in profusion. Passing to Osborne Road and the adjoining thoroughfare the same scenes presented themselves. Clarence Parade and many of the outlying villa residences were elegantly attired in holiday dress. Palmerston road, as anticipated, was the great feature of this locality, as far as decorations went. At considerable expense and trouble triumphal arches were constructed, one opposite St. Jude's Church, and the other at the corner of Clarendon Road. Grove road, Kent Road, and Elm Grove were severally hung with many-coloured banners and other decorations. The large block of buildings situated at the west end of Clarence Esplanade demand especial notice, as from the house tops floated one stream of banners, while evergreens lined the roof. New Southsea, Havelock Park, and the district lying to the eastward was as loyal as the other parts of the suburbs. Bath Square in Portsmouth, and the surrounding houses, the consulate, Messrs. Garratt's etc. joined the general display, while the vessels around showed their colours, even to the wherry plying about the harbour.

At an early hour in the morning the fleet, which had formed in line, was dressed in colours from stem to stern. The ships in harbour were similarly decorated, as were also the yachts and smacks lying close by.

In describing these decorations no doubt that many portions of the borough have been inadvertently overlooked. Suffice it to say, however, that scarcely any locality in the neighbourhood was entirely devoid of decoration suitable to the occasion. The following is as complete a detail as could be obtained of the illuminations and decorations worthy of particular notice.

THE GOVERNMENT HOUSE.

Before the residence of Major-General Lord W. Paulet, there were two transparencies. Upon one were the initials "A. and A.," and the other represented a globe, around which were four figures representing the four quarters, Asia and Africa were on either side, while Europe and America rested on the sphere. The appropriateness of this design was not particularly obvious, and, although the artist doubtless did his best, it was by no means a masterpiece, and scarcely worthy of its situation.

THE GUILDHALL.

The illumination placed in front of this building by Mr. Brown, of the South of England Music Hall, was certainly one of the handsomest and most elaborate in the borough. It was designed and painted by Mr. G.B. Wilson, artist of the Music Hall. The length of the base was 50 feet and the height 26 feet 6 inches. The centre was a transparency of oval form, 14 feet by 16 feet, painted on white silk, the subject being portraits of the Prince and Princess in a medallion supported by Cupid and Hymen, acting as guides and strewing their paths with flowers. On the base of the transparency were the arms of England and Denmark, supporting the Portsmouth arms worked in handsome scrollwork, the sentiments on a white riband, supported by Cupids, being "Hail, happy pair" and "May they be blest with all that heaven can send." On either side was massive scrollwork, lit by gas jets, and interlined with hundreds of white opal lamps. The flags of England and Denmark and various nations were also lit by gas lamps in appropriate colours, the whole surmounted by the Prince of Wales' plume, of gigantic size, containing upwards of two thousand variegated lamps.

VICTORIA PIER.

The Directors of this Company very liberally threw the Pier open to the public free of any charge, and thousands availed themselves of the opportunity during the day and night. The large gate was closed and festooned with evergreens, over which was a transparency of the Prince of Wales' feathers, and on each side the letters "A.E.A." On the other side was another of equal dimensions and brilliancy, lit up with gas, and a profusion of laurel round each case. The small gate was also decorated, with a flag staff on each side. On one was the Royal Standard of Denmark, ordered expressly by the Directors in compliment to the Princess Alexandra, and on the other waved the Royal Standard of England. On the facade hung four iron hoops, tastefully arranged with laurel, containing medallions of the Prince of Wales and Princess Alexandra, with their arms on each side, and under the glass roof was turned into an Arcadian bower, with suspending garlands, the whole illuminated with variegated lamps. Joints of mutton, beef, game, and ham hung in all directions, having been liberally supplied by the Directors for the staff of the establishment and their friends to enjoy themselves with a substantial supper in the evening. Before the illumination of the fleet, the pier was illuminated with a profusion of blue lights.

PRINCE OF WALES'S CLUB.

The illumination at the Prince of Wales' Club consisted of a large transparency showing the Prince of Wales' plume between the initials "A." and "A." and the motto "Ich Dien" under the Crown. The members were to dine on Tuesday at the Club to celebrate their Royal Highnesses' marriage. In order, however, that they might view the illuminations and other interesting sights the Committee postponed the dinner until Tuesday, the 17th instant. Of course, the dinner will still be in celebration of the Royal marriage.

THE POST OFFICE.

A transparency representing the Prince of Wales's plume and motto, flanked by the initials "A." "A." in

Roman capitals, with the rose, shamrock, and thistle at each corner.

Erected a triumphal arch of a very light and elegant character, composed of several kinds of evergreens, the names of "Albert" and "Alexandra" being made of box leaves and spring flowers. The crown of the arch was surmounted with beautifully executed portraits of the Prince and Princess, painted in oil, surrounded by laurel leaves, the corners having four shields with the letter "A" in gilt, on a red ground, and with flags above and beneath, most tastefully disposed. Altogether it elicited the admiration of all.

ROYAL CAMBRIDGE GALLERY OF ART.

Across the road from the Gallery to the Governor's Green was suspended a garland of flowers, 12 feet in diameter. To the poles either side were emblazoned banners of the Prince and Princess of Wales. The front was festooned with white and red roses and evergreens. Over the door there was a figure of Victory with gilded wings, holding a wreath from which coloured fires were lighted during the evening, and a trophy of British flags looped up by two garlands of white roses. There was also a very handsome decoration, which was very creditable to the taste of the artist.

PORTSMOUTH ROYAL SAILORS' HOME

The Chairman of this noble institution intimated to the superintendent of the wishes of himself and the directors to give a dinner to every Sailor who came into the Home on the auspicious occasion. About 51 Sailors sat down to a substantial fare of roast beef, plum pudding, etc., which they appeared to enjoy. The Home was beautifully illuminated.

DOCKYARD GATE. - THE HARD.

The illumination of the principal Dockyard Gate was unfortunately spoiled by the wind, only a portion of it would remain alight. The illumination itself was tasteful and elaborate in design. The centre consisted of the Prince of Wales' plume, with the motto "Ich Dien," and the letters "A. A." on either side. This was surmounted by a large cable, the coils of which were formed by the arrangement of the jets, and it was surmounted by the British Crown, resting on a cushion. On the extreme outside two anchors surmounted the pillars on either side of the gate, the capitals of which were decorated with jets tastefully arranged. In this illumination the gas was so sea laced that had the wind been in another quarter it would have been perfect in detail and very effective. It was designed in Mr. Wood's office. The other Dockyard Gate was illuminated with appropriate designs.

THE GUNWHARF.

The decorations at H.M. Gunwharf were the subject of general attention and admiration. Over the centre gate was placed in illumination a field-piece and carriage, surmounted by the Prince of Wales' plume, supported on either side by the initials "A. A.," while to the right and left of these, two stars surrounded by rays of swords, would have looked brilliant and produced a very pleasing effect, had the supply of gas been sufficient. Against the middle gate stood the effigies of two men clothed in armour guarding a Chinese Mandarin, above whom floated an Imperial flag, embroidered with golden dragons on a blue silk ground. We understand this beautiful flag was taken from Canton, and that the duplicate is in the possession of her Majesty the Queen. About the upper part of the gate and in the recesses suits of antique armour were arranged. The remainder of the facade was decorated tastefully with evergreens and the flags of England and Denmark.

WISH STREET.

Besides any quantity of flags, streaming from almost every house in the street, the ends of it were marked by two arches - the one opposite Mr. Godwin's, a single arch spanning the roadway, gaily garnished with flowers and evergreens, two royal crowns, similarly decorated, surmounted the whole. Opposite to Dr Miller's a very grand double arch, of gothic structure, supporting two lesser ones, they, in their turn, bearing between them a double transparency, on each side of which were the Prince of Wales's feather at the side of these the initials "A.E." "A.D."

The *tout ensemble* was perfect, either from going out of Wish Street or approaching it from Elm Grove. This arch attracted a vast number of admirers throughout the day and evening, when the transparency was lighted, and the Chinese lanterns also. Dr Miller displayed a transparency of the Danish arms, crowned by the plume of feathers, with the Prince's motto, supported by English flags; at the foot "A. A.," entwined with a true lover's knot. The whole was very effective.

THE POLICE STATIONS.

The chief Police Station at Landport was decorated with 28 flags of different descriptions, stretched from poles on the roof to Colonel Ward's house on one side and to a house in Russell Street on the other. In the evening the front was illuminated with 60 lamps, and a gas illumination with the Prince of Wales' Feathers, the initials "A. A." on each upper corner, the Danish flag on one side and the Union Jack on the other, with the words "May they be Happy."

KINGSTON.

At the early hour of six in the morning the bells of the parish church began to send forth a merry peal. At a subsequent part of the day the church Sunday and day school children were treated by the vicar to a good dinner of beef and pudding previously to their march to Southsea Common. A most unaccountable report was circulated to the effect that all the marriages for this day were to be solemnized gratuitously, and that nearly 100 couples were to be married. The consequence was that at an early hour the parish church became densely filled, in fact, it was crammed, scarcely leaving sufficient space around the altar for those that were to be married, amounting in all to eight couples. Several persons who intended to have been married on that day, owing to the report, were deterred, and put off the ceremony to a more convenient day.

PORTSEA ISLAND UNION HOUSE.

The decorations were of a very simple character, merely consisting of a few flags at the top the building. The whole of the inmates who wished it, after being supplied with an excellent dinner of roast beef and plum pudding, had permission to leave the house to see their friends and join in the public festivities outside. The remainder had a liberal supply of tobacco, snuff, and extra tea issued to them as on a Christmas Day. The principal demonstration was made by the schoolchildren, who, immediately after a good and substantial dinner, were formed in procession, and, preceded by their senior boy, bearing a beautiful silk banner, inscribed "Portsea Island Union" on it, and another which attracted much attention throughout the route, with the following lines:-

> Welcome, Alexandra!
> A million voices welcome thee today,
> A million mothers for thy safety pray.
> A million maiden hearts with thee rejoice;
> And every little child that has a voice
> Sings out, and, still unwearied, sings with pride,
> God bless the Prince, God bless his bride!

They joined the other schools of the district and proceeded to Southsea Common. On their return to the house a most bountiful supply of tea, cake, biscuits, etc. the expense being paid out of the public subscription was served to them in their large dining rooms, and, in the evening, it was intended to give them oranges, nuts, etc., but at their request, as they could eat no more, this part of the treat was postponed until the following day. After singing the National Anthem, with three cheers for the Prince and his bride, they were sent to their beds, after a day of thorough enjoyment. All the inmates who did not go out on liberty were supplied, by the liberality of Mr. J.J. Young, with a glass of good ale to drink "Health, happiness, and long life to the Prince and his Bride."

ROYAL MARINE ARTILERY, FORT CUMBERLAND.

The men belonging to this corps were supplied with a good English dinner, after which a series of athletic games, under the patronage of the Colonel Commandant, took place, and were well contested on the glacis of the fort, the games being continued till night drew on. A huge bonfire was then lighted, and a grand display of fireworks was made, at the conclusion of which the men were regaled a substantial supper, and the celebration of the auspicious marriage was kept up with the greatest decorum and good feeling till midnight. Nor were the families of the married men forgotten on this interesting national occasion.

MISCELLANEOUS FACTS.

One mis-called decoration created general condemnation and disgust. A marine store dealer residing near the foundry evinced his loyalty by painting the most horrible heads and profiles on his window. These consisted of death's heads, demons, comical faces, and countenances full of grimace and idiocy. Above these were written the words, "Heads of all Nations." Underneath these ghastly objects the same loyal subject, thinking to make people laugh at his foolery, painted a huge rosette, around which appeared the motto, "God bless the Prince and Princess, or any other man." The person who placed these figures above his door strangely mistook the character of loyal inhabitants when he believed that they would cause laughter and mirth. Their feeling expressed was one of disgust at his want of loyalty and propriety.

THE ADMIRALTY HOUSE, PORTSMOUTH DOCKYARD.

In the evening Vice-Admiral Sir Michael Seymour, G.C.B., Commander-in-Chief at this port, entertained at dinner the heads of the naval departments; and the Captains of H.M. ships in this port. The Admiral himself, however, was unavoidably absent with Major-General Lord Wm. Paulet having proceeded to Cowes to receive their Royal Highnesses the Prince and Princess of Wales on landing at that port. The Prince recognised both of these distinguished officers, and vey graciously introduced the Princess to them.

ST. JUDE'S CHURCH, PORTSEA.

The clock tower was surmounted by flags placed at each angle. An offer was made to illuminate, but it was declined on account of the possible danger.

On Sunday evening the service was preceded by Mendelsohn's Wedding March and concluded with the Danish anthem, performed by Mr. Reeves, the organist, and during the evening a new version of the English National Anthem was sung with enthusiasm by a large congregation.

A ball, at which about 100 were present, also took place at the Portland Hall, Southsea.

A double night soirée was held at the Society's Hall, which was numerously attended.

The Theatre also proved to be an attraction, and the beautiful drama of Jeanie Deans was put upon the stage. It is admirably adapted, well sustained and most effective.

Mr. Bastable gave away 1,000 buns to the poor children on this occasion, and Mr. Gunnell distributed amongst the Landport poor children 1,100 cakes, bags of biscuits, etc.

The inmates of the alms houses, in connection with King Street chapel, numbering about 20, were provided with an excellent dinner on the wedding day, defrayed by the congregation.

The New Gardens at North End were opened on Tuesday, and attracted a large numbers of spectators. The amusements provided were varied, and included an exhibition of fireworks.

About 400 of the elderly poor and children belonging to the neighbourhood of Broad Street, were entertained with tea, cakes, oranges, and nuts, in a large booth erected in Bath Square. A band of music was in attendance and both old and young enjoyed themselves greatly.

A volunteers' ball was held in the factory dining rooms of H.M. Dockyard, on Tuesday evening. About 250 volunteers and their friends were present. Dancing commenced at ten p.m. and continued until four a.m. Permission for the use of the room was given by Captain H. Broadhead, commanding the steam reserve, in the absence of Rear-Admiral Elliot.

A procession of Foresters belonging to courts in this district formed at the railway station at 9.45, and marched round the principal streets, finishing their route about two o'clock. Three cheers were given for the Queen, and three for the "Prince and Princess." The assemblage then dispersed.

Forty-seven widows connected with Wesley Chapel, Arundel Street, Landport, were regaled with a substantial dinner of good old English fare, kindly provided by Mr. R.E. Davies, draper, Landport. Mr. Davies and family, the Rev. J. Smith, and Mr. F. Burt were also present. After the removal of the cloth the Rev. J. Smith delivered a suitable address, and was followed by Mr. Burt. The society stewards returned thanks on behalf of the widows to Mr. Davies.

PORTSMOUTH RAGGED SCHOOL.

In order that there might be no interference with the chance of these children who frequent the above school earning an honesty penny on the public holiday, which in various ways may be down, this event was resumed for the following day (Wednesday) when they were regaled at their rooms, in Oyster Street, with a substantial tea, after which an interesting panorama was exhibited. A little singing was provided and each child (they numbered 360) on leaving was presented with an orange and a little book suitable to the occasion.

THE VOLUNTEERS.

The new boat house in the Dockyard having been fitted up and tastefully decorated with flags, evergreens, and military devices, the volunteers assembled there after the review to partake of an excellent dinner provided for them by their officers. The bands of the various corps were present, and a large number of spectators occupied the galleries. Major Sturdee occupied the chair, supported by the officers of the different corps. "The health of the Queen" was loyally received, and "the health of the Bride and Bridegroom" enthusiastically drunk. Several other loyal and patriotic toasts were proposed and responded to. During the afternoon the health of Mr. Barford, a Dane (a member of the 5th Hants Rifles), was drunk with enthusiasm.

In acknowledging the toast, he said he wished to return them his thanks for the kindness with which the Princess of Denmark had been received in this country, and for the reception her name had met with in that room. He had the honour to be a "countryman of Denmark," which was a Protestant country like this, and he had no doubt, if England should ever need an ally to "fight for freedom," she would find one in the Danes, who would spill the last drop of their blood to help old England. Soon after this the volunteers resolved themselves into a convivial meeting, and spent a very pleasant afternoon together.

1863 – THE TOWN AND HARBOUR OF PORTSMOUTH.

The construction of the fortifications at Portsmouth has just been resumed so a few further details may not be uninteresting in connection with the general view of the town and harbour which makes up our illustration.

The earliest account we have of the fortifications is that left by Leland, who visited Portsmouth about the year 1540 in whose "Itinerary," which he dedicated to

Henry VIII., we find that the towers at the harbours mouth were "began in the time of Edward IV., and set forward in building by Richard III.; and Henry VII. ended them, at the procuration of the Bishop of Winchester." From this it appears that, as well as the round tower now standing at Portsmouth, there was also another where Blockhouse Fort now stands. From those towers, Leland says, "there was a mighty chaine of yron, to draw from tower to tower."

The other part of the fortifications at this time, as it appears from the same author, "was a mud waulle armed with timbre with a ditch without." This was the state of the fortifications in the reign of Henry VIII., as it seems to have been in 1552, when Edward VI. visited the place who, in a letter to his friend, Barnaby Fitzpatrick, complains, that the bulwarks were "ill favoured, ill flanked, and set in unmete places." But, says another ancient author (Blount) "in our tyme, Queen Elizabeth, at great expense, fortified it so stronglee with new works that nothing is wanting to make it a place of greater strengthe; some of the garrison mount guarde day and night at the gates, others the steple, who by stroke of a bell giveth notice what number of horse and foot are approaching, and by a flag which way they come."

In the reign of Charles II., the new work of Elizabeth underwent some alteration, and in that of James II., a line of covered batteries took the place of the fortifications, where in Leland's time "the town was murrod a forough length with a mud waulle," i.e., from the point gates to the "great tourre;" and under William III., the whole was completed nearly as it now is. Very soon after these fortifications were finished, that part which faces the north was in measure rendered useless, in consequence of buildings having been erected on what was before furze common and common fields, then and for many years after called Portsmouth Common, but now the town of Portsea. In consequence of this, and for the security of the Dockyard, in the year 1750 the Government purchased the lands on which are the present Portsea lines, and in 1770 began to erect them; they were not, however, fully completed until 1809.

The introduction of rifled ordnance utterly nullified the confined area of all then existing lines of defence surrounding fortified positions such as Portsmouth Dockyard and arsenal, and the lines had, therefore, to be considerably extended, so as to increase the distance between the points of attack and defence. In the instance of Portsmouth, the northern and southern extremities of its proposed lines of defence (the central fort on Portsdown Hill and the marine forts on the Noman and Horse Shoals) form parts of a nearly circular defensive line, of about nine miles in diameter, between the points named. Portsdown may be considered as commanding all approaches to the port from landward (supposing that an enemy may have effected a landing on any adjacent part of the coast), and the Noman and Horse Forts, through the narrow channel by the Warner Light, from sea; supposing, also, in the latter instance, that the Needles Channel is rendered impassable to any iron fleet.

The position of Portsdown is nearly seven miles in extent, and runs nearly parallel with the line of coast, or the anchorage of Spithead, and in its centre rises to a height of 460 ft. above Ordnance level, and is here at a distance of about 5,000 yards from Portsmouth Dockyard, while the large powder magazines at Tipnor, and the shipping moored in the upper part of the harbour, lie at its very base. The vast importance of such a position and the imperative necessity for including it in the general plan for the port's defence are thus evident; and, although the extent of the plan, including Portsdown, somewhat staggered even Sir John Burgoyne, yet that able officer, in his evidence before the Defence Commission, admitted freely that the defence of the port of Portsmouth would be imperfect without it, and the fortification of Portsdown was therefore decided upon, and has been completed in its first stage.

It is being crowned with seven forts—Purbrook, Farlington, and Crookhorn at its eastern extremity, Wallington at its western, and Widley, Southwick, and Nelson intermediately along its crest, These forts are being constructed on an exceedingly simple plan, being somewhat of horseshoe form, with the toe of the shoe pointing inland and the heel of the shoe towards the sea or Portsmouth, but of strong trace and prodigious strength, the base lines of their figures abutting on a common base line along the hill's crest.

At the east end of the hill the works are the least forward of any, but here may be seen the unusually formidable nature of the "trace." It is commanded by three works—Farlington, Crookhorn, and Purbrook. All three have yet proceeded in their construction but little beyond their formation of parapet and ditch and general outline. Their height reaches 300 ft. above Ordnance level, Farlington commands the eastern point of Portsdown, and will mount eighteen of the heaviest guns on its terre-plein, with mortar batteries in the angles of its surrounding ditches, each battery mounting three mortars. A sunken gallery communicates with Crookhorn, which will mount sixteen guns on its terre-plein, with six guns in the angles of its ditch. A continuation of the same sunken gallery leads from Crookhorn to the main work at this eastern end of Portsdown—Purbrook —which will mount twenty-one guns on its terre-plein, nine guns in caponnieres in the ditch, and three mortars in the ditch's west angle. It has a nearly straight face of 240 ft., looking inland; the open gorge being opposite the west side of Langstone Harbour and the eastern side of Portsmouth Harbour.

The ditches surrounding the three works vary in depth, according to their position, from 35 ft. to 50 ft. Sunken galleries from the interior of the works communicate with the mortar batteries and caponnieres in the ditches. The walls of the ditches themselves are supported in their vertical formation by chalk and brick masonry; and these formidable outer obstructions are carried out generally in the entire line of works along the hill's crest. At Wallington, the fort which commands all approaches to Portsdown at its western end, the arrangements are somewhat different, owing to its position, but continue of the same comprehensive and formidable nature. It will mount fifty-six guns on its terre-plein, four of them being in casemates at the angles. Capponieres project into the ditch, mounting three guns each at each angle, and have mortar batteries in the rear. Sunken galleries communicate between the enceinte of the work, the caponnieres, the mortar batteries, and an advanced covered way on the right shoulder, which mounts three guns, sweeping the line of ditch. It stands at an elevation of 140 ft. above Ordnance level, has a right front of 520 ft., a left front of 326 ft., a right flank of 437 ft., and a left flank of 383 ft. Its gorge is as yet open, like the rest of the Portsdown forts, and looks towards the seacoast.

Although not, strictly speaking, belonging to the line of Portsdown forts, still it must be considered a "Portsdown" fort, as, erected on the low land at about a mile distant from Fort Wallington, and nearer the line of seacoast, stands Fort Fareham, the village of Fareham, which stands at the uppermost head of Portsmouth Harbour, being situated between the two forts. Any attack upon the position of Portsdown from the westward must include Fort Fareham, which must therefore be considered conjointly with the seven hill forts already noticed. It is a work of more than ordinary pretensions. Like the forts on Portsdown, it may generally be described as of horseshoe shape, with five faces of 224 ft., 176 ft., 313 ft., 364 ft., and 400 ft., respectively. It will mount fifty guns on its terre-plein, double Haxo casemates being at each angle. The terre-plein is supported on massive brickwork arches, which give the necessary accommodation for the garrison, and the whole work will have an elevation of 36ft. over the surrounding country, its front being well covered with earthwork. The ditch encompassing the fort is 15 ft. in depth, 119 ft. in width at the top, revetted in brickwork, and with 9 ft. of water.

Portsdown is thus the base of a great polygon of works designed and now being carried into execution for the defence of Portsmouth. South of Portsdown is the anchorage of Spithead, and the proposed sites of the marine forts which are to defend Spithead and Portsmouth from the sea.

While Portsmouth is being thus engirdled with a vast net of fortifications, it is impossible not to acknowledge, on examining the general plan, that in the channel approach from the sea stands the "Achilles heel" of the whole plan. Only five hours' steaming from the greatest military port of another country, there is not at present existing one single obstacle to a hostile squadron steaming into Spithead whenever it may choose, and bombarding and destroying Portsmouth Dockyard, its shipping, and its arsenals at pleasure.

The fortifications for defending Portsmouth from an attack from the sea are old works which would fall to the ground from the concussion of any guns fired from their parapets of sufficient calibre to inflict damage on an iron clad fleet. To show the truth and importance of this statement, it is here necessary to observe that the mouth of Portsmouth Harbour, Southsea Castle, and Fort Moncton form a triangle of which Spithead is the base, with Portsmouth Harbour at the apex, and that the guns at these three points are the only present obstacles to the entrance of an enemy's fleet from the sea.

Southsea Castle is a very old stone-built work, partially covered with earth on its flanks, and is in such a dilapidated state that not a gun has been allowed to be fired from its walls for months past, not even for blank practice. The front face of Fort Moncton, which faces Spithead, and is supposed to crossfire with Southsea Castle, is the weakest part of the work, and would certainly not bear the concussion from the fire of heavy ordnance. In these two points, therefore, at the base of the triangle, there are at present no existing means for the defence of Portsmouth from a sea attack.

The Government plans for the defence of Spithead from a sea attack consist of the three marine forts of the Horse, Noman, and Sturbridge, all three to be constructed on shoals abutting upon the narrow, deep waterways of Spithead. The two first named will lie south of Spithead and be the first obstacles to the entrance of a hostile fleet from the Channel. The Sturbridge (built on the Sturbridge shoal, off Ryde, Isle of Wight) can only be of service after a fleet has forced its way into Spithead, and therefore its use under any circumstances would be very problematical. From its position, even if it missed an enemy's ship, it must strike a friend, its shots in each case would plump either into the town of Ryde or Fort Moncton. It is situated at 4,500 yards distance from the Noman and Horse forts and is about 6,800 yards from the Dockyard. It stands, in fact, or rather is intended to stand, in the centre of the ground into which an enemy's fleet must never be allowed to enter, and by its fire would injure its friends more than its enemies. So well is the futility of this proposed fort understood, that Captain Tyler, of the Royal Engineers, has not hesitated to condemn it in letters to the public press, and proposed in lieu to erect a fort on the Warner Rock, outside the Noman and Horse forts. The three forts would then form a perfect triangle, with the Warner as the apex and in advance, and if constructed and armed as contemplated no iron ship should ever swim past them.

All parties appear now to agree the expediency of constructing these marine forts, provided they are built to carry guns of sufficient power to smash in the sides of any iron ship that may come between them. The Government plans have, however, been severely criticised from the date of the first report of the Royal Defence Commission, and various plans have been submitted, some on evidence before the Commission, and others from non-official sources, either to prevent an enemy from ever entering Spithead at all, or for rendering it so hot after he had got there that he would be glad to quit it again.

Our Illustration shows many of the most noteworthy features of the town. Beginning on the left of the picture, the most prominent object in the foreground is the Nelson obelisk, erected to the memory of the great national naval hero. Then comes the Church of St. Jude, a massive and noble structure, the elegant spire of which towers high above the surrounding mansions. St. Pauls Church, a little further right, is considered one of the finest specimens of Gothic architecture in the kingdom. It was opened for public worship in 1822, having been erected, under the New Church Act, at an expense of £16,000.

The Military Hospital is fitted with every comfort for the sick soldier; and near this are workshops of the Ordnance department, to which belongs the superintendence of all the castles and fortifications in the south-west district of England. The Dockyard covers an area upwards of 118 acres and has been enlarged at various times as the necessities of the public service required. In the masthouse the making of ships' masts, yards, bowsprits, &c., is performed.

Haslar Hospital was projected, in 1742, by the Earl of Sandwich, and was sixteen years in erecting. It contains accommodation for about 2,000 patients. The Royal Clarence Victualling Yard contains storehouses of immense size, used as depositories of bread, beef, pork, and other articles of food, as well as rum, wine, clothing, &c., for the Navy. It covers a large area of ground and is separated from all other buildings by substantial walls.

In the middle of the view is the ancient castle called Portchester, and near it the new railway station. In the foreground is Portsdown Hill, from which our sketch is taken, and on which the operations in connection with the erection of the new fortifications are being busily carried on. From the hill, which is about five miles from Portsmouth, on the road to London, a magnificent prospect is obtained, extending down the English Channel and nearly forty miles over the New Forest on the west; on the east, over the South Downs in Sussex; on the north, over fine woodland country; while on the south the islands of Portsea and Hayling, with Portsmouth and Langstone harbours, Spithead, and the Isle of Wight on the other side of the Solent, complete the view.

Portsdown Hill has recently been purchased for the erection of the new inland fortifications described above, one of the most forward of which is Fort Nelson, on the extreme right of the Engraving.

Sturbridge Sea Fort a Day Before Building Work was Stopped

Victorian Portsmouth – 1860-1869

Victorian Portsmouth – 1860-1869

1863 – THE SPITHEAD FORTS.

The marine forts at Spithead the Horse, Noman, and Sturbrid111ge, present the same appearance as yet that they have done through the winter. In each instance a score of wooden piles has been driven into the shoal, with a huge iron cylindrical pile in the centre, and the whole covered by a wooden staging, on which is erected a timber cabin, with a temporary lighthouse attached, to which someone from the staff of the contractor for the construction of the forts (Mr. Leather) is occasionally sent to trim his lamps and keep watch that no drift runs foul of the staging.

In Stokes Bay, a substantial pier has been run out by the contractor, and fitted with the necessary cranes and purchases for receiving and discharging heavy weights, while, at a convenient distance from the shore and the pier, a village of workshops has sprung up. Looking, therefore, at the preparations made by the contractor, the progress already made with the forts, and the penalties which would be incurred by their abandonment, there cannot be a doubt that when the question comes before the House of Commons it will be decided by a large majority to proceed with the two outer forts, the "Noman," and "Horse," whatever may be otherwise decided upon with regard the "Sturbridge," off Ryde.

While the question of marine forts for Spithead remains thus undecided and favourable weather for the construction of their foundations is being lost, the construction of new batteries, flanking the position of the forts on the Isle of Wight shore, and the strengthening of old batteries in similar position on the Portsmouth shore, is being rapidly proceeded with by the Royal Engineers. Preparations have been nearly completed by the erection of temporary piers on the sea beach and deposit of materials for strengthening the flanks and altogether altering the nature of the defences opposite the Spit buoy, now occupied by Southsea Castle.

On the island shore, the earthworks of a large open redan at Popful Point are being rapidly developed. Popful Point is the most projecting portion of the Puckpool Estate, adjoining St. Clare, where the Prince and Princess Louis of Hesse spent their honeymoon. To obtain possession of the piece of land on which to erect the battery, it has been necessary to purchase the whole of the estate and residence. The work is being constructed for mounting guns of great calibre and range, and will probably have mortar batteries at its angles.

Funeral of William Keeler

1863 – PRINCE ALFRED AT A SAILOR'S FUNERAL.

William Keeler, a seaman gunner, belonging to her Majesty's steam corvette *Racoon*, of which Prince Alfred is one of the Lieutenants, lately fell from the maintop and was killed on the spot, his skull having been fractured. The ship reached Portsmouth on Monday, the 3rd inst., and it was decided by the Captain, in accordance with the wish of the ship's company, that the body of the deceased should be interred in the Portsmouth Cemetery.

The funeral procession started from the Dockyard at two p.m., in the following order:—A firing party of two non-commissioned officers and twelve rank and file of the Royal Marines; then the band of the *Racoon*, twelve in number; a drummer of the Royal Marines; the coffin containing remains of the deceased, surmounted by the union jack, and on the carriage of a field-piece drawn by twenty seamen of the *Racoon*; then the seamen of the ship, ninety in number, all attired in clean white drill frocks and trousers; then Captain Count Gleichon and the whole of the officers, with the exception of Prince Alfred and the First lieutenant, H.W. Miller; then a mourning coach conveying the relatives of the deceased.

On arriving at the cemetery, the procession was joined by Prince Alfred, who had preceded the cortege in a cab, accompanied by Major Cowell. His Royal Highness was attired in undress uniform of a Lieutenant. The corpse was conveyed into the cemetery chapel, and by the grave the burial service of the Church of England was performed by the Rev. William Lake Onslow, A.M., Chaplain of the *Racoon*, assisted by the Rev. C.W. Bohr, Vicar of Redingham, Norfolk. Three volleys were fired over the grave by the firing party of the Royal Marines, and the procession then re-formed and returned to the Dockyard.

When the funeral ceremony was concluded, his Royal Highness, in company with Major Cowell and the Rev. Mr. Onslow, left the cemetery in a cab for the railway terminus.

1863 – MONUMENT TO ADMIRAL SIR CHARLES NAPIER.

A handsome monumental column has just been erected in the centre of Portsmouth, by seamen and marines, to the memory of the late Admiral Sir Charles Napier.

Monument to Admiral Sir Charles Napier

1863 – VISIT OF PRINCE & PRINCESS LOUIS OF HESSE TO THE DOCKYARD.

The Prince Louis of Hesse and Princess Alice of Hesse, accompanied by Prince Alfred and the Princess Helena, paid a visit the Dockyard and to H.M.S. *Victory*, on Wednesday afternoon. Her Majesty's yacht *Fairy* arrived alongside the Dockyard from Osborne shortly before 5 p.m. and the Royal party, disembarking, were received by Vice-Admiral Sir Michael Seymour, G.C.B., and Rear-Admiral Superintendent

The Garrison Church and Font

George Elliot. They first visited the *Royal Sovereign* turret ship, and evinced great interest in their inspection of the work in construction of the turrets both on and between decks. A sectional model of the pilot house was examined with much attention. The steam basin, where the *Hector* iron frigate is fitting, and the basement floor of the steam factory were next visited. Thence the Royal party proceeded to the armour plate workshop, where the processes of heating, bending, drilling, and planing the plates for the *Royal Sovereign* was explained by Rear-Admiral Elliot and the officers in attendance.

The *Royal Alfred*, a frigate, now waiting for her iron casing on No. 1 slipway, was next inspected. Passing along the line of building sheds on which stand the unfinished wooden ships *Dryad*, *Harlequin*, and *Helicon*, their Royal Highnesses crossed No. 10 dock, in which the *Emerald* was receiving a four-bladed screw, and, after a cursory look at the *Black Prince* lying alongside the north jetty, went on board the *Defence*, an iron frigate, lying alongside the jetty adjoining the *Black Prince*.

After going over the ship on deck and below, their Royal Highnesses visited the *Victory*, and were received with the usual honours. They thence embarked in the *Fairy*, and left on their return to Osborne.

1863 – THE GARRISON CHURCH AND FONT.

1863 – WORK IN PORTSMOUTH DOCKYARD.

Mr. J. Stansfeld, M.P., Junior Lord of the Admiralty, has lately been daily engaged at Portsmouth Dockyard in investigating the Dockyard system of account keeping and the mode of carrying out work in the different departments of the yard. The system of keeping the accounts of the yard may certainly be very much simplified, and there is no doubt Mr. Stansfeld will, in the end, have reason to be satisfied with the reforms he may affect. He will, however, be much less at home in dealing with the great question of labour in the yard. It certainly is a matter of surprise to those who frequently visit our great national dockyards that so little work is done in them. The visitor hears thousands of persons employed, and yet sees no work executed to be compared with what he would expect in a private yard of the same magnitude.

This is precisely the situation present in Portsmouth Dockyard. Repairs are being made (a work taken in hand certainly not a day too soon), tramways laid down, sheds, stores, and workshops cleansed and whitewashed, ornamental grass plots formed, trees planted, and hideous old "figure heads" stuck up in different parts of the yard. There are men at work on the *Royal Sovereign* certainly, but she is not more than three parts completed, and thirty-five or more hands have been taken off her during the past week, on the plea that employment cannot be found for them on board. There is a delay in the delivery of the armour plates for her turrets, the officials say, and therefore the men are sent from her to other work.

However, the case may lie between the Admiralty officials and the contractors, certain it is that now, instead of having the *Royal Sovereign* afloat by Christmas, as was looked forward to as a certainty a month or two back, that event is postponed until March next. It is impossible to look at the *Royal Sovereign* without coming to the conclusion that, while the vast resources and labour of Portsmouth yard have been long employed, and are still employed, in simply converting a broadside into a turret ship, Mr. Laird's yard at Birkenhead—a comparatively petty establishment—turned out three new turret ships. Can Mr. Stansfeld grapple with this labour question satisfactorily? If he deals with it on the broad basis of an entire reform of the whole system he may achieve, possibly, a satisfactory result; but if he has only power to deal with it on the ground of "retrenchment" he will fail utterly, as others have failed before him.

The Dockyard "system," like the Admiralty system, is rotten to the core, and to effect any beneficial reform the existing state of things must be entirely swept away and a new one substituted. It is admitted now by all parties, except among those personally interested, that no permanent reform or good of any kind can be affected with the Board of Admiralty until it ceases to be a political board, closely connected with the Ministry of the day. A similar radical change must take place in our Dockyards before any permanent good in them can be affected. Take the shipwrights as an example of the employed skilled labour of the yards. A man receives 4s. 6d. per day; he works in a "gang" of twenty, superintended by a "leading hand," who has over him an "inspector," a "foreman" being over all. Now, one man in this twenty may not earn more than 3s. per day, while the man working next to him may earn 6s., yet both are paid alike. A discretionary power of measuring work is vested in the Master Shipwright, but is never exorcised except when extra hands are placed on a ship and the work is hurried. In such cases, if a man is found to have shirked his work, he is mulcted in his pay according to the established scale of prices. It is needless to say that if a man is found to have done more than his required quantity of work, he is not paid the extra money for it. It certainly seems that here a system of payment according to the work done could be introduced with advantage. It might be so, but not under the present "system." The "leading hand," who has the most immediate charge of the gang of twenty men, is but one of themselves, and receives only 6d. per day over the pay of the men under him.

Another aspect from which the employment of labour in our yards may be viewed is in the repairs of ships in commission, say the Channel Fleet. The fleet, or a part, as is at present the case, arrives at Spithead, and every ship requires repairs of some kind or other which must be carried out by the labourers at the yard. Two, perhaps, of the ships go into harbour, and the necessary work goes on without any loss of time beyond what "routine" and "system" impose. The ships at Spithead must remain there, for the moorings in the harbour are taken up by harbour ships or useless hulks, and therefore there is no room for ships that have come in from sea wanting repairs, however urgently their services may be required, even if an enemy were out in the channel.

All the ships, however, must be repaired, and so men and materials are sent off to Spithead. The amount of daily work which can be done by a couple of hundred workmen under such circumstances is very small indeed, as every Commander of a ship that has lain at Spithead "under repairs" can well remember, to his infinite disgust.

When a war comes upon us with any great naval Power, our "heads of departments" say we should clear off all the old craft up the harbour, even if we shoved them in the mud, and remove the present craft off the Dockyard moorings higher up, so that the moorings off the yard would be available for a dozen ships to come into from sea and lie at during their repairs when not in dock. Now, why should not this be done in times of peace? Why must we wait until war "comes upon us" to provide the necessary means for the due reception our ships in harbour on coming in suddenly from sea for repairs or refit? Why, in fact, should we continue squandering many thousands annually in this one item alone when the remedy is so obvious? Ships and shipwrights have referred to thus in connection with Mr. Stanfeld's visit to Portsmouth yard simply because they are naturally the most prominent features in our Dockyards; but there is no single department in those establishments but what cries out loudly for reform.

1863 – THE CHESAPEAKE MEMORIAL.

We have engraved a view of the Memorial column which has been erected on the Clarence Esplanade by Vice-Admiral Sir J. Hope, K.C.B., and the officers and ship's company of the *Chesapeake*. The memorial consists of a column, of a free Romanesque treatment, with plinth and sub-plinth resting on a pedestal, the summit being ornamented with a naval crown of gilt bronze, elevated on a tripod, also of bronze. The height of the monument, from the top of the raised mound to the summit of the crown, is 25 feet. The sculptured capital, the base and band of the column, the sub-plinth, and the die of the pedestal and the step, are of Portland stone. The base of the tripod and the cornice and plinth to the pedestal are of the grey Forest of Dean stone. The shaft of the column is in red Aberdeen granite, polished, and the plinth is of grey granite, also polished. The plinth has on its representation in bronze of the attack on the Taku forts. The sculptor who executed this portion of the

The Chesapeake Memorial

work was Mr. T. Phyffers. The north face of the pedestal bears the following inscription:-

In memory of their comrades
Who fell in battle,
Or died from disease and accident,
During an eventful commission of four years,
This column was raised
By
Vice-Admiral Sir James Hope, K.C.B,
The Captain, Officers, and Ship's Company
Of
H.M.S. Chesapeake."
1862.

The central band on the column is of Portland stone, with the word "Chesapeake," in ornamental letters, carved thereon; and on the moulded base of Portland stone standing on the plinth, are the words, Pelho, Calcutta, Jeddah, and Pekin, raised on each face.

The stonework was executed by Mr. G.P. White, of London, from the design and under the superintendence of Messrs. Wilson & Nichol, architects.

1863 – DEFENCES OF THE ISLE OF WIGHT.

It will be in the recollection of our readers that we published some time back, a series of Illustrations of the fortifications in course of construction for the defence of Portsmouth Dockyard, accompanied by ample descriptive particulars of these extensive works. To render this account more complete, we this week publish some Engravings of the fortifications now in progress at the back of the Isle of Wight, which are designed to cover the Portsmouth approaches, and are in strict accordance with the recommendation of the commission appointed to consider the defences of the United Kingdom.

The commissioners were of opinion that it was of the utmost importance that the necessary measures should be taken; firstly, for the defence of the Needles passage; and, secondly, to prevent an enemy obtaining a footing upon the Isle of Wight, as it was evident that in the event of either points being left unprotected our anchorages in the Solent and at Spithead could be rendered untenable. After recommending the construction of certain batteries to provide for the defence of those parts of the island between Cliff End and the Needles, and others in the neighbourhood of Brook and Brixton, and at Atherfield Point, the report proceeds to speak of the works necessary to be constructed at the most vulnerable point of all—namely, Sandown Bay.

"This," the commissioners say, "affords the best and, indeed, the only good landing place for an enemy on the whole of that part of the island between the Needles and Spithead to the southward. The beach here, which is sandy and generally clear of rocks, is about 2,000 yards in extent, 600 yards of which is available for landing at all times of the tide, whilst there are five fathoms at low water within 550 yards of the shore. There is in existence for the protection of this bay an old bastioned fort, which is now very much out of repair, and is only provided with a stone parapet four feet thick. We recommend that a new permanent work, secure against a *coup-de-main*, should be substituted for this, and that batteries, secured by keeps in their rear, should be placed, one

The South-Eastern Defence of the Isle of Wight at Sandown Bay to Cover Portsmouth Approaches

on the rising ground near Yaverland, another on a projecting point near Languard, and a third at a point below Sandown Barracks, so as to flank the beach. It is advisable that the three latter works should be constructed before any steps are taken towards the removal of the old fort in the centre of the bay, which we consider should meanwhile be made available to afford some protection to this portion of the coast, by providing it with an earthen parapet armed with heavy guns bearing to seaward; on each side of the work should be placed permanent batteries of about five guns each, bearing on the offing and flanking the beach. The works at the eastern side of the bay would, however, be subject to be taken in reverse from Bembridge Down, if a small force of the enemy succeeded in landing at White Cliff Bay; it is therefore necessary to occupy the summit of the down by tower which would also be of considerable value to cut off the access of any force which might have gained a footing on the shore of the peninsula, between Brading Harbour and White Cliff Bay."

1864 – EASTNEY BARRACKS AND THE EXTENSION OF PORTSMOUTH DOCKYARD.

In the House of Commons on Monday night, Colonel Barttelot rose to call attention to the situation of the new Marine Artillery Barracks at Eastney. These barracks were erected in the very eye of the Channel, and no ship going into Portsmouth harbour to attack Portsmouth but must fire into them. There could have been no communication between the Admiralty and the Defence Commission in designing these barracks. They were in a most untenable position. It might be said that this was the only spot where the Marine Artillery could practise the large guns, but the Admiralty might have got a better site inland, where the soldiers and their wives and children who were to lodge in the barracks would have been safe. They were close to the shore, and between two small forts, which were bombproof. But the barracks were three stories high; they were not bombproof; and if shot or shell were fired at them, they would not be tenable for a quarter of an hour. He would admit that the barracks were built on a very good plan, but the Admiralty

View from Yaverland Fort

ought to have taken the trouble to secure a sufficient space around them for their defence.

Public houses and other dwellings were, however, allowed to be built close up to the barracks. The noble Lord at the head of the Government had made himself responsible for the fortifications at Portsmouth, and it was his bounden duty to see that all the works for the defence of the port were in harmony and concert with each other.

Lord C. Paget said that the barracks were placed on the best site that the Government could procure for the purpose which they had in view. One weighty reason which had influenced the site was that the barracks were close to the sea and had a very good range for heavy guns. It was necessary that the young Marine Artillerymen, who were constantly practising at this range, should reside in the neighbourhood of their guns. Another reason which influenced the site was that the Admiralty obtained it at very little expense. The barracks were close to Fort Cumberland, and formed a chain of defence from that fort to Southsea Castle, so as to occupy the whole of the beach. The barracks had a very strong breast work in front, and all round the rear was a crenelated wall, so that they were capable of a very creditable defence. It would not be occupied by any very great number of men in time of war, as marine artillerymen generally embarked for distant service.

The barracks were, in fact, considered a place for the education of young recruits in time of peace. They were certainly exposed at present, but, when the Spithead Forts were completed, the Admiralty trusted that Spithead would be pretty well defended, and that the works within Spithead would be comparatively safe. Then the Hon. and gallant gentleman said these barracks were surrounded by public houses. Unfortunately, that was true, but all our barracks were equally surrounded by public houses. Build them where they might, there was no escaping the evil. He wished they could put a stop to it.

Sir F. Smith expected to hear a better defence than had been made by the noble Lord. In the whole course of his military experience, he had never found a barrack worse situated. (Hear, hear.) It was said it was a link in the defence, but it was a link of sand. A heavy weight striking that barrack would carry all before it. It could not stand for a minute before the broadside of a man of war. Let it not be called a defence then. His Hon. and gallant friend stated that there could have been no communication between the Admiralty and the War Department on the subject. But if that were so, and if there had been no consultation with the Defence Commission, it was a most flagrant instance of neglect. (Hear, Hear). If considered as a defensive work it was one of a most discreditable character; and if it was not a defensive work then it was placed in the wrong position, and was a waste of public money. (Hear, Hear). He believed the total amount was to be 167,801l. But what he most found fault with was that those who had devised this plan had placed the officers under a bombproof building (Lord C. Paget. - That is only partly the case), while the troops were put into that pack of cards house.

Mr. Whitbread thought the fort on the Horseshoe Sand had been left out of sight by the gallant officer. Did any officer suppose it would be an agreeable position for any vessel to lie near that fort for the purpose of shelling the barracks? The barracks were built, in the first place, because the site was an eligible one, and, secondly, because it would afford great facilities for practice in gunnery. The gallant officer was mistaken in supposing that the Admiralty had not communicated with the authorities at the War Office.

Lord C. Paget said the gallant officer ought to have known better than to talk of the officers being placed in a bombproof building while the men were exposed in the barracks. There was the full complement of officers with the men.

Sir F. Smith said he went upon the estimate.

Captain Jervis asked what was the good of having an unprotected barrack between the two forts. The noble Lord said they had got merely recruits, women and children there. (Lord C. Paget explained that what he meant was that, in time of war, they would probably have but a small number of Marine Artillery there. They would go on shipboard.) And leave their wives and children behind. The great object should be to have the barracks out of range of shot.

Colonel North said when he had inquired who were to defend the fortresses which they had constructed, he was told the Volunteers and Militia. But the volunteers were never intended to man these forts, except when the country was invaded. There they were, night after night, voting vast sums of money, and now it appeared that instead of men for the defence they were to have women and children.

Lord C. Paget said the barracks were not for the artillery, but for the Marine Artillery in time of peace. If there was a war tomorrow the probability would be that every able-bodied man in the Marine Artillery would be on shipboard.

Colonel Dickson asked whether they were to understand that they were to lay out these enormous sums on barracks as to which in time of war, when the Marine Artillery were on shipboard, it did not matter a jot whether they were to be blown in pieces or not.

Mr. Lindsay wanted to know whether this 7,500l. was to be expended on the Pesthouse fields, and if so, was it to be done by way of preparing for the extension of the Portsmouth Dockyard. He was not aware that the House had sanctioned any extension of that Dockyard.

Lord C. Paget said the 7,500l. was to be expended partly on the Pesthouse fields. The Portsmouth Dockyard was extremely confined. There were piles of timber in the Dockyard which they wanted room for elsewhere. The War Office had given the Admiralty a fine site which would be available not only for timber but for a naval barrack, and also, perhaps, for the extension of the basin and dock accommodation.

Captain Jervis wanted to know how much money had been spent on those barracks, and how much on the officer's quarters.

Lord C. Paget replied that the total estimate for the work was 167,000l., the amount already voted was 67,000l., and the gross sum already expended on it was 56,000l. The sum taken for the present year was 30,000l., and the further estimate for completing the work was 73,000l. He could not at the present moment say what were the particular sums out of that amount to be expended on the officers' quarters and on Fort Cumberland.

Colonel Barttelot inquired, in the event of the Marine Artillery now in Fort Cumberland going into ships, what officers and men would then garrison that fort.

Lord C. Paget said that in the event of such an improbable matter as the bombardment of Spithead, Fort Cumberland would be garrisoned, in the absence of the Marine Artillery, by the Militia.

In reply to Sir F. Smith, Mr. Childers said that it would be impossible to stop the works now, which were completed to a considerable extent, without the loss of all the money expended upon them under the sanction of the House during the last three years.

Lord C. Hamilton wished to know whether, supposing it to be inexpedient to alter the plan of the officers' and men's quarters, as far as it had gone, there was not yet time to locate the women's and children's quarters in a place not so very dangerous.

Mr. Childers presumed that the noble Lord would not propose that the women and children should be placed in a different spot from the place where their husbands and fathers were located.

Colonel Barttelot said that he should have divided the Committee against the item if he had seen the barracks sooner. The officers' quarters were unroofed.

Sir F. Smith noticed that the former estimate for constructing additional barrack accommodation at Plymouth was 76,600l., and in the present estimates the sum of 80,000l., was put down for their further extension and completion. He thought that some explanation was necessary on this point. It was deceiving the House to bring forward a supplementary estimate larger than the one originally proposed.

Lord C. Paget observed that every day, improvements were being made in the construction of barracks for the army, navy, and Marines, by means of additional ventilation and in other ways. Again, the Marines had been increased from 15,000 to 18,000 men, and consequently, additional barrack accommodation was required for them. At Chatham, for instance, the barracks had been increased, and in order to furnish additional barrack accommodation it was sometimes necessary to throw down existing buildings.

Sir F. Smith thought the noble Lord's explanation quite satisfactory.

1864 – CHRISTMAS TREAT TO RAGGED SCHOOL CHILDREN.

The Sunday scholars at the Portsea Free Ragged Schools have not been forgotten this festive season. It is undoubtedly the case that in the homes of many of these children there is an absence of that enjoyment which most of us look for at Christmas. The ladies and gentlemen who devote their time to teaching those children very generously determined that they should have a Christmas entertainment, and subscribing liberally themselves, and obtaining the aid of friends, they were enabled to give the children a treat on Monday afternoon, which will not be soon forgotten by those who participated in it. Upwards of 100 boys and girls were provided with a bountiful supply of tea and cake in the lower school, which we need scarcely say full justice was done. The teachers and visitors waited upon the children, and were most assiduous in ministering to their wants. After tea the children sang several of their songs in a very spirited manner. They then proceeded to the upper school, which presented a very gay appearance, being hung with flags, and tastefully decorated with evergreens, &c. Two magic lanterns with a large number of slides, which had been lent for the occasion, were exhibited, and afforded much amusement.

Great praise is due to Commander Vine, who not only lent the flags and sailors to hang them, but was present with his galvanic battery, and afforded all who would venture a slight sensation in the shape of an electric shock. Among the visitors were the Revds. T.D. Platt and J.B. Wilkinson, Major Roberts, &c., &c.

After the children had enjoyed a very pleasant evening, they sang the hymn "Jesus meek and gentle;" the Rev. Mr. Wilkinson pronounced the benediction, and the juveniles departed to their homes, with happy hearts and joyous faces, highly delighted with the entertainment which had been so kindly and considerately provided for them.

1864 – OPENING OF THE NEW CIRCUS AT LANDPORT.

On Wednesday evening this edifice, which is situate in Surrey Street, was opened for Divine service. The new circus has a frontage in Surrey Street of 66 feet and a depth of 70 feet, with an additional building at the back about 24 feet by 19 feet, containing vestry, gallery, &c., and connected with the building by a large elliptical arched opening. The internal height of the building is 40 feet in the centre; it is divided longitudinally into three spaces by two rows of cast iron columns which support the galleries, (which are very high) and take part of the weight of the roof. There is a gallery at each side and at the end nearest to Surrey Street, besides the singers' gallery, at the opposite end, already referred to.

The ventilation has been carefully attended to, the ceilings over the side galleries being filled with ornamental perforated openings. The centre space is covered with a ceiling at a higher level than those over the galleries, with horizontal glazed panels for the admission of light. Provision for ventilation has also been made in the centre ceiling.

There are three entrances from Surrey Street to the ground floor, opening into a spacious lobby, and two separate entrances from the same street to the galleries, with separate staircases. There are two entrances at the back to the ground floor, and one to the galleries from Church Path.

The principal front has kiln brick facings with Bath stone quoins and Portland cement dressings. The openings have semi-circular heads with arches in gauged brickwork. The whole is surmounted with an ornamental cornice, the central portion of the elevation having a pediment following the lines of the roof. The ground floor will seat nearly 900 persons, and the galleries about 900 more. The seats are open benches of deal, stained and varnished, with sloping seat and back.

The schoolroom, which adjoins the main building and communicates therewith, has a frontage to Surrey Street of 28 feet by a depth of 68 feet, and is capable of holding some 600 children. The style of the church is Italian, the architect is B. Tabberer, Esq., of 10, Basinghall Street, City, and the contractor, Mr. T. Backhurst, of Landport. The cost of the land, building, &c., was nearly £4,000, of which sum the Rev. J. Martin, the minister, has subscribed £1,000 and undertaken to collect £500 more, and the congregation have raised £1,300. Nearly one half of the sittings will be free.

At the service on Wednesday evening, to which admission was gained by ticket, the building was crowded to excess in every part. The evening service was read by the Rev. J. Martin and the sermon was preached by the Rev. John Knapp, incumbent of St. John's Church, Portsea, who, it will be remembered, founded the old Circus church. The Rev. gentleman preached a very eloquent and impressive sermon from Ephesians, chap. II, verses 21 and 22.

At the conclusion of the service a collection was made at the doors in aid of the building fund.

1864 – EMPLOYMENT OF CONVICTS IN THE DOCKYARD.

It was rumoured a short time ago that the convict prison adjoining the Dockyard was about to be abolished, and the work in the Dockyard, which had been hitherto done by convicts, was to be performed in future by ordinary hired labourers in the employ of the authorities or by contract.

Since the appointment of the present superintendent of the yard, however, these rumours have died away. The numbers of convicts in the prison have been increased, and they have been employed in the Dockyard more freely than ever, and have certainly, under the rigid superintendence to which they have been subjected, done a large amount of work, the benefits of which will be felt for many years to come.

In the days of wooden shipbuilding, the convict could always be fully employed in transporting timber, and in setting up the ship's framing as required by the skilled workmen of the yard. Now, however, that no ships are being built in the yard, it was necessary, if the convicts were to retain their position as part of the available labour of the yard, that some other kind of work should be found for them, and this Rear-Admiral Elliot found without difficulty on assuming his command of the yard.

For many years past the roads in the Dockyard have been so rough and uneven that the general work of the establishment has been much delayed, owing to the great difficulty and loss of time attending the transport of material from one part of it to another. In a very short time, however, a fathom of uneven paving or of mud or water in the road or footway will not be found throughout the yard, and all the improvements will be accomplished by the convicts. The whole of the paving has been taken up and re-laid, and tramways of old iron ballast have been laid down the centre of each, owing to which measures material may now be transported from one part of the yard to another in one-half the time and with one-half the labour expended formerly.

In addition to this, a party of convicts are now engaged in the yard manufacturing for their own use, when on labourers' work in the yard or outside their prison walls, carts, wheelbarrows, picks, spades &c. The work these men are now engaged upon will, however, soon be completed, and it will be necessary to find them other employment. It is believed that they will be employed on some part of the works comprised in the extension of the Dockyard, and the creation of the docks and basins which are about to be commenced.

1864 – GARIBALDI'S VISIT TO PORTSMOUTH.

The public movements of the Italian patriot in the Isle of Wight were this day brought to a most brilliant and satisfactory termination. Mr. Seely, believing it would afford his guest a paramount pleasure to visit and inspect the docks of Portsmouth, organised in the quietest possible manner such a visit. It was a profound secret, as far as the public were concerned. However, questions were rife overnight as to the movements of Garibaldi, and it was not until the Admiralty yacht, the *Fire Queen*, having on board Captain F. Scott, aide-de-camp to Her Majesty, and flag captain of the *Victory*, and Staff Commander Paul, was observed moored off West Cowes in the morning, that anything like suspicions were aroused. This fact of course soon became known, and before Mr. Seely with Garibaldi arrived, many persons had assembled on the esplanade eager to get a glimpse of the world-renowned patriot.

The morning was beautifully fine, and the water calm as a lake. Upon a sudden the *Fire Queen's* boat darted from her moorings and proceeded towards the shore, announcing that Garibaldi had arrived. In a moment all eyes were concentrated on Garibaldi, who sat in the stern of the advancing boat. As he approached the steamer, all hats were raised, but not a voice was uttered. Upon gaining the steps of the gangway, Captain Scott extended his hand, and assisted the general to mount them. In a few minutes afterwards, all those privileged to accompany the general had gained the deck, and the *Fire Queen* at once again steamed out of Cowes Roads.

Shortly after getting well under weigh, the *Fire Queen* passed close alongside a fine Dutch barque, whose crew cheered and dipped the colours of Holland. The General acknowledged the compliment by waving the right hand. Garibaldi appeared especially interested when Osborne House was pointed out to him as the "residence of the Queen." He steadfastly gazed on it, and then inquired if she was still staying there?

A little before twelve o clock, the *Fire Queen* steamed into Portsmouth harbour amidst the cheers of the people, who had assembled on every available spot of terra firma commanding a view. The crews of the gigantic men-of-war, the *Victory*, the *Duke of Wellington*, the *Royal Sovereign*, and the training-ship *Excellent*, were crowded on the decks and in the portholes, eager to catch a glimpse of the patriot as he stepped from the *Fire Queen* into Admiral Seymour's barge, which was in attendance under the command of Flag-Lieutenant Seymour, to convey him and his suite ashore. The harbour and its surroundings presented a scene of the liveliest animation and excitement, and loud cheers mingled with the waving of hats and pocket handkerchiefs, greeted Garibaldi as he landed at King's Stairs. Here Admiral Sir Michael Seymour, K.C.B., Lord William Paulet, Captain F. Scott, Captain H. Caudwell, Captain Seccombe, and Captain Key, and the heads of the dock departments, were in attendance, and received him with the most cordial welcome.

Giuseppe Garibaldi

Admiral Seymour briefly told him of the pleasure he experienced at receiving him, to which Garibaldi replied, "I thank you; I thank you."

They then proceeded to inspect certain departments of the Dockyard, within the gates of which the workmen had assembled in hundreds, and directly they caught sight of the hero, one of the most genuine and spontaneous bursts of hurrahs that perhaps ever issued from the lips of men rent the air. This compliment the general acknowledged with a wave of the hand, and the words, "I thank you; I thank you." Admiral Seymour then conducted him on board the *Royal Sovereign* cupola ship, which, when finished, will be one of the most formidable long-range warships afloat. It has on its decks four revolving turrets, one of which in the fore part of the vessel contains two Armstrong 300-pounders, and the other three, revolving at respective distances, one 300-pounder. The General was much pleased with the invention, and devoted a good half hour in inspecting it. He spent some time in the blockhouse, and then passed through the steam machinery department, at which he expressed himself highly gratified. He was then conducted across the yard to the *Excellent* training ship, and in his journey was much struck by the gigantic overhanging crane that is capable of lifting 60 tons at one lift. Having gained the steps, the Admiral's barge was again in attendance, and the General and his suite and the other members of the party were conducted on board the *Excellent*. Here he spent a considerable time. Captain Key had the men put through a series of evolutions, and shot and shells ranging from a calibre of 68 to 150 to 300-pounders, were fired at the target with wonderful accuracy—in one instance, a 300-pounder passed completely through the target at a distance of 2,600 yards. During this practice the General stood steadfastly watching the delivery of the shots from a porthole, and every now and then exclaimed, "Beautiful, beautiful!" The first shot that was fired had a wonderful effect upon him. That softness of expression so peculiar to him at once disappeared, and his countenance flashed with interest and delight. Captain Key gave an order for a concentrated broadside to be fired, which was accomplished with such precision that it caused him to absolutely laugh with gratification, at the same time exclaiming, "I have never in all my life seen such a thing!"

He then proceeded on board the *Resistless*, where some practice with the Armstrong gun was gone through. At the conclusion of the firing, he went up to several of the men and officers, and heartily shook hands, congratulating them upon their efficiency in drill.

The party then adjourned to the house of Admiral Seymour, where a luncheon was served; after which Garibaldi, accompanied by Captain Scott and suite, went to Portsea in the Admiral's barge, for the purpose of visiting an old friend, Mrs. White, the mother of his youngest son's former governess; there he also received a most cordial welcome from the inhabitants, who assembled in strong force on the pier and along the esplanade. The hero then returned to the *Fire Queen* amidst a perfect ovation, and reached Cowes at five o'clock.

1864 – GUNPOWDER AT PORTSMOUTH.

The Dockyard at Portsmouth and the town of Portsea are joined to the town of Portsmouth by the Ordnance wharf and Arsenal. Inside the walls of this establishment stand four large magazines, which at present, in addition to a large assortment of rockets and other missiles of war, contain upwards of 8,000 filled, or as they are expressively named in technical language, "live" shells, the majority of which are for 8-inch guns. When these magazines were first erected, they were, no doubt, constructed with all possible care, and were isolated from all other buildings the companionship of which might be dangerous. Within the past 18 months, however, a change has taken place. The magazines now stand within a few yards of the roaring furnaces of the boiler house of a newly erected Royal factory for the repair of Armstrong guns and their carriages - a Woolwich on a diminutive scale. A narrow cart road and some 20 or 30 feet of this new factory only separate its boiler house furnaces from the four loaded magazines. The only sane course to follow under such circumstances would be to remove the magazines and their dangerous contents to some more safe and isolated locality.

1864 – ADDITIONS TO OUR IRONCLAD FLEET.

The progress lately made in constructing ships of war is enormous, and in reality, it is not more than ten or eleven years since the fatal truth broke upon men that wooden ships were no better in naval battle than just many chip boxes. It was at Sinope that we first learnt that the being able to fire shells horizontally, and set fire to a whole navy in ten minutes, would

Government Magazines at Gunwharf

Unloading a Powder Cart

render necessary the reconstruction of all our naval armaments. The French were the first to appreciate the force of the lesson the Turks got from the Russians and we, following their example, succeeded at last in producing four as ugly plated tubs as anybody ever imagined. They were called the *Glutton, Meteor, Trusty*, and *Thunderer;* to them were afterwards added the *Erebus, Terror, Thunderbolt,* and *Kina*.

They were never intended for sea boats, and will never be able to do more than protect the mouths of rivers and harbours. The *Thunderbolt*, in fact, has been moored in the Thames as a stationary battery for some time past. The next and most important step was the construction of vessels which could attend the sea, and yet be protected from shot. The *Warrior*, as everybody knows, was our first real experiment under the new order of things. She was built of iron by the Thames Iron Shipbuilding Company, from a design of the late Chief Constructor of the Navy, and has certainly, although our earliest attempt, been a complete success. Three other vessels, the *Black Prince*, the *Resistance*, and *Defence* have been built essentially upon the same principle of that adopted in the *Warrior*. They are all plated in the centre only; and there is doubt that, in this respect, they are defective. The *Achilles*, just finished and commissioned, was originally meant to be a sister ship to the *Warrior*; but the Admiralty have, since Mr. Reed's accession to office, introduced in her, most important alterations, with a view of collecting the evils which experience had revealed in her predecessor.

The *Achilles*, like the *Warrior*, is completely protected in the centre only; but then all along the line is carried a band of iron effectually fortifying the vessel at the most vulnerable part, the next variation is offered by the *Hector* and *Valiant*, where the plating is carried over everything from stem to stern, with the exception of a portion of the water-line at each end. This arrangement is objectionable simply for the reason that it repeats the fault of the *Warrior*, and adds to the weight of the ship. In the *Northumberland*, *Minotaur*, *Agincourt*, and in the wooden vessels of the Prince Consort and Royal Oak class, the plating carried all round. This perfect protection is gained, however, not without great disadvantages. Buoyancy is lost to a very great degree, and it must never be forgotten that a ship has to swim in all weathers as well as to fight.

After Mr. Reed became Chief Constructor, a great step in advance was made. To keep up a fleet of *Warriors*, even if they could do what was required of them, would be out of the question, simply because of the expense. Mr. Reed, therefore, in his *Research* and *Enterprise*, tried to discover if it would be possible to protect small ships which should prove good sea boats, and might be sent anywhere. He has perfectly succeeded. It is true that the *Enterprise*, of 310 tons and loaded with iron, can never be so fast under steam as an old wooden frigate of 2,000 tons which had nothing but her engines and guns to carry, but nobody in his senses ever thought they would. Nine knots' an hour were all that the Admiral ever hoped from the *Enterprise*. She can do ten; and we ought to be perfectly satisfied. The *Warrior*, it is true, can do fifteen; but then the *Warrior* is six times the size of the *Enterprise*, and increase of tonnage is increase of proportionate engine power and increase of speed.

Another style of naval architecture—the cupola-ship, invented by Captain Coles and adopted extensively in America—has also been much under consideration of late; but, we have only one specimen of this style—the *Royal Sovereign*—and as she has been declared by the Admiralty to be designed and adapted only for purposes of harbour defence, and not for seagoing, we need not specify the peculiarities of Captain Coles' system, particularly as the whole idea has already been fully explained and illustrated in our pages.

1864 – LAUNCH OF THE ROYAL ALFRED.

The launch of this frigate, which took place at Portsmouth on Saturday last, and of which ceremonial we publish the accompanying Engraving, the Admiralty have sent afloat another vessel which, when she has been clothed with her armour and fitted with her machinery, will be added to the list of England's ironclad fleet, and become one of the total number, which comprises some nine or ten descriptions of vessels, varying in all the extremes of tonnage, speed, and mode of construction which now form our somewhat heterogeneous collection of ironclads. The *Royal Alfred* is one of the Prince Consort and Royal Oak class, their frames designed and prepared as 92-gun screw line-of-battle ships, but afterwards cut down to a frigate's battery, altered in form at the bow and stern, and strengthened considerably in every part to carry the weight of 4.5 in. armour plating.

The *Royal Alfred* was ordered to be built as a line-of-battle ship in October, 1859, of the following general dimensions: Length between perpendiculars, 252 feet, length of keel for tonnage, 213 ft. 2 in.; breadth extreme, 58 ft.; breadth for tonnage, 57ft. 2 in.; breadth moulded, 56 ft. 4 in.; depth in hold, 19ft. 10in.; burden in tons, 37156294.

The ship was accordingly laid down and nearly completed in accordance with these orders, when, after the work had been suspended on her for some time, just the period when wooden liners had become universally acknowledged useless to compete with ironclad frigates, a second order relative to the ship was issued from the Admiralty in June, 1861, which on this occasion directed that the ship's upper deck, so far as it had been constructed, should be removed, and the necessary alterations and strengthening of her frame carried out, to complete her as an iron-cased frigate.

Under these new conditions, the *Royal Alfred* has been sufficiently completed to be launched from off the ship way on which she has been constructed; her hull shorn externally of all aids to her beauty, her bows without the "figurehead" which has existed as part of a

Launch of the Royal Alfred

Launch of the Royal Alfred

ship from the times of the Phoenicians, or the curved lines of headrail and cutwater, and her stern without the ornamental quarter-galleries, and reduced to a bare conical termination, the apex projecting over and protecting the fixed screw and rudder. Her length is now increased beyond her original dimensions to 273 ft. between perpendiculars and 233 ft. on her keel, and her tonnage increased to 40452694, while her breadth remains the same.

On Saturday last, as, previous to launching, she lay on her blocks, with her vast hull painted black, and without other ornament than the gaily-decorated bottle of wine suspended from the stem for the "christening," she looked like some antediluvian monster. A few minutes before ten a.m. Miss Alice Cradock, the daughter of the Master Shipwright, was led forward, and, with great grace, broke the bottle against the ship's stem, at the same time uttering the customary wish, "Success to the *Royal Alfred*." The ship was named, but not yet quite freed. Some ten blocks under her keel remained to be split out, but the most of these were soon dealt with, and Miss Cradock, having a small mallet placed in her hands, struck a blow on a sharp chisel held against the cord on the ship's stem which kept suspended the iron dogs, when the latter descended in their grooved channels and knocked clear the dogshores, which alone now held the ship on the ways. A few moments only of suspense, accompanied by groaning and creaking sounds, and the ship started and slid with a gentle rush into the water, amid ringing cheers from thousands of spectators.

Like others of her class, the *Royal Alfred* does not look much handsomer afloat than she did on the blocks; but in the absence of beauty there is evident fitness for fighting purposes as a broadside ship, looking at her superficially as she lay broadside on to the building shed, and brought up in that position by her anchor immediately after being launched.

If the launching scene be now left, and the reader transported on board the *Royal Alfred*, the ship may be inspected from another point of view. The upper deck is at present clear fore and aft, after the fashion of our best specimens of wooden screw-frigates, with the exception that a forecastle is being constructed at the fore end of the deck and lines are laid out for the erection of a poop at the after end—the first being a covered-in space of the deck, which may be appropriated to the accommodation of the crew; and the second a similar space, for the accommodation of an Admiral and his suite—the *Royal Alfred* being destined as a flag-ship—thus meeting the difficulty hitherto experienced in providing such accommodation for the officer commanding a fighting fleet.

The upper deck of the *Royal Alfred* is composed of the ordinary wooden planking; but this is laid upon an iron deck of half-inch boiler plate, which, strengthened and tied by edge and butt straps of iron of equal thickness, and fore and aft stringer rows of plates, rests upon rolled iron beams which span the ship at short intervals Descending from this upper to the main or gun deck below, the ship is here found to give, from appearances, her greatest promise of future efficiency as a man-of-war; and at the same time, on close examination, she exhibits her inefficiency such in common with her sisters of the same class. The deck, from beam to floor, is of good height; there is ample room for working the guns of the battery fore and aft; the means of ventilation for carrying off the smoke in rapid firing are good; and, to crown all, the entire deck, round the stem and stern, as well as on the broadside, is protected by 4 in. rolled armour plates, from the Atlas Works, Sheffield. So far for efficiency.

As to her inefficiency, all this capital arrangement of gun battery, roomy quarters, and ventilation, protected by the best of all armour plating, is supported only by some eighteen inches of timber, without any inner iron lining, and the consequences in action would be that steel shot from guns of any power would go completely through the side of the ship fired at and knock off the armour plates from the opposite side, and if only cast-iron shot were fired from the ordinary 68-pounder smooth-bore gun, although the shot would not penetrate into the ship, yet the splinters flung off from the unlined ship's side internally, the impact of the shot upon the armour plates, would be sufficient to disable all the men at the guns.

Descending lower into the ship, workmen are found busily employed fitting the mess, berthing, etc, for the crew; and still lower may be seen the preparations made for the reception of her machinery. Neither machinery nor amour plates yet form parts of the *Royal Alfred*, and both will have now to be fitted in dock or in the floating basins of Portsmouth yard, as may be required, according to the progress of the ship's outfit. The engines will be of the united power of 800 horses, nominal, from the establishment of Messrs. Maudslay, Field, and Co., the latter fact being a sufficient guarantee for their excellence. The lower masts of the ship are splendid specimens of iron manufacture, from the works of Messrs. Finch, of Chepstow. The *Royal Alfred* is pierced for thirty-five guns, but, with the rapid strides now being made in the calibres of naval ordnance, it would be useless to speculate upon what her armament may eventually be.

1864 – THE CORONATION HOLIDAY.

A very large number of excursionists visited Portchester Castle on Tuesday last. As many as a hundred boats and yachts from Portsmouth, Gosport, Isle of Wight, &c., arrived with visitors during the day, but the bulk of the pleasure seekers came by road and rail. Great preparations and excellent arrangements had been made for general accommodation by Mr. John Binsted, of the Castle, and we were pleased to see that his exertions were appreciated, and rewarded with much patronage. The band of the Hampshire Artillery Militia was in attendance, and made the old ruin reverberate with musical echoes. There was capital play on the cricket ground, and many a crack shot made the targets ring at the rifle butts. In the archery department the arrows were whizzing through the air intermittingly. Croquet and football had many patrons and admirers, and the swings and donkeys were going all day long.

It was gratifying to see that the humble cottagers, who exhibited very generally the manuscript mementos of "Tea made here," met with a harvest of custom, most of the woodbined snuggeries being crowded during the after part of the day. The "hostelries" also were well filled, and great was the call on each Boniface and his attendants. Notwithstanding the lowering clouds that constantly threatened rain, and in some degree damped the pleasure, the scene was very animated. Almost all seemed determined to be merry, though the sky would not smile on them.

Hundreds in succession mounted to the platform on the top of the Great Tower, from which a magnificent prospect is obtained of Portsdown Hill, the celebrated Forts in course of construction on its crest, the harbour of Portsmouth with its Dockyard and noble ships, and in the far distance the lofty Downs of the beautiful Wight. We enjoyed this wide and varied scene amazingly, as also did a gentleman at our side, who was busy with his pencil and tablets. He was evidently fresh from "Dreamland," for he handed to us an effusion on Portchester Castle.

1864 – SUSPENDING OPERATIONS.

Instructions were received here on Tuesday from headquarters to suspend all further operations upon the Sturbridge Shoal in the construction of the foundations for one of the three proposed marine Spithead Forts. This course, says the *Times*, has no doubt been adopted by the authorities owing to the insuperable difficulties which exist in finding any foundation of sufficient strength to carry a part of the weight requisite to carry ordnance of the "Big Will" class, which is supposed to be the smallest description of gun with which these iron cased granite works will be armed.

Whatever cause, however, may have led to the abandonment of the work, it is understood to be intended now to erect a fort on the Warner Rock, where three forts would then stand together in a triangular position at the very throat at the narrow entrance to Spithead from the sea. Since the Spithead forts have become an acknowledged necessity, this is really the only position in which the three retained forts ought to be placed. It is the gateway to the only direct entrance to Spithead from the sea, and the bolts and bars fixed to secure it cannot well be too strong.

Inside this gateway the enemy must be met and fought, if the bolts and bars are forced and he is still afloat, by our own ironclads. The Sturbridge shoal lies off Ryde, and visitors to the island will remember the mass of staging which rose above the water at about a quarter of mile's distance from the pier head, in the direct track of the steam packets running between Ryde and Portsmouth, encircling a huge iron cylinder, which was being sunk down through the shingle forming the shoal, and surmounted by an odd-looking combination of staging, cabin, and an embryo lighthouse. These form the now doomed works, which were erected for the construction of the foundations of the Sturbridge Fort.

1864 – THE WARRIOR DECOMMISSIONED.

The *Warrior*, this fine frigate, the most successful of our iron clads afloat and after a commission of no more than three years, has been stripped and dismantled, and her crew paid off. No fault can be found with the Admiralty for paying her off, as she has been in commission the usual period, but what reason there could be for dismantling her to her lower masts and clearing her out entirely, we are at a loss to understand.

The vessel was inspected by Admiral Sir M. Seymour, G.C.B., Port Admiral and Commander-in-Chief, on Monday. The Admiral was received by Capt. the Hon. A. Cochrane, and conducted over every portion of the vessel, and expressed his entire satisfaction with her appearance. The motto carved on the ship's wheel, "The Princess is much pleased," did not escape Sir Michael Seymour's attention.

The history of the motto is this. On the occasion of the *Warrior* escorting the Royal yacht *Victoria and Albert* from Flushing to the Thames, with the then Princess Alexandra of Denmark on board, signal was made from the yacht the *Warrior*, at the conclusion of the run across, by special desire of the Princess, "The Princess is much pleased," and the officers of the frigate adopted the signal as the future motto of themselves and their ship while they remained together.

The paying off took place on Tuesday, under the superintendence of Rear-Admiral S.C. Dacres, C.B., Commander-in-Chief of the Channel Squadron. The arrangements were most creditable to all concerned, the whole process only occupying one hour and ten minutes. The following men received gratuities and rewards:—William Percival, chief captain of the forecastle, good service medal and £15 gratuity; Robert Bone, coxswain of the launch, good service medal, £24 pension, and £7 gratuity; and John Tozer, quartermaster, £24 pension.

During the period of her commission, several accidents have occurred on board the *Warrior*. One seaman fell from the maintop, and broke both his thighs; another was knocked down in a coaling ship and broke his leg and collar bone, and another fell from the topgallant yard. All these men have been thrown, by these accidents, into crippled helplessness for life, and with true generosity the crew of the *Warrior*, on receiving their pay, deposited each a trifle for their three unfortunate shipmates, and in this way the sum of £50 6s. 11d. was unostentatiously subscribed.

1864 – YACHTING SEASON AT RYDE.

Our Engraving, entitled "The Yachting Season at Ryde," is from a sketch made by our own Artist on the Ryde Pier, which offers the gay and pleasant spectacle of a numerous company of well-dressed ladies and gentlemen promenading its floor, at certain hours of the afternoon and evening during the time of the great aquatic festival at Ryde.

The tradesmen of Ryde, who naturally take an interest in the proceedings of the Victoria Yacht Club, had subscribed for a handsome piece of plate, constituting the first prize, which was sailed

Yachting Season at Ryde

for on Tuesday week. It was a vase, designed and manufactured by Mr. Thurlow, silversmith, of that town. One side of the vase is sculptured with yachts in full sail, surrounded with a border of waterlilies; the other bears a shield, with a suitable inscription; the cover is surmounted by a figure with Neptune's trident in one hand and a wreath of victory in the other. The race for this prize was contested by ten vessels—schooners and cutters of different sizes. It was finally won by the *Aline*, of 214 tons, belonging to Mr. C. Thellusson, Commodore of the club. The *Albertine*, 153 tons, belonging to Lord Londesborough, came in ten minutes later; but all the other yachts, which, except the *Galatea* (Mr. T. Broadwood's), were of much smaller dimensions, lagged a long way behind. The next day's proceedings consisted of the sailing of the yachts belonging to the club, in divisions, under flag officers, and the annual dinner at the clubhouse in the evening.

1865 – THE SOUTHSEA BEACH MANSION.

The foundation stone of the Southsea Beach Mansion, situate at St. Helen's, was laid by the Mayoress (Mrs. R.W. Ford), on Wednesday afternoon. A more delightful site could scarcely have been selected in the whole district, for the Mansion will command an uninterrupted sea view, taking in the Isle of Wight, Spithead, St. Helen's, and the Culver Cliffs. The Mansion will be erected from the designs and under the superintendence of Mr. Whichcord, of Wallbrook, London, the architect to the Grand Hotel, at Brighton, the Clarence Hotel at Dover, and other extensive establishments of a like character, and will be completed in time for the summer season of 1866. It will be arranged as an Hotel and Boarding House, and will comprise, on the ground floor, a spacious gentlemen's coffee room, ladies' coffee room; on the first and second floors, reading room, saloons and bedrooms for invalids, saloons, sitting rooms and bedrooms, which are so planned that families may occupy them en suite. The third and fourth floors will be entirely devoted to bedrooms.

The Mansion will be so constructed that it may, if desired, be subdivided into three distinct buildings, and occupied as several superior boarding houses or mansions, as at Brighton. The kitchen, servants' hall, and necessary adjuncts will be fitted up with all modern improvements, and placed in a well-lighted basement. The structure will contain 110 rooms, including 85 bedrooms. The design is of a plain Italian character, with bay windows and balconies, admirably adapted to gain the fine sea view which the site commands. The contract for the erection of the building has been taken by Messrs. Sims and Marten, of London.

About half-past one o'clock the company began to assemble; and the Mayoress, accompanied by the Mayor, the chairman of the directors (Mr. H.B. Norman), and a large number of ladies and gentlemen, ascended the scaffolding for the purpose of laying the stone.

The proceedings were opened by Sir James Elphinstone, M.P., who said he thought it was of some advantage to the undertaking that the ceremony was somewhat of an apocryphal description, for the company would be happy to see that the building had reached the first floor, and he trusted that the success of the undertaking would be commensurate with the progress already made. They deposited under this stone a number of coins, and a portion of the press of the day, together with other documents which would enable - not he hoped the New Zealander who, it was supposed by some, would stand at some future period on London Bridge - but those who might dig up those documents from the debris, to form some idea of the manners and customs of the persons who now deposited the stone. On the laying of this stone, he wished every success to an undertaking which was likely to prove of great benefit to Southsea.

The Architect described, in humorous terms, the contents of the bottle about to be placed under the stone. The bottle contained several coins of the realm, a copy of a local journal, and a scroll. The bottle having been duly deposited, the stone was "laid" by the Mayoress, who was certainly deserving of the praise subsequently bestowed for the skilful manner in which the tools were handled. The Rev. J. Knapp offered a brief prayer, after which Mr. Norman, on behalf of the directors, presented an elegant silver trowel to the Mayoress in acknowledgement of her services, expressing a hope that the trowel would not only be handed down to the family, but that in time to come they would see this a prosperous undertaking, and, as the Rev. gentleman had prayed, a place in which those in search of health might find it.

The Mayor briefly acknowledged the compliment, after which three cheers were given for the undertaking, and the band of the Royal Marine Artillery played the National Anthem. At the close of the ceremony the company proceeded to the pavilion adjoining the site of the Mansion, where an elegant dejeuner had been prepared, under the superintendence of Mr. Smith, of King's Terrace. The wines were supplied by Mr. Weston, of the Sussex Hotel.

1865 – THE NAVAL FESTIVAL AT PORTSMOUTH.

The brilliant series of festivities at Portsmouth in honour of the meeting of the French and English squadrons in that port commenced on Tuesday week. Just before noon that day the booming of the cannon at Spithead announced the arrival of our foreign guests. For some little time previously the vessels composing the French squadron had been visible in the offing from as high as the narrow entrance to the harbour, and it was evident that they were steaming at a pretty smart pace. They did not get up sail, though the wind, during the previous hour or so, had gone round from N.W. to N., and from N. nearly to N.E., a most favourable change for them had they availed themselves of it.

The Emperor's screw yacht *Reine Hortense* and the Queen's paddle yacht *Osborne* led the squadron; the *La Gloire* was apparently next. Then came the *Solferino* and *Magenta*, two twin iron-cased double-decked ships, and they soon attracted general attention with their ponderous *eperons* or beaks, by which they are to strike their adversaries beneath the water line. The squadron steamed slowly up to the places appointed for the vessels which composed it, and to which they were guided by pilots, they presented a very imposing spectacle.

The Emperor had sent to Portsmouth no less than nine large ironclads. There were the *Solferino* and *Magenta*, two-deckers; the *Normandie, Couronne, Invincible, La Gloire, Provence, Heroine,* and *Flandre*, frigates; with four small vessels, the *Caton, Ariel, Faon*, and the *Reine Hortense*. The officer commanding was Count Bouet-Willaumez, Vice-Admiral-in-Chief, on board the *Solferino*. The *Reine Hortense* conveyed M. de Chasseloup-Laubat, the French Minister of Marine, with his Staff; and M. de Lome, Chief Constructor of the Navy.

Admiral Sir Michael Seymour, Naval Commander-in-Chief, in attendance on the Lords of the Admiralty, had by this time arrived at Spithead in his paddle yacht, the *Fire Queen*. Steamers of all sizes and descriptions, too, were cruising about the roadstead, while a fine fleet of schooners, yachts, yawls, and cutters belonging to the Royal Victoria Yacht Club came out from Ryde Roads and darted to and fro by

Arrival of the French Fleet

Returning the Salute of the French Fleet

Waiting for the Fleet to Arrive

the line in which the English ironclads lay at anchor, in as yet silent and grim array. Their numbers had been increased by the arrival from Portland of the *Research*, an iron-cased sloop.

On reaching Spithead, she took up her position on the line west of the *Prince Consort*. The remaining English vessels of war lying at Spithead to receive the French fleet, anchored in a line from N.W. to S.E., were the *Edgar*, screw wooden line-of-battle ship, on board which was hoisted the flag of Rear-Admiral Sir. C. Dacres, K.C.B.; the *Hector*, iron frigate; the *Defence*; the *Black Prince*, iron frigate; the *Achilles*, iron frigate; the *Royal Sovereign*, turret ship; the *Liverpool*, wooden frigate; the *Salamis*, paddle wheel dispatch vessel; and three screw wooden gunboats, acting as tenders. It will be seen by this list that the English fleet was very powerfully represented at Spithead, consisting, as it did, of twenty vessels, with a combined tonnage of 38,187 tons, and a nominal horse power of engines of 9,750.

There are few places in which a naval spectacle can be seen to greater advantage than the broad expanse of water separating the Isle of Wight from the mainland, in which this splendid squadron lay moored. It was here that the nine most powerful ironclads in the navy of France, accompanied by four frigates, steamed slowly in and each dropped her anchor opposite to one of her English sisters. As soon as the *Solferino* had anchored, the *Osborne* and the *Hortense* stood towards each other and, meeting midway between the two fleets, dipped their flags in salutation. The English ships were then, with almost magical rapidity, manned at every yard, and a more stirring scene than that which greeted the spectator, both on shore and afloat, as they did so it is not easy to conceive. A vessel with her yards fully manned is always a pretty sight; but when, as on this occasion, a whole squadron contributes to the effect, it is a most animated and interesting spectacle. The *Reine Hortense*, followed by the *Osborne*, then made for Portsmouth; and as the former rounded the Spit Buoy, the flag of the Minister of Marine received a salute from the *Victory*, stationed in the harbour. This salute the *Solferino*, not wishing to be outdone in courtesy, returned with rigid punctuality, belching forth flame in rapid flashes, each discharge succeeded by a brief silence, which, although it might convey no compliment, was extremely grateful to civilian ears. But the land was not to be outdone in this great strife of sound, and accordingly the roar of the garrison artillery went booming across the water, dying away in reverberations which grew fainter and fainter until at last they totally ceased, and the vexed air was quiet once more.

Reception on Board the Victory

By this time, too, the smoke created by the firing, which hung over the water, began to drift before the wind and to break into light fleecy clouds, each of which took its own way into the heavens, leaving the atmosphere immediately over Spithead perfectly clear. Then might be seen, lying harmlessly by one another in the roadstead, such an array of ironclads, constructed on the most deadly principles, as had never been seen assembled together before. Hundreds of boats immediately clustered round them, and loud cheers continued long after they anchored to greet the appearance of the French officers and sailors on the decks of their respective vessels.

The official programme, which had been arranged by the French and English naval authorities in accordance with the rules of naval etiquette, was observed in the exchange of formal civilities between them. When the last ship of the French squadron had anchored, the Duke of Somerset and the members of the Board of Admiralty, accompanied by the Naval Commander-in-Chief, the Lieutenant-Governor of Portsmouth, and the Admiral Superintendent of Portsmouth Dockyard, visited the French Minister of Marine. The visit was returned by the French Minister and Admirals, who went on board the *Edgar*. When the French Commander-in-Chief had returned to his ship he was visited by the English Commander-in-Chief, who, on leaving, was saluted with seventeen guns. The French Commander-in-Chief then returned the English Commander-in-Chief's visit on board the *Victory*, Nelson's celebrated flagship at the Battle of Trafalgar. Here Admiral Bouet-Willaumez was sainted with seventeen guns. After the French squadron had anchored, the Rear-Admiral commanding the Channel squadron visited the officer commanding the French squadron and the junior French flag officers, who afterwards returned his visits. No more salutes were fired, but the steamers passing round the fleets repeatedly sent forth peal after peal of cheers, which were courteously responded to by counter-cheers from the French ships. In the evening the Duke of Somerset entertained at dinner, on board the *Duke of Wellington*, the French Minister of Marine and the flag officers and captains of the French fleet.

Next day the French Minister and Admirals inspected the Dockyard, accompanied by the Duke of Somerset. A visit was also paid by them to Nelson's celebrated flagship at the Battle Trafalgar—the *Victory*. The spot on the quarter-deck where the great Admiral received his death wound, and the cockpit in which he breathed his last, were shown

Receiving Admiral Seymour on the Reine Hortense

to the representatives of that naval Power which he repeatedly defeated, and never more decisively than the day of his glorious death. These recollections of the valour and the prowess of the most formidable adversary whom France ever met upon the ocean cannot have failed to excite in the breasts of the French Admirals profound emotion. The *Victory* is always visited by Englishman with pardonable pride, but Frenchmen may equally regard that memorial of the greatest of our naval heroes and of our naval victories with those feelings which ought to inspire one brave nation when paying a tribute to the gallantry of another.

On leaving the Dockyard the French Minister, with the flag officers, accompanied by the Duke of Somerset on board the *Enchantress*, and shortly afterwards the Admiralty yacht steamed out of the harbour in order to make a few hours' cruise in Southampton Water and the Solent. In the evening a grand banquet was given by the Lords of the Admiralty to the principal officers of the French fleet at the Royal Naval College. The Duke of Somerset presided at the table, the French and English guests being, in alternate order, ranged, according to their degrees in the service, on his right or left hand. Four toasts were proposed—"The Emperor of the French," "The Queen of England," "The French Navy," and "The British Navy." Just as the health of her Majesty had been proposed by the French Minister, the signal for the commencement of an illumination of all the ships was given by the discharge of a rocket from the *Victory* and the firing of one of her guns.

As if by magic, every ship in the allied fleets was illuminated. A salute of twenty-one guns was fired from the fleets, and, as the echo of the last shot died away, every ship in the two squadrons was so illuminated, by means of red, white, and blue lights placed in every port, at both broadsides, and both yardarms, that the object which only a few moments before looked, even at a short distance, so grim and shadowy became at once transformed into a ship of light, revealing to view the outline of her slenderest spar. Rockets were then sent in clusters from the whole of the fleet, which, as they burst in the heavens, expanded into bouquets of red, white, and blue, and then gradually melted away in the still air, but only to be followed at short intervals by other clusters of rockets bursting and descending in an equally-brilliant shower.

As the long lights only burn for a couple of minutes, three were lighted in succession in each port, and as each set of lights died away, and the illumination seemed to be coming to an end, the

Illumination of the Fleet

full blaze of its splendour was again restored with the same magical rapidity with which it was first created. When the three sets of long lights were nearly burnt out a bouquet of twenty-four signal rockets was fired from each ship, and immediately after the fleet faded from the view of the thousands of spectators who lined the ramparts at Portsmouth, and all was again comparative obscurity at Spithead.

The illumination lasted for about twenty minutes, throughout the whole of which time the *St. Vincent*, the *Duke of Wellington*, and the other men-of-war in the harbour, displayed lights at every porthole, causing the gentle ripple on the waves to sparkle like diamonds. The town itself was also most extensively and brilliantly lit up during the night, the combination of the illumination of the houses near the Dockyard gates with the magnificent illumination over the gateway itself shedding a radiance like that of a bright summer sun at noon on the roadway and pavement below. No grander spectacle of this kind could scarcely be conceived.

Banquet Given to the Officers of the French Fleet

The Crowds on Southsea Common

Ball Given to Naval Officers

Reine Hortense Leaving Portsmouth Harbour

French and English Sailors

Decorations in Commercial Road

The French Minister and officers of the French squadron were entertained on the Thursday with dejeuner, a promenade concert, and ball, given by the town of Portsmouth, the Duke of Somerset being also present; and there was a grand display of fireworks on Southsea common. Thursday night's ball took place in the grand pavilion erected for the entertainments on Governor's Green. The ball of Friday night, was given by the Lords of the Admiralty at the Royal Naval College. The French squadron left Portsmouth the Saturday forenoon.

1865 – THE PURIFICATION OF PORTSMOUTH.

We are enabled to congratulate the inhabitants of Portsmouth on the prospect of a speedy reformation of the sanitary condition of the borough. After years of labour, and persuasion almost amounting to importunity, the reason of the great majority of the inhabitants was convinced. They admitted the necessity of sanitary purification, and the adoption of the Local Government Act by the Borough Council was the result of this great change in public feeling. Of course, so important a change did not take place without some opposition, but it was of a trivial character, and was not supported by any of the classes upon whom the burden of sanitary improvement will most heavily fall.

We have now reached the second stage in this work of sanitary reformation, by the ratification of the plans submitted to the Local Board, and we are entitled to say that every precaution which forethought and prudence could suggest has been adopted by the Local Board to prevent any failure of the great work which they have undertaken. A careful examination of the plans has been made by Mr. Hawkshaw, one of the most competent authorities in England on questions of engineering science, and the propositions of Mr. Angell have received his unequivocal assent. So far, nothing, perhaps, could be more satisfactory.

The plans were subsequently approved by the Secretary of State for the Home Department; and we have the satisfaction to observe that tenders have now been advertised for the carrying out of the work. With regard to the cost, there appears to be no reason to suppose that the estimated sum of 90,000l. will, to any considerable extent, be increased. This sum, of course, will be borrowed and repaid by instalments extending over a period of thirty years. By a wise provision embodied in the Local Act the annual rating for the carrying out of these works cannot exceed 2s. 6d. in the pound, and we understand that this sum will be sufficient to meet not only the general expenses of the board, but also the annual instalments for the repayment of the whole of the principal and interest on the money proposed to be borrowed within the thirty years.

Taking into account, therefore, the taxes levied by the old boards of commissioners for the purposes of local improvement, and the great work which remains to be accomplished under the new regime, the taxation of the borough on this account cannot by any means be considered excessive. The task is a great one; but the results will materially affect the social as well as the physical health of the inhabitants, and their influence cannot be overestimated.

1865 – CENTENARY FESTIVAL OF NELSON'S SHIP, THE VICTORY.

The *Victory*, Nelson's flagship at the Battle of Trafalgar, hallowed by the memory of his death, is still extant, as a hulk, in Portsmouth Harbour. On Wednesday week the centenary festival of this famous ship, which was launched at Chatham, in July, 1765, was celebrated by her present commander, Captain Francis Scott, C.B., with a ball, which he gave, on the upper deck, to a party of some four hundred guests, including Admiral Sir Michael Seymour, with Lady Seymour, and the chiefs of the various departments in the Dockyard, with their families, besides many of the naval officers and of the neighbouring gentry. The upper deck, as shown in our Illustration, was covered in with a sort of awning and tastefully decorated with the flags of all nations, and with festoons of evergreens around the masts, while some pots of beautiful flowers were ranged on the poop.

The ship had been brought alongside the Dockyard for the convenience of access. The dancing commenced at three o'clock in the afternoon and ended at seven in the evening. The company were therefore in morning costume; and some of the ladies wore their bonnets or hats all the time. The naval officers appeared in their blue frock coats, with laced sleeves, or scarf to denote their rank; and the military gentlemen were in their undress frock coats or braided shell jackets. Refreshments of the choicest description were provided upon the main deck, where the table was handsomely laid. Three wine glasses

The Centenary Ball

used by Nelson himself were among the furniture of this repast, and many of the guests were permitted to drink from them to the immortal memory of the great English naval hero. The whole entertainment passed off with entire success.

1865 – PRESENTATION OF THE VICTORIA CROSS ON SOUTHSEA COMMON.

The Naval Commander-in-Chief at Portsmouth, Admiral Sir Michael Seymour, G.C.B., presented the Victoria cross to a midshipman and two seamen of the *Euryalus*, on Friday, the 22nd ult., in the sight of a large assembly, on Southsea Common.

The Illustration we have engraved, from a sketch by Mr. F.L. Bedwell, represents this interesting scene. A battalion of Royal Artillery, and one of the Royal Marines, were on the ground, besides a field battery of seamen with Armstrong guns, and a strong brigade of seamen, the *Excellent* contributing the largest contingent. The naval brigade was under the command of Captain A.C. Key, C.B., of the *Excellent*, and consisted of small-arm parties of her Majesty's ships in port and at Spithead. The artillery and marines were commanded by Colonel Tate; the general direction of both brigades was entrusted to Lieutenant and Adjutant Colomb, R.M.A.

The forces were drawn up in line parallel with the beach in the following order:—Field battery on the right, brigade of seamen, Royal Marine Light Infantry, and Royal Marine Artillery, which formed the left flank. The crew of the *Euryalus* were drawn in two divisions, right and left of the saluting point, opposite the other line.

On the arrival of the Admiral, after a salute and marching past, they formed a square, within which the performance of the ceremony took place. The Admiral said a few words to each of the brave fellows as he affixed the cross to his breast. They had earned this distinction by individual acts of gallantry in the storming of the Japanese stockades at Simonosaki, on the 4th of September 1864. The first was Mr. Duncan Gordon Boyes, a midshipman, who at Simonosaki carried a colour with the leading company, and kept in advance of all in the face of the thickest of the fire; his colour-sergeants having fallen, one mortally, the other dangerously, wounded; and he was only detained from proceeding yet further by the orders of his superior officer. The colour he carried was six times pierced by musket balls.

The second was Thomas Pride, captain of the after guard, the survivor of the two colour-sergeants who supported Mr. Boyes in the rush which he made in advance of the attack; and the third was William Seeley, an ordinary seaman, also of the *Euryalus*, for the intelligence and daring which, according to the testimony of Lieutenant Edwards, commanding the third company, he exhibited in ascertaining the enemy's position, and for continuing to retain his position in front during the advance after he had been wounded in the arm.

The performance of the ceremony was notified by the firing of a Royal salute from her Majesty's ship *Victory*, the troops at the same time presenting arms. The brigades then formed in line of contiguous columns in the same order as before, and, advancing in review order, gave a general salute to the Commander-in-Chief, and so the ceremony ended.

1865 – THE GREAT TEA QUESTION.

Singular disagreement between the Poor Law Board and the guardians of the Portsea Island Union, comprising the parishes of Portsmouth and Portsea, has just culminated in an act of open rebellion against the authority of the Poor Law Board. It appears that for many years past it had been the practice of the guardians, at their fortnightly meetings, to adjourn for tea about five o'clock, the public business generally occupying their attention some four or five hours. Fourteen out of the twenty-one guardians have been the average attendance at tea, and the character of the meal may be inferred from the fact that the cost per head has not exceeded 2½d. or 2¾d., and that the entire cost per quarter has never been £3. This sum has for many years been paid out of the funds of the union, although not without remonstrance on the part of the Poor Law Board.

During the time Mr. Hoskins was poor law auditor we understand that the item was not challenged, but subsequent auditors have objected to it, and the guardians signing the cheques have for the last twenty years invariably been surcharged, although the surcharge has been remitted. The Poor Law Board has, however, frequently intimated that, if the practice were continued, they should enforce the recovery of the money from the guardians who signed the cheques. At a late meeting of the guardians a letter was read from the central authority, in which it was certified that the item was again disallowed, and the rebellion then commenced. It was argued by several of the guardians that the strictest economy had been observed, for they had had nothing with their tea but bread and butter, and that, after spending four or five hours in the discharge of public business, such slight refreshment ought not to be objected to.

The chairman (Mr. J.F. Pratt, J.P.) declared that he would be taken before the Magistrates rather than pay the money they had been surcharged, and announced that he had made up his mind not to attend the board again unless the same were allowed. At the close of the discussion, it was unanimously resolved— "That, the Poor Law Board having refused to allow the guardians to take tea at their meetings,

Presentation of Victoria Crosses

and having surcharged certain members of the board with the amount, the members of the board positively refuse to attend any future meetings to administer the poor law until the Poor Law Board withdraw their opposition thereto." The guardians present attached their signatures to the resolution, which was duly forwarded the Poor Law Board.

A reply was shortly afterwards received from London, signed "Enfield, Secretary," in which it was stated that, if an auditor considers any expenditure which may appear in the accounts submitted to him to be illegal, he is compelled to disallow them, and that if the Poor Law Board, on appeal, should be of opinion that the auditor was right they were bound to confirm his decision, having no power to issue any order or regulation which would make such illegal expenditure lawful. But it was also intimated that if the guardians were not satisfied with this decision, they had the right of appeal to the Court of Queen's Bench, through any guardian who might have been surcharged, and that it was competent for the Court to order the costs of the persons prosecuting the certiorari to be paid by the union.

A private meeting of the guardians was subsequently held, at which no fewer than twelve members signed their resignations, and it was understood amongst the body that no more duty should be performed until there was some satisfactory adjustment of the question. The consequence was that on Wednesday week not a single member of the board was present, and the clerk, the governor of the union house, and the relieving officers were the only persons in possession of the boardroom. The clerk stated that it would be his duty to notify the Poor Law Board how matters stood, and he advised the relieving officers also to write to that board for instructions with regard to the outdoor relief. Fortunately, the outdoor relief on this day was unusually light; but no cheques were signed, and next day the relieving officers were unable to administer any pecuniary relief to the poor, who clamoured at their door?

Several of the guardians were visited with similar result; and, as the guardians began to discover the consequences of their act, several of them met, during the morning, at the offices of the clerk, and signed cheques for the dispensation of outdoor relief. The fact of the revolt was communicated to the Poor Law Board, and a letter has since been received from that body, in which they point out to the guardians that they have no power to resign, and remind, or rather inform, them of the severe penalties to which they will render themselves liable if their conduct involve serious consequences to any of the recipients of poor law relief. Thursday week was the day appointed for the acceptance of what are called "the long contracts" for the supply of provisions to the union workhouse for the ensuing quarter, and of clothing for the half-year; but the guardians again absented themselves, and no contracts were taken. On Wednesday last the old contracts were at an end, and, unless the guardians change their determination, or the governor accept the contracts on his own responsibility, the latter will be in the awkward position of having about 1,500 persons to feed and clothe, without having either food or raiment at his disposal.

1866 – EXPERIMENTAL FIRING AT THE ROYAL SOVEREIGN.

The H.M.S. *Royal Sovereign* was the first turret ship built for the British Navy on the plan of Captain Cowper Coles. On Friday, the 15th inst., this ship was subjected to the severe ordeal of having her turret fired at thrice by H.M.S. *Bellerophon*, with one of her great rifled guns of 9 in. calibre, at the distance of 200 yards; the object being to try two important questions—first, that of the vulnerability of the turret; and, secondly, the liability of the machinery on which it revolves to injury either from a shot striking the rollers or from splinter from the side of the ship so injuring them as to render the turret practically useless.

The experiments took place in the waters of the Solent, off the coast of the Isle of Wight, at St. Helens, where the two ships were moored. The Duke of Somerset and other Lords of the Admiralty, with Admiral Robinson, Comptroller of the Navy, witnessed the proceedings from on board the steamer *Osborne*. There was a great number of spectators on board the excursion steamers and the private yachts which lay as near the *Bellerophon* as they were allowed.

A brief description of the thickness of the turret and of the size of the shot directed against it will give some idea of the nature of the trial. The bullseyes, about 1 ft. diameter, are on the right and left of the port, the centre of the former being at a distance of about 2 ft. 9 in. from the edge of the latter, and at a height of about 2 ft. 3 in. from the raised plating (forming a sort of combing) which surrounds the turret. This plating is 3 in. in thickness, and gradually slopes for a distance of about 3 ft. For about 6 ft. on each side the port (and the bull's-eyes were within this distance) the thickness of the turret is about 2 ft. Outside is a 5 in. plate; then comes a 4 in. plate, which is backed by 14 in. of teak; and the inner skin is iron plate; the whole forming a compact circular wall, 24 in. in thickness.

The shots or bolts (composed of steel) were 246 lb. and 250 lb. weight, and were 17 in. or 18 in. long, and 9 in. diameter. They were fired from the 121-ton rifled Armstrong gun, mounted on the main deck battery of the *Bellerophon*, with charge of 43 lb. each, and at a distance of 200 yards.

The gun and carriage belonging to the after-turret of the *Royal Sovereign* had been removed, and a skeleton supplied in their place with ballast equal to the weight of the ordinary gun and carriage. Against this proceeding, however, Captain Coles protested, contending that it was unfair to remove that which might be an excellent barrier in the event of a shot entering the port.

The Board of Admiralty, having on their arrival inspected the turret, retired to the *Bellerophon*. The deck of the *Royal Sovereign* having been cleared, the first shot of 246 lb. was fired at a canvas target surmounting the turret (the gun being at an elevation of 12 mins), and a portion of the canvas was carried away. This shot, however, was fired with no other object than to obtain an accurate range, but it was speedily followed by a second for a very different purpose. This was also a 246 lb. shot, and was fired at the bullseye on the turret. With tremendous force the shot struck the left edge of the port, and penetrated the 5-inch plate; but, on reaching the 4-inch plate, it glanced off, crossed the port, caused a slight indentation on the right side, and was shivered into a dozen pieces. The skeleton gun and carriage were broken into fragments; the plate iron next to that on which the bullseyes were painted was forced out several inches; a portion of the top of the turret was carried away; and the whole of the bolts in the neighbourhood of the target mark were started. The revolving machinery was then tested, and it was found that it had not sustained any injury, the turret moving with as much ease as before the shot was fired. A revolution of a quarter of a circle was then made, and this exposed the thinnest side of the turret (there being only a single plate of 5 in. at this point) to the *Bellerophon's* fire.

The next shot was of 250 lb. weight, fired at an elevation of 12 mins. It entered the turret at a junction of two plates, and made a clean breach through and separated them. The shot passed through the 5 in. plate, splintered the teak immediately behind it, and, taking an upward direction, forced up the top of the turret, and remained in the teak, the hand of the shot projecting from beneath the plate. The bolts were started, but the machinery on which the turret revolves again escaped damage.

The last shot (of 250 lb.) was a glancing shot, the elevation being 9 mins. Striking the deck at a distance of about 6 ft. from the turret, and at a point where there is thickness of 6 in. of wood and 1 in. of iron, the shot glided along the deck, tearing up the planks in its progress to the plate surrounding the turret, which it slightly bent. The shot then glided on to the side of the turret, caused an indentation about 17 in. long, 9 in. wide, and 3 in. deep, and flew away on the port bow, a cutter yacht at a distance of some 800 or 1,000 yards narrowly escaping the shot as it passed. For the third time the machinery

Experimental Firing of the Bellerophon at the Royal Sovereign at Spithead

was tried, and the turret revolved on the rollers as easily before.

This closed the experiments of the day, and Captain Coles was at once surrounded by a large number of officers and friends, who warmly congratulated him on the success which had attended the trial. The gun was trained by Jonathan Boning (a gunnery instructor on board the *Excellent*) with admirable accuracy.

1864 – SWEDISH BRIG WRECK AT SANDOWN.

The weather of Friday evening last was very wild and threatening till about eight o'clock, when the wind blew a gale from the southwest, so that foot passengers along the open space between the two lower hotels could hardly keep the road at all, being forced against the hedge, and roughly assailed by driving rain and foam; men hurried by with uncertain steps, and soon a boisterous night set in.

Observation was fearfully directed seaward, where three or four large vessels could be seen slowly but surely drifting towards the coast. By half past eight o'clock, one had stranded, and remained in an upright position to meet the full fury of the sea, but little anxiety was felt by the experienced in nautical matters, because the shore was favourable, and a ship of ordinarily substantial build, it was believed, could weather the storm till morning should relieve the crew; hence not even an attempt was made to put off a boat to rescue the distressed on board.

As time passed, the two other ships were seen close in land; a few minutes and it appeared impossible but that they must drive in; happily, however, they succeeded in clearing the first danger, and escaped altogether at last the dreaded dangers of the rocky lines about White Cliff. In the meantime, groups of men watched, by turns, the fated *Fahle Bure*, doubting a little the first opinion of safety, and fearing a worse mischance. By one o'clock, the danger was imminent, and from among the 200 watchers several proposed manning a boat of succour. Mr. Bunt, master boatman of the coastguard, and his men had been for hours watching and signalling the distressed, and now launched out their service boat, unfitted as she was for such an enterprise. Cries for help from the ship were distinctly heard; gentlemen offered rewards; and brave men stood still, plainly not because they were insensible to the cry, but because they had no suitable vessel to embark in, or apparatus to accompany them; one man is wanted for the coastguard boat to complete its crew, will any volunteer? One of the crowd steps out, entirely unprepared as he is, and the boat pushes off on its errand of mercy, but it is thrown back and again, and that effort failed. Now the shrieks became heartrending, for the ship had parted

Wreck of the Swedish Brig

completely asunder, and the crew were drowning. A boat's crew was quickly formed, determined to render all the help that a small boat, skill, and British courage could afford. A messenger was despatched to Ventnor for apparatus, and again the coastguard boat is set off to accompany the intrepid few just started farther off; tossed about and nearly swamped, the two boats approach the wreck, and each secures an increased living freight.

The coastguard boat makes first the land, and leaves the rescued men, to return for others; the little boat has done the same, and, after many attempts, the men who risked their lives for fellow creatures are made the happy instruments of saving lives, and receiving a reward money cannot purchase—the proud title of brave men. The *Fahle Bure* is a total wreck, and everything lost of cargo and clothing, but the twelve men, her crew, are all saved. They were taken to the Sandown Hotel, and were hospitably received, while willing hands surrounded them, and thankful hearts were glad to render help.

The vessel was a Swedish brig, laden with salt, upwards of 500 tons burden, under Captain Skogland. The hull, spars, ropes, &c., are to be sold in lots by public auction, on Thursday, March 30th, on the shore opposite the coastguard station, to which the wreck drifted with the tide. This is the second wreak in the bay this season, and lives might have been sacrificed, although six hours elapsed after the striking of this last ship before she broke up. Is it impossible to start a life boat fund to prepare a little for the future?

1864 – THE CHURCH BELLS OF PORTSMOUTH.

The bells in the tower of the church of St. Thomas, Portsmouth, forming a peal of eight, which had long been silent, have at length been re-hung by Messrs. Mears and Stainbank of Whitechapel, and again give out their peculiar melody. The weight of the tenor is 22 cwt., and its note in E somewhat flat. The following are the inscriptions on the several bells:

> Prosperity to all our benefactors. A.R., 1703.
>
> Peace and good neighbourhood. A.R., 1703.
>
> God save Queen Anne. A.R. 1703.
>
> John Prior, William Snook, Churchwardens 1737.
>
> Abraham Rudhall of Gloucester, cast us, 1703.
>
> God save our Queen, Prince, and Fleet. Anno Domini, 1703.
>
> Thomas Mears of London. Fecit 1794. Wm. Butler and John Parker, Churchwardens. 1794.
>
> Messieurs James Yeatman. Nicholas Horwood, Churchwardens. W. Bartlett, R. Phelps, Fecit, 1730.
>
> We good people all
>
> To prayers do call;
>
> We honour to King
>
> And brides joy do bring;
>
> Good tidings we tell
>
> And ring the dead's knell.

With regard to the history of the bells, the subjoined brief particulars which I have gleaned from various sources, may be somewhat interesting.

According to an "inventory of the church, taken A.D. 1636," there were then "four bells in the tower," and "One saints bell on the top of the church." It appears, however, that in 1702 the old tower was pulled down, and the present one erected. During the same year, "at a vestry of the inhabitants, they came to a resolution of raising a cupola on the tower of the church, which was accordingly done." It is in a later account stated that "over the cupola is a lanthorn with a bell in it, formerly employed to give notice how many ships appeared in the offing for which purpose a watchman was kept there." I may add that the bell is still retained in the lanthorn or turret, but it is now employed in case of fire.

Now, about the year 1702, when the present tower was erected, five ancient bells were presented to the parish by Prince George of Denmark, who, at the request of Sir George Rook, M.P., had them removed from the Roman Pharos, or watch tower within the fortifications of Dover Castle. Assuming then, that the four bells described in the above inventory, dated 1636, were still retained, there must have been nine bells belonging to the church in question about 1702, besides the fire bell.

And I believe that in 1703, Abraham Rudhall, the famous founder of Gloucester, a predecessor of Messrs. Mears, re-cast those nine bells into a complete peal of eight of which the first, second, third, fifth and sixth, still hang in the tower; and were certainly made by him. The fourth, seventh, and eighth, called the tenor, were subsequently cracked, and then re-cast by different founders, as indicated by the respective inscriptions.

1866 – PORTSMOUTH AND GENERAL STEAM BISCUIT COMPANY.

This Company has been formed for the purpose of extending a business already in active and profitable operation, commanding a large and increasing trade at Portsmouth and the neighbourhood.

The Directors have entered into contract for the purchase of the well-known premises, consisting of Freehold Land, Buildings, Steam Machinery, and other plant, situated at Fratton, Portsmouth, and known as "Gunnell's Steam Biscuit Factory." The present factory is fitted with a patent travelling oven, coal ovens, steam engines, rolling, pressing, stamping, and steam lifting machinery, capable of doing large business, which will be materially improved by the outlay of additional capital. As it is situated at Portsmouth, and is also contiguous to Southampton, the Company will have every facility, through its local connections, for entering into contracts with the various shipping agencies at these ports for Colonial consignments, and also with the Navy, and the numerous steamers sailing from Southampton.

The great demand for biscuits, and the absolute certainty of immediate sale to wholesale and other houses, independent of the present Business, which has been established 6 years, takes this Company, as it were, out of the region of speculation, and makes it at once a *bona fide* investment. The Directors, in recommending the same to the public, feel certain that it only requires the necessary capital to make it a source of large profit to the Shareholders; and, from the estimates in their possession, which can be inspected at the Offices of the Company, they have every reason to believe that the profits will exceed 30 per cent.

The Company, in addition to acquiring the eligible site, and freehold premises at Fratton, have also secured the valuable services of Mr. W. Gunnell, as Manager, whose practical experience in Steam Biscuit Baking, for the last fifteen years, is a guarantee that the Company's goods will be second to none in the Kingdom.

A careful inquiry has been made into the operations of the works at Fratton, and the result is of a highly satisfactory character. With only a limited capital, a trade is being transacted which yields the above large net profit after deducting all outgoings, and the Manager states that he has been compelled to refuse orders to a very large amount from want of the necessary capital, from which fact he computes that no less than fifteen hundred customers could be secured at once, in addition to those already on the books. With additional means this difficulty can be surmounted, and the business can be augmented to almost any extent.

As the Company will be in receipt of the income of the business immediately on taking possession of the premises, an early dividend may be relied on.

Prospectuses and Forms of Application for Shares may be had of the Bankers, or at the Offices of the Company. The Plans and Elevations of the Factory can be inspected at the Offices of the Company.

1866 – OYSTER CULTURE IN THE AREA.

In the times when the Romans held their *portus magnus* in the upper waters of Portsmouth harbour and anchored their galleys under the walls of the fortress whose remains may now be traced in the ruins of the Norman castle of Portchester, the estuary of waters which extended east to nearly the walls of Regnum, or Chichester, as the ancient city was afterwards named, was famous for its oysters and the almost endless varieties of fish found in its many creeks and inlets. This reputation holds to the present day, but the improvidence of man has, in many instances, extirpated the oyster from grounds it had held since first covered by tidal waters, and on others has so reduced its numbers that, dear as all sizes of the bivalve now are, from the three months oysterling to the full-grown native, the dredge will scarcely pay for the labour of working it.

The banks surrounding Spithead and extending for miles east and west of the anchorage, were equally prolific with the inland waters of Langstone, Emsworth, and Chichester, but they are now becoming equally barren. For very many years past all the grounds available to the dredger have been ruthlessly worked, and everything of the oyster kind, from the spat clinging to the stones, brought up in the dredge, to the patriarch of unknown age, has been carried off, the eatable portion sent to the market, and all small stuff carried off to Whitstable and other places, to stock private ponds.

But this has not been the worst evil the oyster has had to contend with in fighting for existence on the great shoals of the Horse, the Dean, and others on the Isle of Wight shore and off Chichester Harbour. About ten years back certain portions of Portsmouth Harbour and the harbour channel were deepened by steam dredging machines, and an immense quantity of black mud was conveyed out of the harbour in the contractors' barges and discharged on these shoals, the result being that the greater part of the oysters, as well as the spawn of other fish, was poisoned, and invaluable fishing grounds converted into a barren waste. Thus, what with over-fishing by the fishermen and the poisoning of the banks at the hands of the Government, the extensive range of banks outside Langstone, Emsworth, and Chichester Harbours were nearly denuded of their fish, and the inner waters of the harbours with their preserved grounds suffered accordingly.

There is still, however, an abundance of oysters on the outer banks to stock them thoroughly, if the waters could only be placed under a strict conservancy, and we will take two extreme points of the grounds in proof of this assertion. On the line shore which extends about 4,000 yards from the west side of Langstone harbour's mouth to Southsea Castle, it is still possible now for one man to collect on the first flow of the tide after a south-east gale a bushel basketful of fine clean oysters. These have been rolled over the Horse and Dean Shoals by the scour of the water in the gale, and where they came from undoubtedly there are others. The other illustration is that about seven miles out seaward from Southsea beach there are three small shoals lying in a triangular form in 4½ fathoms at low water. These three shoals have been fished from time immemorial, and until the recent scarcity of oysters in the market the dredge would always bring up at the least one half full of oysters, the remainder being clean round boulders about the size of a man's fist. A fisherman hauling up his dredge could tell by the size of the oysters in which part of the shoals he was working without looking at his marks.

A few years since these oysters fetched 3s. per tub, but they are now sold at 18s., and the yield per dredgeful has therefore lessened naturally from the overworking of the shoals, but still the banks fill up again with the fish from an inexhaustible source. The collection of spat and oysterlings on public fishing grounds for laying down in private ponds for growth and fattening has been carried out at Emsworth and Langstone, as in a number of other places on our coasts, for many years, but no attempt was made at oyster culture proper until France set us the example.

In 1845 M. Curbonel read a paper at a meeting of the French Academy in which he urged the necessity of taking steps to restock the oyster beds then becoming exhausted. In 1849, Professor De Quatrefages urged the same thing, and the Government ordered M. Coste to report on the subject. In 1855 M. Costes's report was received and published, and in 1861 a second edition appeared recounting the state in which the natural beds had been found and the means taken to restock them. In 1863-4-5 M. Coste's method was introduced, not altogether successfully, at Herne Bay and Southend, by means of companies formed for the purpose, Mr. Buckland in 1865 expressing an opinion that the system of M. Coste, so successful in France, was not practicable in English waters owing to the difference in temperature and the lesser amount of the Gulf stream in the English than in the French waters.

In June, 1865, Mr. G.W. Hart, the present manager of the South of England Oyster Company, visited the west coast of France, and inspected the oyster beds at St. Brieux and Ile de Re, and other places, and came to a conclusion contrary to that of Mr. Buckland. The South of England Oyster Company was immediately afterwards formed, and it is to the proceedings of the company to this date that we wish to draw attention, as very few persons will deny that all facts connected with oyster culture in this country are of interest, and that our knowledge of the subject, which at present is very limited, will be best extended by open discussion. The company have secured a large space of ground as oyster beds for the future close to the village of Havant, on the north-west shore of Hayling Island, which will give three beds, of about forty-six acres in all. The defunct Hayling Island Railway has cut off this land from the sea, but sluices have been provided in the railway embankment for necessary admission and discharge of water. These beds are yet, however, incomplete.

At the opposite extremity of Hayling Island, at the entrance of Chichester Harbour, the company have made their first great experiment in oyster culture, and their success so far has been most startling, the supply of spat in their breeding lake having proved almost unlimited, and this, too, at a time when there is a universal failure of spat at Whitstable, Herne Bay, Poole, and other places on the English coast.

The company are also engaged in preparing a portion of their grounds for breeding lobsters and other Crustacea; but it is with their endeavours to introduce successfully oyster culture on the Continental plan into this country that this notice more particularly deals. As Mr. Frank Buckland says, in "*Land and Water*," "All must be rejoiced to hear the good news; the success of this experiment in oyster breeding does the highest credit to the ingenuity of the gentleman who had the planning and superintendence of the works."

The gentleman referred to by Mr. Buckland is Mr. George W. Hart, the manager of the company; and we can bear witness to his courtesy and also to the great interest which attends a visit at the present time to the oyster farm of the South of England Oyster Company at Hayling.

1867 – A MUCH NEEDED IMPROVEMENT.

A great improvement, the want of which has been seriously experienced for many years is about to be made in the way to and from Southsea Common, through King William Gate. The road was for some time since widened and heightened at the extreme end near the guard house, but as the bridge still continued to be only of sufficient width to admit one carriage, the traffic at that particular point was often much impeded, and it is to avoid this that the improvements referred to are contemplated.

The bridge is to be extended on either side to the width of the roadway near the gate and that beyond it, and it will also be heightened to the same level. The work has been entrusted to Messrs. Simms & Marten, and it is now progressing. When they are busy, they might as well take away the arch, which is a great nuisance without being of any use in the world.

1867 – IMPROVEMENT OF THE NAVY.

Of all the steps which have been adopted of late years for the improvement of the morale of our navy, none have been so successful as the establishment of canteen recreation and reading rooms on board our larger men-of-war, where the seamen can amuse and enjoy themselves without being driven ashore to the temptations which formerly surrounded them in the slums of the seaports at which they happened to be stationed.

A writer in the *Times* gives the following account of a visit in October last to the *Duke of Wellington* receiving ship at Portsmouth:

"We found the canteen open on the main deck, with men footing it merrily forward to the sound of the violin and tambourine, others smoking and looking on gravely and critically at their shipmates' gymnastic doings, the seats around the tables on which games of various kinds were being played all filled, and lookers-on and would-be players standing round, waiting their turn, the "reading room" with upwards of a hundred men seated at its tables, some wading slowly and thoughtfully through the leading articles of a newspaper, and others deeply absorbed in the pages of *All the Year Round*, or any other periodical that luckily came to hand in turn. Over all this was a blaze of light from numerous lamps, giving a sense of comfort and warmth on a cold, damp October evening; and through all was an evident decorum of manner pervading the rough fellows' enjoyment of their pipe and their beer, their dance, their games of backgammon, chess, the races, &c., and their conning over the contents of the newspapers and periodicals. There was no doubt then of the complete success of the scheme, but a twelvemonth's experience has proved its success to a much greater extent than was then anticipated, and it now stands a self-supporting and permanent institution on board the seamen's receiving ship in Portsmouth harbour, and must remain so if supported and encouraged by those in power.

No man contributes any sum, however trifling, towards the cost of the newspapers, periodicals, or the games on the recreation tables. The whole thing, as have already observed, is self-supporting, and it is managed in this wise. The beer is supplied in casks from some brewery on shore at the trade price, and is retailed to the men at the ordinary retail price. The profit on the beer sold is placed in a fund in charge of the captain of the ship as treasurer, and this fund supplies newspapers, periodicals, and games. In all matters of expenditure from this fund Captain Fellowes has always taken the opinion of the men as expressed to him by the petty officers of the first class."

1867 – THE NAVAL REVIEW.

The grand naval demonstration on Wednesday, at Spithead, in the presence of the Queen, and in honour of the Sultan, passed off with all the éclat which could have been anticipated considering the boisterous weather. There was a large fleet of men-of-war; there were fleets of yachts, fleets of pleasure boats, and royal and illustrious visitors in numbers. Nothing was wanted to ensure success but fair winds and clear skies. The morning broke fine and clear, but with a wind violently high, and the sky and the horizon marked with that ominous grey watery tint which always forbodes a summer gale. The mist thickened as the wind freshened, with angry squalls of cold, biting rain. The sea came rolling in heavily on the beach at Southsea, where it broke in clouds of spray, and the ships heavy swells outside were dipping to their anchors in a way which showed it was impossible for small boats to get off from or to come alongside the huge craft in the distance. The review was, therefore, impossible. Some minor evolutions of the gunboats were gone through, and the fleet itself manned yards and saluted as the Sultan passed, saluted again as her

Majesty came by, but this was nearly all. The fleet did not raise their anchors.

The Queen embarked on board the *Alberta* at Trinity pier at a quarter before eleven o'clock, and went out to the *Victoria and Albert* yacht, Captain H.S.H. the Prince of Leiningen, in Cowes roads, when the Royal yacht steamed round to Osborne bay, where she remained until the *Osborne* arrived with the Sultan on board.

The strength of the fleet under review was of vessels of war (exclusive of armed troop ships, &c.) forty-nine, mounting 1,092 guns, and having an aggregate of horsepower of 22,500 horses, and a burden of 102,000 tons. The ships were moored in two lines, extending nearly east and west from within a short distance of the Spit buoy to a little beyond Ryde pier. The port, or left-hand, division, looking eastward, consisted entirely of wooden vessels, and included the following ships:—*Terrible, Victoria* (flag), *Donegal, Revenge, Duncan, Irresistible, Lion, St. George, Royal George, Mersey, Liffey, Liverpool, Phoebe, Sutlej, Dauntless, Nymph, Daphne*; while the starboard line was composed altogether of ironclads, and showed the following formidable array of vessels of the new era :—*Gladiator, Minotaur, Achilles, Warrior, Black Prince, Bellerophon, Lord Clyde, Valiant, Pallas, Research, Royal Sovereign, Prince Albert, Wyvern, Viper, Vixen, Waterwitch*. The whole fleet was under the command of Admiral Sir T.F. Pasley, who hoisted his flag on board the *Victoria*, while the starboard division was under the direction of Admiral Warden, whose flagship was the *Minotaur*.

As soon as the *Osborne*, having the Sultan and Viceroy on board, reached the Spit buoy and bore to pass through the fleet, the leading ships began to fire a Royal salute and manned their yards, an example which was followed in due order by all the other vessels of the squadron.

The discharge of the first few guns speedily wrapped the fleet in smoke; but, while the view was

Embarkation of the Sultan at Clarence Yard

uninterrupted by this dense screen, it was a pretty sight to see the men lying out upon the yards in their white frocks and ducks. Almost all the ships carried the Turkish ensign at the fore, and all had the white ensign, now the distinguishing mark of the vessels of the Royal Navy, flying from their other masts. As the *Osborne* passed between the ships the squall increased in severity until the blinding rain obscured the atmosphere and prevented anything like a critical examination of the noble vessels that lined her pathway. The Imperial yacht, however, steamed straight through the fleet, followed by the *Helicon*, the *Enchantress*, the *Ripon*, and the *Syria*, and continued her course to Osborne bay, where her Majesty's yacht, the *Victoria and Albert*, was moored.

Soon after this position was reached the weather cleared up, and the smooth slopes and green woods of the Isle of Wight, which had hitherto been shrouded by impenetrable mists, shone out in the bright sunlight. Some little time was lost here, but so varied and animated was the scene presented to the gaze that none but the most inveterate grumblers were disposed to cavil at the delay. Looking seaward, the eye ranged over the long line of ships through which the yachts had just passed, and whose massive hulls and taper masts were clearly relieved against the green water or the clear blue sky; landward, there was presented a lovely prospect of swelling uplands and deeply-tinted woods, with Osborne House in the background; and immediately at hand, the eye was delighted and the attention engaged by the rapid movements of a numerous squadron of yachts, which followed in the wake of the Sultan.

At half-past two the Queen's yacht steamed between the lines from the west, with her Majesty, the Sultan, the Viceroy, the Prince of Wales, the Duke of Cambridge, and other illustrious persons, on board. Another Royal salute was fired, the yards were manned, and even the trucks of some vessels. The Queen was vociferously cheered as she passed down the lines. A signal was given after the Queen had passed the *Minotaur* to engage the enemy, and then a grand cannonading ensued, lasting until a signal to discontinue firing was hoisted from the *Victoria*.

The operations of the day concluded with an attack by the gunboats upon the seaward fortifications of Portsmouth. These small vessels were originally moored in a line of their own on the port side of the squadron; and, upon the hoisting of the signal, they stood in towards the shores, and engaged the whole line of works from Moncton Fort to Southsea Castle.

About four o'clock, before the gunboats had ceased their attack, the Royal yacht weighed anchor and proceeded towards Osborne, saluted as usual as she passed, and a race took place between all the vessels to keep pace with the *Victoria and Albert*. Princely provision had been made on board the *Ripon* for members of the House of Commons,

The Naval Review

and just previously to the *Ripon* coming alongside Portsmouth Dockyard, Lord Ernest Brace said he had been requested, as the oldest House of Commons' man present, to express their cordial acknowledgments to the directors of the Peninsular Oriental Company for the admirable manner in which the arrangements for the comfort of all on board had been carried out. Mr. Bayley, in returning thanks, said the directors had been anxious to do all in their power to contribute to the enjoyment inseparable from so grand a national display.

On board the *Syria* the members of the House of Lords paid the same company a similar compliment, on the proposition of the Earl of Dudley. The fleet was illuminated at nine o'clock, when the wind had moderated, although it continued to blow in thick rain squalls. During the first part of the display the ships at Spithead were indistinctly seen. The *Duke of Wellington*, the *St. Vincent* and the *Victory* in the harbour presented a splendid appearance with their illuminated tiers of ports and long lights. During the second part the weather cleared for a short time, the fleet showed magnificently, covered in outline with long lights, the *Minotaur* being lit up with red fire over every spar aloft, and the *Victoria* with red and white. The general effect, and more particularly that of the discharges of rockets, was however, greatly marred by the weather.

A fatal accident took place at Blockhorn Fort to a gunner of the 16th Brigade of the Royal Artillery, who was shot from the gun whilst in the act of ramming the charge.

At the close of the inspection the Queen expressed the greatest gratification with the day's proceedings, although the weather had proved unfavourable, and the Sultan and Viceroy expressed the same feeling, but in still more forcible terms.

1867 – TELFORD'S REMINISCENCES OF PORTSMOUTH.

We take the following account of Telford, as foreman in Portsmouth, from Smiles's life of the great engineer, just published:-

"We find him, in July, 1784, engaged in superintending the erection of a house, after a design by Mr. Samuel Wyatt, intended for the residence of the Commissioner (now occupied by the Port Admiral) at Portsmouth Dockyard, together with a new chapel, and several buildings connected with the yard. Telford took care to keep his eyes open to all the other work going forward in the neighbourhood, and he states that he had frequent opportunities of observing the various operations necessary in the foundation and construction of graving docks, wharf walls, and such like, which were among the principal occupations of his after-life. The letters written by him from Portsmouth to his Eskdale correspondents about this time were cheerful and hopeful, like those he had sent from London.

His principal grievance was that he received so few from home, but he supposed that opportunities for forwarding them by hand had not occurred, postage being so dear as scarcely then to be thought of. To tempt them to correspondence he sent copies of the poems which he still continued to compose in the leisure of his evening. One of these was a "Poem on Portsdown Hill." As for himself, he was doing very well. The buildings were advancing satisfactorily; but "above all," said he, "my proceedings are entirely approved by the Commissioners and officers here so much so that they would sooner go by my advice than by my master's, which is a dangerous point, being difficult to keep their good graces as well as his. However, I will contrive to manage it."

The following is his own account of the manner in which he was usually occupied during the winter months while in Portsmouth Dock: "I rise in the morning at 7 (February 1st), and will get up earlier as the days lengthen until it comes to five o'clock. I immediately set to work to make out accounts, write on matters of business, or draw until breakfast, which is at nine. Then I go into the Yard about 10, see that all are at their posts, and am ready to advise about any matters that require attention. This, and going round the several works occupies until about dinner time, which is at 2; and after that I again go round and attend to what may be wanted. I draw till 5; then tea; and after that I write, draw, or read till half after 9; then comes supper and bed. This is my ordinary round, unless when I dine or spend an evening with a friend; but I do not make many friends, being very particular, nay nice to a degree. My business requires a great deal of writing and drawing, and this work I always take care to keep under by reserving my time for it, and being in advance of my work rather than behind it. Then, as knowledge is my most ardent pursuit, a thousand things occur which call for investigation, which would pass unnoticed by those who are content to trudge only in the beaten path. I am not contented unless I can give a reason for every particular method or practice which is pursued. Hence, I am now very deep in chemistry. The mode of making mortar in the best way led me to inquire into the nature of lime. Having, in pursuit of this inquiry, looked into some books on chemistry, I perceived the field was boundless; but that to assign satisfactory reasons for many mechanical processes, required a general knowledge of that science. I have therefore borrowed a MS. copy of Dr. Black's Lectures. I have bought his "Experiments on Magnesia and Quicklime," and also Fourcory's Lectures, translated from the French, by one Mr. Elliot, of Edinburgh. And I am determined to study the subject with unwearied attention until I attain some accurate knowledge of chemistry, which is of no less use in the practice of the arts than it is in that of medicine."

He adds, that he continues to receive the cordial approval of the Commissioners for the manner in which he performs his duties, and says, "I take care to be so far master of the business committed to me that none shall be able to eclipse me in that respect." At the same time, he states he is taking great delight in freemasonry, and is about to have a lodge room at the George Inn fitted up after his plans and under his direction. Nor does he forget to add that he has his hair powdered every day, and puts on a clean shirt three times a week.

1867 – THE EMPRESS OF THE FRENCH.

The Empress of the French arrived at Portsmouth on Monday before reaching Osborne, and spent nearly two hours there, but her presence was known only to very few persons. The Imperial yacht *Reine Hortense* reached Spithead earlier than was anticipated, having made the run from Havre in eight hours, and as the royal visitor was not expected to arrive at Osborne until three o'clock, the Empress, attended by a distinguished suite, landed at the Southsea pier. A telegram was forwarded from "The Countess Reinhardt" (under which name the Empress is travelling) to the "Emperor of the French," announcing the safe arrival of the yacht and the freedom of the passengers from sea sickness, and the telegram was also forwarded to Osborne. The Empress spent some time on the pier, and afterwards walked on the Esplanade, and witnessed the movements of some of the troops, who were going through a series of evolutions on Southsea Common. She then proceeded to the Southsea Pier Hotel, where luncheon was served, and afterwards returned to the pier, when she was conveyed on a launch to the *Reine Hortense*, and proceeded to Osborne.

A great deal of gossip is afloat concerning the private visit of the Empress of the French to Osborne. The immediate purpose of the visit is quite confidently stated to be the delivery of a message from the Emperor to Her Majesty, informing her that with great reluctance he will be obliged to go to war with Prussia, and hopes the Queen will not be less friends with him because he will be in antagonism with a nation to the throne of which the husband of her eldest daughter is the immediate heir.

1867 – UNFOUNDED RUMOURS.

It generally happens that groundless reports follow any great calamity in quick succession, and during the past week all sorts of idle stories and rumours in reference to the Fenian designs have been in circulation. In a large arsenal like this it is, of course, a matter of serious importance that every available means should be adopted to protect public property from the attacks of evil-disposed persons, and it is satisfactory to know that there has been no lack of the necessary precautionary measures. We hear that the naval Commander-in-Chief, Admiral Sir T.S. Pasley, Bart., has received a letter, purporting to have been written by one of the Fenian brotherhood, informing him of a plan devised by Fenians to destroy the ships in Portsmouth harbour. He states that arrangements have been made to blow up the ships by means of torpedoes fixed to balks of timber, which were to float in with the tide, strike against the ships, explode the torpedo, and hurl the vessel hit into the air, and that the torpedoes were being manufactured in Ireland, but that there was one manufactured not ten miles from Portsmouth. The writer gave as his motive for divulging the plot that he had two sons on board ships in harbour at Portsmouth, but it is probable that the letter is the production of some individual gifted with a vivid imagination.

1867 – COMPETITION IN THE DOCKYARDS.

The half-yearly competition of boys for the situation of apprentice in the government Dockyards and engineer student in the steam factories has lately been held at the various yards by the Civil Service

Commissioners. There were 172 candidates for the former class of situations and 75 for the latter. At the same time occurred the large annual competition amongst the Dockyard artificers for promotion to the higher grades. These examinations also are now, at the request of the Admiralty, conducted by the Civil Service Commissioners, the test consisting partly of exercises in arithmetic, &c and partly of practical questions prepared at the Admiralty. The number of competitors on the late occasion was 649.

1867 – THE CONDITION OF THE KINGSTON BURIAL GROUND.

A vestry meeting was held in the vestry room adjoining the parish church, and thence by adjournment to the neighbouring schoolroom, on Monday afternoon, for the purpose of "considering the present dilapidated and neglected state of the Kingston Churchyard, and to adopt such measures as the vestry might determine towards keeping the churchyard in repair." The Rev. J.V. Stewart, the Vicar, presided, and there was a tolerably good attendance. Mr. S. Hogg officiated as vestry clerk.

The Chairman, in introducing the matter, said he did not think it necessary that he should say much upon the subject, but he would preface his remarks by observing that if there were any gentleman present who wished to be convinced as to the state of the burial ground, he should feel obliged if he would walk over it and see the state it was then in. And if, after an inspection, they were not all thoroughly persuaded that something was necessary to be done, and that without delay, he (the Vicar) would be really very much surprised as to the feelings of those whom he was addressing.

A ratepayer interposed, and asked if the present condition of the graveyard was the result of natural decay or wanton mischief?

The Vicar said he would answer that question presently. The question for the meeting now to determine was, after making themselves thoroughly acquainted with its present condition, what remedy they could devise, and what those who were interested in the question proposed to do was this. They had already had recourse to the best means in their power in order to keep the churchyard in more decent order. Constables had been in the yard from time to time, but as their stay was necessarily short, it followed as a natural consequence that the depredations were continued during their absence, and consequently without the probability of detection. It was the practice for boys to come, not singly, but in squads, and as soon as one body was removed, unless someone were constantly there, another came, and the result was that they were perpetually being annoyed by sights which were anything but satisfactory to the feelings of a Christian person.

And so general had this state of things become, that the churchwardens and himself (who were equally interested in the movement) felt themselves placed in the position that it was their duty to call the meeting together, trusting that this unhappy state of things would be at length brought to a close. They would remember, while considering this question, that they were not calling upon the meeting to contribute in the same way as they would if a church rate were levied towards the support of the church, but that they were appealing to their better feelings to contribute in accordance with the provisions of an Act of Parliament which rendered it obligatory for them, not only to keep in a becoming and proper state the church ground, but also the walls of any ground which had ceased to be used in consequence of the formation of another. From the terms of the Act (the 18th sec. of the 18th and 19th Vict., chap. 198), it was clear that it was the duty of the Burial Board or the Churchwardens to keep the ground and walls in a proper and decent state, and so thoroughly were the Burial Board agreed upon the necessity of the matter receiving attention, that it was in entire conformity with their feelings and wishes that the subject was brought under the consideration of the vestry meeting some two years since, when it met with opposition.

It was quite true that it was the duty of the Churchwardens to keep the burial ground in order, and that if they neglected the discharge of their duties then the Burial Board would take it in hand, but neither were disposed to expend the money requisite without first having the sanction of those who would be called upon to contribute to it. And who was there amongst them who would object to the expenditure of a little money for such a purpose? It was evident that it was necessary something should be done without delay, and if they were all agreed upon this point the next question would be how they could best accomplish it. He would suggest - and having lived for some time in the neighbourhood he could speak from experience - that if they wished to perform the work satisfactorily, they must have someone continually on the spot, otherwise all they did would be in vain. They could, perhaps at a small cost, secure a cottage in the locality where the person selected and his wife could reside, and if he were a pensioner his remuneration need not be large, so that the whole of the duties could be performed at a trifling cost. The person selected would act first of all as a constable who would have the opportunity of contending with any difficulty which might occur, such as that of removing persons who might conduct themselves with impropriety; secondly, he could act as porter or keeper of the gates, who would open them to all respectable people, to the exclusion of those who were known to be disorderly; and thirdly, he could also occupy his time as a labourer, by cutting the grass and performing such other acts as would be necessary in a place of that description.

If such a course were adopted, he believed the result would be that the sacred spot would hereafter be highly satisfactory to the parish generally, and if a few shrubs and plants were introduced it would be an attractive spot for persons to retire to consult their feelings over the graves of their departed relatives and friends, and would prove a credit to the parish and would be accomplishing an object which they must all desire as a Christian community.

Mr. Bayne had taken some interest in this question, and had recently taken the trouble to go over the ground and ascertain the extent of the wilful damage to the graves and other resting places of the dead. He could give them a number of instances of the most disgraceful acts in this sacred spot. Of six brick graves, one was entirely filled with rubbish, and the tops of three others had been torn off and removed. Twenty of the vaults had been most shamefully defaced and destroyed, and the iron railings round 16 of them had been torn off and removed whilst 13 head stones were thrown down, broken, and lying in all directions over the ground.

A voice - Are they public or private property?

Mr. Bayne could not say anything about that, but it was a fact that the ground was in the condition he had described, and he would ask the gentlemen seriously whether they thought that was at all creditable to a place like Portsmouth? Worse than this, too, the churchyard was the resort of the worst classes, and most of them were aware that things took place there which were of the most immoral character, and which could scarcely fail to call for the sympathies of all who respected the ashes of the dead.

A ratepayer confirmed Mr. Bayne's statement, and added that recently a boy was seen in the neighbourhood of the Kingston burial ground with a human skull under his arm, which he was beating with a human shin bone which he had in one of his hands. Was there any person present or in the parish who would like to know that the skull or legs of their departed friends had been removed in this disgraceful way from their last resting place?

Mr. Thunder thought that as the vaults were private property, they should be repaired by those to whom they belonged, or that they should be confiscated and pulled down. He was occasionally called upon to pay for the repair of stones and graves in which he was interested in another part of the county, and had even been threatened with county court proceedings in the event of there being any delay in the payment; and if that were law in one county or borough why should it not be in another?

The Vicar thought Mr. Thunder had made a mistake. The parish churchyard was the property of the ratepayers, and they, or the churchwardens who represented them, were bound to see that it was kept in a proper state of repair. It was true that the owners were liable to repair defects arising from age and decay, but it was not so with reference to acts of wanton mischief.

Mr. Kidd fully endorsed the Vicar's explanation, and added that so far as his knowledge of the law went, he believed that if he had owned a vault and it had been wantonly destroyed, he should have felt justified in bringing an action against the responsible persons if it were not repaired. He knew that was the position of the present Burial Board, and he did not see why the same law should not apply to the churchyard.

Mr. Hatch spoke in support of some immediate steps being taken for the purpose of avoiding the many disgraceful scenes which were now witnessed.

A ratepayer asked if the money which would be necessary for the purpose would come from the poor rates or the burial fees?

The Vicar - It comes from the poor rates through the overseers.

Mr. Kent said this was a matter he had taken great interest in for many years past, and therefore he was pleased to have the opportunity of taking part in the proceedings on this occasion. The condition of the burial ground was a source of vexation to him when he occupied the position of churchwarden, but as he did not like personally to take the responsibility of the thing the question was from time to time deferred, and that would account for its present disgraceful condition. Now, however, that there was an evident desire to do something in the matter he thought they could soon overcome the difficulty at a trifling cost, if they were to adopt the course suggested by the Vicar, by having a person living on the spot. He thought that the present dead house (which was now perfectly useless) could at a trifling cost be converted into a residence for a man and his wife, and with the addition of a small weekly remuneration, they would always have a person on the spot, and thus obviate that which had hitherto occasioned so much pain and annoyance to those who were interested in the parish burial ground. Believing that some such course as this was about the best they could adopt, he was prepared to propose a resolution on the subject, especially as they could get the services of a competent man for about 7s. or 8s. a week. Mr.

Kent then proposed the resolution, which was to the effect that this meeting acknowledged the disgraceful state of the churchyard, and consented to the Burial Board, with the Churchwardens expending a sum not exceeding 100l., to put it in a proper state of repair.

Mr. R.F. Jolliffe seconded the motion.

Mr. Kidd suggested whether it would not be as well to embody in the resolution something with reference to the employment of a person, at a weekly salary, to look after the place?

Mr. Kent assented, and it was arranged that the words "and that a person, to be selected by the Burial Board or the Churchwardens, shall be appointed to have general charge of the ground," should be added to the resolution.

In its amended form (it being thought desirable to leave the question of remuneration to the discretion of the Churchwardens), the resolution was put to the meeting and carried by a large majority, eight only voting against it

On the motion of Mr. Bayne, seconded by Mr. Kidd, a vote of thanks was awarded to the Vicar, and the latter, in reply, said he was very glad to see that the vestry had adopted the resolution, because he believed it would be highly satisfactory to the parish to know that the ground would be kept in decent order, which it would be.

1867 – THE PORTSMOUTH PANTOMIME.

The popularity of pantomime, remarkable, and to some extent inexplicable though it may be, is an assured fact, and the glances of Yuletide holiday seekers are instinctively directed to the advertisement announcing its production. The sternest legitimist who at the bottom of his heart hates opera, and at the top of his voice denounces the modem sensational drama, would as soon think of hooting Hamlet or Macbeth from the stage as of prohibiting the appearance of Harlequin and Clown at Christmas.

Portsmouth play goers will be glad to learn that Mr. Rutley has provided for their delectation at the approaching festive season a pantomime from the practised pen of Mr. R. Soutar, entitled "Ding Dong Bell, Pussy's in the well," or "Harlequin who Killed Cock Robin!" The brilliant success of previous pantomimes raises expectations which we expect will be fully realized, and we believe that on no former occasion have the pantomime preparations at the Theatre Royal, Landport, been on such an extensive scale. The pantomime is to be played for the first time on Monday evening next.

1867 – STATE OF THE ROADS AT FRATTON.

A very crowded meeting of the inhabitants of Highfield, Delhi, Bishop, and Gliddon Streets, and Curtis Terrace, was held on Wednesday evening at Mr. Newall's, Bishop Street, Fratton, to take into consideration the disgraceful state of the roads in that locality. Mr. S. Smith, who was voted to the chair, said they all knew the object of the meeting. It was to court no favour, to seek no privilege, but to ask from the Local Board that which they, as respectable inhabitants, were warranted in expecting.

They were aware that the state of their roads had been noticed by the local papers, and that petitions had also been sent to the board, but nothing definite was decided. What position would they have been in last summer, during the visitation of cholera, if it had not been for the hand of Providence, which was more thoughtful towards them than the Local Board. In case of such a visitation half their homes would have been desolated by sickness. They were now cherishing and cultivating disease at their very doorsteps; they were driving all respectable people from their neighbourhood, and getting a lower class—that was, they were turning their houses into barracks. They had to pay extra for all cartage; medical gentlemen were ordering their patients away, and bakers refused to call upon them.

Such was the present state of things, and he felt they were justly entitled to one of three things. Either let the Local Board repair their roads or cause them to be done or strike them off the roll and never let them see the face of a collector. It was proposed by Mr. Allen, seconded by Mr. Notting, and resolved - "That a deputation of five, selected from this meeting, wait upon the Local Board to receive a definite answer to our petition, and if their reply is not favourable, immediately to obtain the signatures of all the medical gentlemen in this borough to a petition, together with the inhabitants, and forthwith send our real grievances to the highest authority, in London."

A vote of thanks to the chairman brought the meeting to a close.

1867 – SOUTHSEA IMPROVEMENTS.

It is truly gratifying to see how rapidly improvements are now being carried out in this neighbourhood, but more especially in Southsea. The esplanade and Common have been greatly improved during the last few months, and now that the Southsea Pier Hotel is open, and the additions to the Queen's Hotel are approaching completion, the Common itself seems to have acquired a sudden transformation.

The terrace adjoining the Southsea Pier Hotel is complete, some of the houses are let, and, altogether, Southsea has had such a complete "lift" as to render it one of the best, if not the best, watering places in England.

This, of course, refers more especially, to the west end of Southsea Common but the desire for building first-class houses has manifested itself at the extreme eastern end. The "Southsea Beach Mansion," containing upwards of 140 rooms, is progressing rapidly and the land adjoining will shortly be built upon. It may, therefore, be fairly presumed that before long the whole of the north side of the Common from west to east will be bounded by handsome buildings, commanding an uninterrupted and unrivalled sea view.

Great and manifest as these improvements are, they only serve to render further extension necessary, to effect which it is indispensable that an easy and rapid communication with the Railway should at once be made. This can only be effected by means of a tramway worked by horse traction, as the Board of Trade have the strongest objection to level crossings, although, in this instance, but two lines of road would be crossed, namely, that which is known as Albert Road, leading from the east end of Elm Grove to Highland Road, and that from Southsea Common to Cumberland Fort.

A company will shortly be formed to carry out these improvements, with the title of, the "East Southsea Tramway and Pier Company." It is their intention to make application to Parliament in the coming session for permission to lay down a double line of tramway, with all recent improvements, communicating with the present railway at and under the footbridge of the footpath leading from Fratton to Milton, crossing the old canal by means of a bridge, Albert and Southsea Common roads, as before stated, on the level, and terminating at or near the Coast Guard Station at the east end of the Common.

This communication with the railway could be effected at a moderate cost, as it would only be necessary to erect a small station at the spot before mentioned, and at which the whole of the arrival tickets could be collected with greater advantage than as hitherto at the Landport Terminus. The line proposed, for the greater portion of its length, would be carried over land which is literally "landlocked," and has no communication with the highways beyond that which is afforded by occupation roads. This alone, it is confidently believed, would induce the owners to dispose of their land at a moderate remuneration, as by means of the road proposed the remainder of their land would become much more accessible, and would be rendered immediately available for building purposes.

The tramway, however, would form but one portion of the scheme, as it is intended to make it a building speculation as well, for which purpose it is proposed that the new roadway should be eighty or a hundred feet in width, which would leave ample space for a carriage drive, and a footpath on each side of the tramway, with building land two hundred and fifty feet in depth on the east and west sides. At certain intervals, too, it is proposed that crossroads should be set out, the effect of which would be that the whole of the adjoining land would be well opened for building purposes generally, and good corner sites would be obtained for the erection of handsome residences. This description applies only to that portion of the new road which runs on the north side of Albert Road (leading to Highland Road, Cumberland Fort, &c.) The remaining portion would run immediately between the roads on the east and west sides of "East End House," and terminate at the north side of the residence, formerly known as Lump's Mill. The only house property necessary to be purchased would be Beach Farm, situate on the north side of Albert Road.

It is also intended that a row of trees should be planted on each side of the new road. The new road will communicate with Fratton, at or near the railway bridge, by means of a road which will be carried along the southern bank of the old canal. It is believed that the sale of the land thus acquired, laid out principally in frontages of 100 feet each, would prove highly remunerative; and that, on account of the roadway being of so extensive a width, speculators will be ready to commence the erection of first-class villa residences on each side.

In addition to this it is proposed that a promenade pier should be built immediately opposite the new Coast Guard Station at East Southsea, and that steamboats of light draught should ply between such pier, Southsea, Victoria, and Albert piers, and the proposed new pier at Gosport at a minimum rate for transit.

1867 – THE PORTSMOUTH FEMALE PENITENTIARY AND SOCIETY FOR THE REFORMATION OF FALLEN WOMEN.

A public meeting to commemorate the union of these two excellent institutions was held in the Portland Hall, Southsea, on Wednesday afternoon. There was a tolerably good attendance, and several ladies occupied seats in different parts of the hall. J. Deverell, Esq., of Purbrook Park, presided; and amongst those present were Mr. Sergeant Gaselee, Admiral Sir Thomas Pasley, Bart, the Port-Admiral, Admiral Sir H.D. Chads, Bart., and others.

Prayer having been offered by the Rev. A. Lowry, the chaplain to the institutes, the Chairman opened the proceedings. He said they were assembled together on this occasion to communicate to the meeting the union which had been recently effected between two institutions in this locality which had for their object the reclaiming and reformation of those unfortunate women who had fallen into sin and misery. Now, as their worthy chaplain had so appropriately said, this was a great and important work, and no one had had a better opportunity of forming an opinion than he had, as the chaplain of the hospital, and this institution, of the importance and value of the work in which they were engaged.

They were all pleased and grateful that this union had taken place, and from it they were induced to believe would follow the most happy results. He believed they would find that the society at Landport (the Penitentiary) had not previously prospered as they could have wished; but now that they had succeeded in obtaining the good services of an excellent lady, who had not only devoted the whole of her time and Christian services to the work, but who had also nobly given her money for the support of this institution, under God, it had prospered; and he (the Chairman) was pleased to think and believe that it would continue to prosper.

However, he believed they were all of one opinion that a work of so much importance should be increased in usefulness; and the committee were resolved, God blessing them, that this institution, which had already done so much good, should now have increased support given to it. They had called the meeting together this day for the express object of appealing publicly to the inhabitants on the subject; and notwithstanding the meeting was thinly attended and by this he meant that the meeting was not so large as the importance of the work warranted, yet he was induced to hope that from it would result a great effort, not only within this immediate locality, but without it, to reclaim those poor unhappy women.

It was at all times a delicate subject to speak upon, but yet it was one, the importance of which, they must all feel and thoroughly appreciate and there could be no question that the sphere of usefulness had been considerably enlarged in consequence of the increased number of lock wards at the hospital, which, as they were no doubt aware, resulted from the passing of an act of parliament, with which he (the Chairman) was pleased to think he had something to do with. With reference to this act, he believed he was one of the first who agitated the question. He had urged upon one of the Under Secretaries of State the desirability and necessity of passing in parliament a measure which would arrest and restrict the progress of crime in this and other seaport and garrison towns.

He well remembered that when he first mentioned the subject to the gentleman, to whom he referred, he started, and said, "It won't be possible to put the thing in operation." He (the Chairman), however, continued to explain his reasons upon the subject; and the result was that at the close of the conversation between them he took a different view of it. He (the Chairman), succeeded in removing some of his objections to legislative interference; and at the close of the season an imperfect act was passed, which was brought into operation in this town, Plymouth, Aldershot and one or two other places.

That act worked so well that the Admiralty in conjunction with the War Department, determined upon increasing the accommodation in the lock wards in the hospital at Landport, and in the following year an amended act was passed giving greater facilities for these unfortunate females into that institution. Of course, it was useless to consider that the Government in this respect were influenced by charitable feelings to protect our sailors and soldiers; with them it was purely a question of economy; but the result was that these poor creatures were there provided for and attended to according to their several wants.

Then it was – as he heard it urged with considerable force and earnestness at a large meeting in Willis's Rooms, in aid of the funds of the London Lock Hospital, last March two years ago, and which was attended by men of all shades of political opinions – that the question arose as to what should be done.

It was, however, useless to think that the evil would to any extent be abated, unless some interest were manifested towards these poor creatures upon recovery, and it was then resolved that something should be done, and he believed that by the introduction of such institutions as these, the great work had been commenced.

Well he repeated that, accommodation having been increased in Portsmouth – he believed to the extent of 60 beds, and a still larger increase of accommodation was to be provided – the question arose, "What shall we do for them when they leave the hospital?" and that was just the question he wished to put to those present and to the public generally.

They had, as he had previously intimated, succeeded in getting Mrs. Colebrook to come and reside in the Penitentiary, and under her kind efforts they had hitherto been enabled to receive all who were willing to come. But the funds were low, and in an exhausted state; and were it not for the pecuniary sacrifice Mrs. Colebrook had made, they would now have been aground. Now, was that a state of things which the inhabitants of this neighbourhood were disposed to permit? He would ask some of them to walk through the wards of the hospital, and cast their eyes upon some of those unhappy woman - he could hardly call them women either, for many had not advanced beyond childhood - and their hearts would bleed when told how they were led astray, and how willing they were, if an opportunity offered, to come out of the hospital and lead a decent and respectable life.

But what, he would ask, was, their position? In passing through those wards they found that a vast number of these poor creatures were girls, and were they to be left alone, uncared for and without the chance of entering a place in which they could enjoy the advantages of a reformed life? They had now, through the suggestion of Mr. Gillman, himself and others, a superintendent of those lock wards - a Christian woman, whose business and desire it was to direct their attention to better things, and to that holy influence which could lead them from sin and misery to a better walk of life. But there was something far more required. These seduced and poor women were away from friends - how they had been brought here it was impossible to say; but it should be, and in many instances was, the desire of good Christian people that they should not again return to their former abodes of wretchedness and vice.

He was quite aware that in some instances there was a degree of prejudice to overcome - and this was one of the principal difficulties they had to contend against when urging the claims of these women before the sympathies of some people could be wrought upon. But should they allow prejudice to prevent them from stretching out the hand of love and charity, to assist a fallen sister? Would they, through prejudice, allow these unfortunate females to wander from one town to another till they found themselves again in the lock wards at the hospital, and permit them to remain there uncared for? He thought there were few right-minded people who would wish to do that; but if there were no accommodation in the shape of properly conducted Christian homes, this must inevitably be the result. So soon as these wretched objects of charity were outside the walls of the hospital, so soon were they trapped by those who harbour them and live upon their immorality and vice, in those dens of iniquity, which reminded him of some of the horrors of the slave trade.

And, therefore, unless such institutions as those he was now advocating were supported, nothing but an early grave awaited these abandoned women when discharged from the hospital. Now, it might be asked, "How can we assist in this good work?" Well, first of all, they could help pecuniarily with their subscriptions. It was proposed to enlarge the asylum, and this subject had already been seriously considered; but even supposing they succeeded in raising the necessary money for this purpose, it would be of little or no use unless they saw a prospect of obtaining sufficient subscriptions to maintain the extra beds which would thus be provided. And this was really one great question which they were called upon to consider; and those who would come forward with an annual subscription to support the beds would encourage the committee to proceed with the alterations, and he would undertake that the committee proceeded to enlarge the home.

There was another way, too, by which the usefulness of the institution could be extended and enlarged, and this depended entirely upon the assistance of heads of families. If, for instance, people would go to the Home and ascertain from Mrs. Colebrook those who are willing and competent to go into domestic service, and engage them, it would, of course, materially relieve the institution, and would also secure for the person selected a comfortable residence away from the influences of their former vice. Again, others could assist in providing work. The women in the Home were actively employed - he meant with needlework, but principally with washing – and as the produce added considerably to the revenue, he hoped that the institution in this respect would meet with increased support.

Apart from all this, however, the one great and important question they had to decide was as to how the women could be disposed of after leaving the home. That was a question which had occasioned a great deal of anxious thought, and he (the Chairman) had directed his attention to emigration. He had made some enquiries, but he was not at present in a position to anticipate that it would be attended with any successful result. This would be a scheme, if practicable, which would be of great advantage; but then the difficulty was in selecting a colony where such women would be welcomed, and in raising a fund to convey them there. This was a question of very great importance, and there was considerable difficulty in arriving at a conclusion as to what should be done in the matter. However, they already had a home, and it was for those who sympathised with the unfortunate women referred to to support the Christian efforts of Mrs. Colebrook in her work of faith and labour of love. Were those present, he asked, willing to see Mrs. Colebrook work single-handed? If they were disposed to take any part in this great work, and would undertake to strengthen those who were at present engaged in it, then it would indeed be apparent that they had not met together that day for little purpose.

Again, referring to the want of accommodation, the Chairman said he had got his builder to prepare an estimate of what it would cost to erect an additional ward, and he found that it would be a comparatively small sum - about 250l. Half of that sum had already been promised, and the committee would like to proceed with the work next autumn; but then came the question - How were the beds to be maintained and supported? He believed it cost, after deducting the earnings, about 15l. yearly for each bed; and taking into consideration the nature of the work in which they were engaged, he was induced to hope that money would be forthcoming to enable them successfully to proceed as soon as convenient with the alteration.

Mr. Gillman read the report, of which the following is a copy:-

The institution long known as the Portsmouth, Portsea, and Gosport Female Penitentiary, established in 1831, has been for some time in cooperation with the Society for the Rescue of Fallen Women, more recently established in Portsmouth, and it has been decided by the committees of the two societies that the same should be considered as one institution, and in future designated the "Portsmouth Rescue Society and Home for Fallen Women," to be located in the premises of the Penitentiary at Landport.

In the report of the Penitentiary last year, it was stated that Mrs. Colebrook had, at the request of the committee, kindly taken charge of the institution in June, 1865, to which she added the Home established by her at King Street, Portsmouth; and the value of her Christian services cannot be too highly appreciated.

At that time the combined institutions contained 33 inmates. Since then 130 have been admitted, and 17 re-admitted, making a total of 180, who, have been disposed of as follows:-

Sent into service - 45
Sent home to their friends - 28
Left at their own request – 56
Sent to the Hospital - 8
Sent to the Union House –
Married –
Emigrated to New Zealand –
Died –
Remaining in the Home - 37

The inmates are occupied in washing and needlework and trained for domestic service. The returns for washing from 1st July 1865, to 30th June 1867, are 478l. 0s. 10d., being for the last twelve months at an average rate of 23l. 12s. 3d. per month. The sum of 32l. has been also received for needlework.

The total receipts in subscriptions and donations by the united institutions since they have been under the charge of Mrs. Colebrook, from 1st July, 1865, to 30th June 1867, a period of two years amount only to 638l. 8s. 3d.; those resulting from washing and needlework, during the same period, amount to 505l. 0s. 10d. making a total of 1,143. 8s 1d. The expenditure during the same period amounts to 1,235l. 0s. 1d., the deficiency having been met by the devotion of Mrs. Colebrook, whose desire it is to rely on the aid of Almighty God to raise up the means whereby she may be enabled to carry forward her beneficent plans.

The balance at present in the hands of the treasurer of the Penitentiary is 29l. 15s. 9d. only, and the funded property is expended.

It must be obvious to every friend and well-wisher of this greatly needed institution that this state of things must not be allowed to continue, and it is, therefore, necessary to make an urgent appeal to the public for an increase of funds, not only to support the present number of inmates, but also to increase the accommodation so much needed in the Home.

The number of beds occupied in the Lock Wards of the Hospital is now 60, and unless a refuge is offered to the poor objects of charity on quitting the Hospital, they have no alternative but to fall back on sin, and end their wretched lives by an early death.

An estimate has been made for enlarging the asylum, and providing a much-needed bath, at a cost of 250l., or thereabouts. More than half of this sum has been promised; but the committee do not feel justified in proceeding to enlarge the building without first obtaining the promise of additional subscriptions to enable them to support the inmates.

The Home is conducted on principles of the strictest economy, which must be manifest to everybody, for it can be shown that the annual cost of the maintenance of each inmate is only 15l. 10s. 9d.

Mr. Norman read the balance sheet of the late institution in Portsmouth, known as the Society for the Reformation of Fallen Women. At the annual meeting in May the balance was 10l. 17s. 1d.; the contributions since then had amounted to 55l. 1s. 1d.;

and a balance still remained in the treasurer's hands of 7l. 10s. 3d. This, Mr. Norman explained, was a much smaller account than had hitherto been presented, but that, he thought was not in any way to be accounted for from a falling off of sympathy on the part of those who had from the first, taken an interest in the work, but rather from the fact that in consequence of the present state of things at Landport, many of the friends had given their contributions there in a quiet manner to forward the good cause.

The Venerable Archdeacon Wright had very great pleasure in moving that the report be received, adopted, and printed. They were assembled there to express their sympathies towards those who might have been, under better and more favourable circumstances, happy members of happy families, and this, he thought, was sufficient to excite the sympathy of any heart which had the slightest amount of feeling in it. While he expressed his earnest wishes towards any institution, which under the blessing of God, had a tendency to mitigate the evils by which they were surrounded, he thought that their one great object to be to remove, as far as possible, the causes which produced these evils.

For instance, they could all show, from the cottage to the house of the wealthy, and from the conduct of the Magistrate and those who acted for the Government in this place, their sympathy towards a movement like that which they were now considering, and endeavour, as far as possible, to alleviate the evils that exist; but he still thought that the grand thing for them to consider was the desirability of going to the fountain head, and thus preventing those poor creatures coming to that condition which was so terrible to consider and which all present, no doubt, much lamented.

Take, for example, as a cause, the accommodation afforded in the cottage, and it would be seen that several persons were perhaps huddled together from early childhood, and were thus from their infancy initiated in those very vices which they were now endeavouring to mitigate. Then, again, take a class of men who were regarded as respectable tradesmen - a class of brewers, who, had the possession of capital, and to what extent were these liable for the growing evils of which they complained? Take the haunts of vice these men bought up, look at them as they pass to and fro and see the collection of poor creatures under the roof of their own property, and yet complacently behold it, to attend, perhaps, their places worship, and to be found at such meetings as these!

Did these brewers, when they went to bed, ever think of these poor creatures, and that it was upon these they were in reality living, and that they themselves had some share, at least, in the cause of the evils which this meeting was lamenting. Having referred to the existence of one particular house in Portsmouth where girls from 14 and 15 were harboured, and were compelled to secure for the landlord of the house the expenditure of as much money as possible for drink, and thus, of course, adding to the income of the very men to whom he had referred, the Venerable Archdeacon Wright asked the meeting if they did not think they were beginning at the wrong end?

Then, again, what influence had the Magistrates in a question of this kind, and to what extent could they exert themselves either for good or for evil? Take a body of Magistrates sitting together, and an application is about to be made for a spirit license. Signatures were to be got - and there was no difficulty about, that! - and when these were obtained, the license, perhaps was granted upon the representation that one was required, when there were one, or two, or four, or ten, as the case might be, within a stone's throw of it, and thus another house was added to which these poor creatures could go, for it was notorious that they always went to drink to drown their care and sorrow. He made these few remarks as one on the outside, as a sojourner amongst them for a time; but at the same time, while speaking of these causes, let him express his warmest sympathy with the holy work in which they were engaged. It did not to him signify who they were or to whom they belonged - they might be Buddhists, or Mahomedans, or members of this denomination or that, but while they engaged in a work so holy as that of administering to the happiness, comfort, and well-being of a poor, wretched class of women, so long were they entitled to his sympathy and support.

The Rev. J.G. Gregson, in a speech of some length, seconded the resolution. He thought in dealing with a question of this importance they should trace the source – drink - and having found the monster they should put their foot on its head so that it should sting no more. These poor creatures trusted man and fell. She was branded, poor creature! but the seducer was free. She was despised, she was an outcast, and an inmate of the lock ward at the hospital; he - the seducer - could continue to associate in good society, was allowed to keep company with decent people's daughters and talk to their wives, and what was the difference between them? If one was unfortunate, the other was a moral murderer. And both should be alike branded. And now with regard to the remedy. It was no use attending meetings of this kind and delegating the duties to a committee. They were all personally responsible; and if they really wished to check the progress of this lamentable sin, they must individually exert themselves in the matter. The consideration of this question reminded him of the effect of a sojourn with the heathen – either heathenism affected Christianity or Christianity affected heathenism. And so, it was with reference to the sins of this world; and if they wished to see a change for the better, they must all exert themselves to their utmost in their efforts to save or reclaim poor fallen women. The resolution was agreed to.

The Rev. J.C. Martin proposed the next resolution, which was to the effect that the meeting desired to acknowledge the Divine influence vouchsafed to the institution, and especially to recognise God's goodness in securing and continuing the valuable services of Mrs. Colebrook, as the superintendent of the Home. Referring to the influence of the Magistrates, he said he was pleased to see that their worships in Portsmouth had determined upon putting the law in proper force and he trusted that if it became necessary to fine persons for harbouring prostitutes upon a second occasion, the Magistrates would do it in such a way as to teach these people that so far as they were concerned, there was a positive determination to put it down.

The Rev. J.W. Banks seconded the resolution, which was agreed to.

Mr. B.W. Carter, from the body of the hall, desired to inform the meeting that a letter had been received from Mr. W.H. Stone, in which that gentleman expressed his regret that a prior engagement prevented his attendance today. The other member for the borough (Mr. Gaselee) was in the room, and perhaps he would speak for himself.

The Chairman said he must apologise for having omitted to notice the receipt of the letter referred to by Mr. Carter. He knew Mr. Stone was a warm supporter of this institution, and that he would have been present could he have made it convenient.

Mr. Serjeant Gaselee, M.P., said he had been a subscriber to the institution for many years, and he was pleased that he had the opportunity of supporting it. He was pleased to hear that there was a prospect of the society increasing in usefulness. He and his friend Mr. Stone amalgamated - they found, too, that there were other judicious amalgamations - and he had been always favourable to the amalgamation of these societies. Indeed, he thought it would be a good thing if there were a few more such amalgamations. He did not come there to speak, and should not have done so had he not been referred to by Mr. Carter; but now that he was speaking, he could not help saying that he was not over pleased with the manner in which the proceedings had been conducted.

They didn't want any preaching; what they wanted was money, and how they should get that was all they need care about. They were not there to listen to an attack upon the Magistrates and the brewers. They were not responsible for the conduct of those who sold the beer. The real point for them to consider was, "How can we get money?" They did not come there to a hear what was the cause of prostitution; they all knew it, and deplored it. They were not there because they believed the result to be so horrible that it was their duty to do all in their power to check its progress; but after all, the great practical question was how to get money, and it was that to which the speakers should have directed their attention.

They were called together to see what could be got from them. They wanted to get hold of people who would say, "I'll give 5s.," and see that they got 5s. – and "I'll give 10s., 20s., 40s." - or anything else, they liked, and look and see that they got the money. That was the way to do business. They didn't want to hear all these horrible tales, and to listen to eloquent harangues. What he would suggest was that before they talked about enlarging the building, they should see that they got money enough to support the Penitentiary as it was at present. He was afraid they would be going too far; and his suggestion was to get the money first, and enlarge the place, if it was wanted, afterwards. He was quite sure his friend Mr. Stone would come down handsomely, but they should also come down handsomely themselves. He thought that before they called upon the members, they should do something themselves. They shouldn't be so free in following their members but allow the members to follow them. He quite sympathised with the movement, but as they wanted nothing but money, he should advise them to lock the door and allow none to leave till they had put their name on paper and promised to contribute something.

The Venerable Archdeacon Wright desired permission to make one or two observations. He must confess that he scarcely anticipated the pleasure of having addressed a member of the House of Commons, and that, of course, he did not expect to be censured by one; but if he wished to select one for this purpose, and one who could do him no possible harm; he certainly should have selected Serjeant Gaselee. He denied having heaped abuse upon the publicans as a body, but what he did say, and what he was prepared to repeat, was that there was a degree of responsibility attaching to the owners of those houses which he had specially alluded to as haunts of vice.

So far, too, from there being a cause to censure the Magistrates, they were just informed by one of their own members, and he was pleased to hear it, that they have determined to take the matter in hand. He repudiated the insinuation entirely; and the only happy thought to him was that it came from Serjeant Gaselee.

The Rev. Mr. Martin said he was in a position to state that so far from Mrs. Colebrook wishing this to be purely an effort to obtain money, she was directly opposed to it, and believed that it was God's work, and that He would sustain her in it.

The Chairman remarked that he thought it was but fair to one of the leading brewing firms here to state that some few years ago, when sitting as a Magistrate at Gosport, they agreed to enter into an arrangement with their tenants, stipulating that if any of them were known to encourage prostitution they would be turned out of the premises there and then.

The Venerable Archdeacon Wright asked the Chairman if his remarks did not justify what he (Archdeacon Wright) had previously said?

The Chairman – Quite so.

The Rev. J.G. Gregson said that recently the Mayor handed him a paper with a list of 45 public houses in the borough in which prostitutes were known to be harboured. He (the speaker) went to a public house – and not one of the lowest order either – yesterday, and he there saw a prostitute who was dying.

After some remarks by Vice-Admiral Chads (who suggested that circulars should be issued and advertisements inserted, containing appeals for increased assistance), the proceedings were brought to a close by the adoption of the usual vote of thanks to the Chairman.

A collection was made at the door in aid of the funds of the united institutions, which amounted to 8l. 17s. 4d.

We may add that 150l. has been subscribed towards enlarging the Home.

1867- CONVICT LIFE IN PORTSMOUTH PRISON.

We take the following interesting personal narrative, (slightly abridged) of convict life in Portsmouth prison from a capital article in *Chambers' Journal*, entitled "*Twenty Years' Penal Servitude*":-

I can scarcely remember the first few days after my sentence; I woke up, as it were, in Millbank Prison. I awoke, to the tortures of my punishment. 0 those weary days: the tread mill, the grinding mill, the oakum picking, the ceaseless routine of labour, the eternal silence. They soon affected my constitution, and by the recommendation of the doctor, I was sent to another prison, where the work was outdoor. Hitherto, I had been separated from all association; but in the prison I was going to, l was to work in company with a gang. Strange to say, I preferred separate confinement. I hated the thought of associating with thieves and pickpockets - I, a gentleman, with refined and honourable feelings - I, who would not wrong a child, to have to herd with the scum of society! I felt it bitterly, for I did not look on my own crime as morally wrong; illegal, I know it was, and I know the law cannot make distinctions.

By the time I got to Portsmouth prison, the numb feeling which I had after my sentence was wearing off. I was beginning to observe things more closely, and, alas, daily to feel them more keenly. I shall never forget the journey by rail in a third-class carriage, with eleven others, handcuffed together, with a heavy bright chain drawn through rings in our horrid bracelets. I sat quite silent; the rest, probably hardened wretches, were willing enough to converse, which they did at every opportunity when they could escape the sharp eyes of the warders. At last, the train stopped, and we got out amongst the crowd of passengers; we saw the kind greetings of meeting friends, and the happy faces around us. I hoped that I should not be recognised at this station, where many a time I had stepped out of a first-class carriage to spend a season at Southsea. But now what a change - a felon, chained and handcuffed! As the people gazed on us, I fancied I was particularly stared at, and that everyone knew my story. It was only fancy. My dearest friend could not have recognised me in my convict's dress. A van took us to the prison, and as I heard the ponderous gates bolted and barred behind me, I felt sick at heart, and mentally prayed for death to take me. The recollection of this past so oppresses me, that, as I write, I feel as if I could scarce proceed further with my relation. However, for the sake of all who read this story, I will show the horrors of my punishment, as a warning against temptation to go astray.

Immediately on our reception inside Portsmouth prison, we were marched, still handcuffed and chained, into a small yard, where we were placed in a row, and our irons removed; our names were then called over, and we were then told to stand to 'attention.' In a few minutes the doctor appeared, and examined us to see if we carried any contagious disorder with us. I suppose we were all right, for none of us were detained, but were marched at once into a long passage, on one side of which was a blank wall with a stove, and on the other, cells with a door and a barred gate at each. Here we found complete suits of clothing, which we were told to put on; but before doing so, after removing the clothes we already wore, we were stripped and subjected to a most minute examination; our mouths, and even under our tongues, were examined. This over, we dressed in our new suits, and were then taken away to the cells. Having had our mid-day meal, we were again mustered, and marched off to another yard, where we listened to the articles and rules of the prison read aloud by the governor. On our way to and fro through the prison, I observed that several of my companions were well known to the warders, and they, my companions, appeared to take a pride in showing themselves to be acquainted with the localities and the routine. After the governor had finished with us, we were again marched off for the doctor's inspection. This inspection was also very minute, and not made by the same medical officer. He inquired into our previous state of health and general history; name, age, and occupation were noted down, as well as height and weight, which were taken by an attendant warder. I answered every question (they were put as humanely as possible) truthfully, except when asked what was my 'previous occupation.' I answered 'a labourer.' I could see by the doctor's expression that he guessed I held a higher position, but he said nothing, and entered what I told him in his register.

We had not yet done with inspections. Being dismissed by the doctor, we were taken before the chief warder; when again in a complete state of nudity, we were rigorously examined, every mark or mole, natural or artificial, was noted; our eyes, hair, speech, in fact everything that would serve to identify us, was copied in a book. This, at length, was finished, and I was thankful to hear a fellow prisoner say that it was the last ceremony of the kind, adding: "I ought to know, for this is the third time I went through 'em." We then were returned to our cells, ready to enter on the ordinary routine of the prison the following morning.

To save repetition, I will detail as shortly as possible the rules that governed my daily life.

The prison is divided into four halls, distinguished respectively as A, B, C, and D halls; and their occupants are divided into four classes, called respectively first, second, third, and probation classes. Each class occupies as far as numbers can be accommodated, a distinct hall, the first class, which is also the highest, belongs to D hall, the second to C, the third to B, and the probation to A. These classes are formed on the principle of time and good conduct. The probation class being dependent on time, all prisoners on first admission are placed in it for a certain period, their promotion altogether depending on themselves. Good conduct is estimated by there being no reports against them, and by their assiduity at their work. A man who is fortunate enough never to have had a report against him during the whole period of his gradations, is entitled to certain privileges during the latter part of his imprisonment. Such cases are very rare for often a report is made for an imaginary fault and the officer reporting is generally believed rather than the prisoner. These reports are made to the governor, who sits every day to judge and adjudicate. First offences, if not heinous, are generally 'admonished' but a repetition of an offence, no matter how trivial, is always punished. In awarding punishment, the powers of the governor are limited to solitary confinement in a cell, light or dark, on bread and water, and with or without bodily restraint for three days. In cases where the governor thinks that this punishment is not adequate to the offence, he reports the prisoner to the director, who at his periodical visit examines into the case, the witnesses being sworn. The director has in is power to award corporal punishment to the extent of thirty-six lashes and solitary confinement in irons for six months with punishment diet.

The incentives held out to good conduct are the class privileges, of which not the least is the improved diet, and the remission of sentence on ticket-of-leave. Formerly, when first penal servitude took the place of transportation beyond the sea, this remission was very much a matter of chance as to its extent; but latterly, by a system of marks, which are allotted by fixed rules, the period of remission is determined accurately, and is known perfectly well to the prisoner.

The rule for remission of sentence is this: Three-fourths of the sentence have been undergone; and if at that period the prisoner has earned the full number of marks, he is set free on ticket-of-leave; but if not, he must remain until he has done so. The marks are obtained by labour, at seven or eight hours a day, according to his capability and earnestness; but whether he works or not, as in illness or under prison punishment, he is accredited with six marks a day. But he is liable at any time to lose, in punishment, any or all the marks previously earned, and also to be degraded to any stage or class. The maximum daily number that can be earned is eight, and the minimum number awarded is six.

The labour at Portsmouth is, in a general way, what is known as navvies' work, the prisoners being employed in and about the Dockyard, a small party being sent to Southsea Common, and formerly to Gosport. The hours for labour differ, of course, at different seasons of the year; but, in a general way, the day is divided as follows: First bell rings to get up at a quarter-past five, from which hour until six o'clock the prisoners are employed washing, cleaning out cells, and making-up beds. Breakfast at six o'clock, forty minutes being allowed. Directly after breakfast comes chapel service, which occupies half an hour, after which they proceed to labour; in winter, a little later. Dinner is at noon, for which meal seventy minutes are allowed, and then labour again, until six o'clock in summer, and four o'clock in winter. Prayers, a supper, school, and making down beds, take up the rest of the day, until eight o'clock, when lights are put out, and the prisoners are locked up for the night.

At three different periods of the day - namely, six a.m., noon, and on return from labour, the medical officer attends at the dispensary, to prescribe for out-patients and casual sick.

Besides the 'ordinary labour,' there is 'light labour,' which consists in picking oakum, and is carried on indoors. Only those prisoners are thus employed who are unfit for ordinary labour, on medical grounds; A few words on the meals, and I think I shall have put the reader in possession of a general idea of prison life. The dietary is classed under four heads - namely, for hard labour, for light labour, penal class diet, and punishment diet. The first two are respectively for those working at hard and light labour; the third is given to prisoners on prison punishment for a protracted time; the fourth, which is only bread and water, is given only to those whose prison punishment does not extend beyond three days.

The dietary for convicts at hard labour is: breakfast of bread and cocoa. Dinner - Sunday, bread and cheese; Monday and Saturday, stewed beef and potatoes; Tuesday and Friday, beef, soup, and potatoes; Wednesday, mutton and potatoes; Thursday, suet pudding, and potatoes. Supper - gruel. With each meal bread is given amounting altogether to nearly a pound and a half daily. Those who are engaged in light labour have the same diet in every respect, except quantity, which is reduced by about one-fourth.

The penal class diet consists of milk porridge and bread for breakfast and supper, and dinner of bread and potatoes. In all cases water *ad libitum*.

I had been accustomed to early rising at Millbank, and I was already awake when the great bell clanged a quarter-past five; and found the morning routine pretty much the same: the same rattling of innumerable locks and banging of iron doors, the same sharp orders in sharp tones and the same dreary sombre look of the surroundings; the same half-cold feed – I cannot call it breakfast, the same stereotyped, cold chapel service. Then the parade, and then (new to me) the marching out to work.

The morning was raw and cold, and the place which we worked on exposed to the cold sea breeze. I was placed with a gang who were levelling a piece of ground; and my part was to wheel the barrows full of clay from one spot to another. At first, I did not mind this much; but soon the unaccustomed strain began to tell on my arms and back, and before evening I was ready to drop with fatigue. This barrow work I found was detested almost more than any sort of labour, and various expedients are made use of by the prisoners to get out of it; sickness feigned and induced being the commonest. Indeed, almost every day someone or other of the prisoners desired to be brought before the medical officer with feigned illness. If they do not succeed in deceiving the doctor, they are sent out and punished. Inducing illness is also very common amongst a low class of prisoners - especially London pickpockets. The most effectual way of ensuring their admission to the infirmary they find is by making sores on their legs. To do this, they scrape their shins with a bit of slate or broken bottle, and to the abrasion thus formed they apply a paste, which is composed of lime, soap, and soda, all of which articles they can easily obtain. As a result of such malpractices, I have seen sores of a most serious nature, entailing confinement to bed for several months. Of course, if found out in these misdemeanours, they are punished; but they are very cunning, and always pretend that they are the result of an accident. Often, too, they take advantage of a real accident, such as a brick or stone scraping the leg; and on this wound, which is seen to be accidental, they carry out their designs.

During the first week of my work, I thought each day that I should be really sick, and have to give in. How I envied some of my fellow prisoners, to whose hard hands and brawny arms the work that was almost killing me seemed like play! I thought then, and I think now, that it is not fair to put a gentleman to the same work as a labourer, their crimes being equal; for the crimes being equal the punishment should be equal - and that cannot be the case where a man, who has perhaps never carried a heavier weight than a gun all his life, is put at the same labour as a man who is accustomed to it from boyhood.

My previous healthy life, and well-nourished and good constitution, however, stood the trial; in a short time, as my muscles grew hard and accustomed to the work, I began to find it not so fatiguing; and before 12 months had elapsed, I was as good a workman as any navvy. During all this time, I had not one report against me for idleness; but an officer, who, I fancy, never liked me, reported me for having a penny in my possession. I picked up this unfortunate penny whilst at work, and without caring for nor thinking about it, I put it in my pocket. For this crime, I was only admonished; but was told that a repetition of the offence would be followed by bread and water and close confinement. This little incident awoke to bitterness my half-resigned feelings. I felt what a mere automaton I was; never to move without being told; speech and action no longer my own; it was horrible. The eternal presence of a keeper fretted me also beyond anything. If I had to proceed from one part of the prison to the other, although surrounded by high walls, I could not stir a step without a warder close to me.

I had been about twelve months in prison since I left Millbank, when a conspiracy broke out among a number of the prisoners. I believe it was a question about food. I know that some of the officers were assaulted, and one seriously injured. It was quelled, however, without difficulty; and the ringleaders, seven in number, were sentenced to undergo corporal punishment in the presence of the rest of the prisoners.

I had never seen corporal punishment administered, and I felt a sort of horror at being forced to witness it. I applied to the governor to be allowed to be absent, but he would not hear of it. The punishment was to take place at ten o'clock in the morning, so, at half-past nine, we were mustered in a hollow square, in one of the large yards. As I stood there, looking at the preparations, I felt a cold shiver run through me. The bright steel triangle with its straps stood in the centre, and near it were two stalwart men, with their coats off, and the horrible cats in their hands. A dead silence reigned through the place. The warders, at regular intervals, stood in front of the prisoners with their staves in their hands; and a party of the prison guard stood near the triangle with bayonets fixed. At last, the silence was broken by the unlocking of a gate; the governor, medical officer, and chief warder entered the square; and, in a few minutes, the prisoner was marched in between two warders. On approaching the place of punishment, he was told to halt. The governor then read aloud his offence and sentence, and desired him to strip. The unfortunate wretch looked very a pale whilst taking off his upper garments, which alone were removed. A band of stiff canvas was then tied round his waist, and another round his neck; his feet were stretched apart, and strapped to the base of the triangle; and his hands, fastened together, were drawn above his head, and the punishment began. With a deliberate stroke, applied with the whole force of a strong man's arm, the knotted cords descended on the victim's bare shoulders; each stroke was deliberately counted, the executer of the sentence smoothing and disentangling the cords each time; and thus, the unfortunate wretch received three dozen. His white skin was soon a mass of purple, blue, and red wheals.

But all through this dreadful punishment he never uttered a cry, and when let free, walked away without showing the slightest appearance of suffering, we had to stand and watch the whole number going through this revolting punishment. Some took it bravely - some screamed as if for their very life; only one man fainted. Among the spectators, however, many fainted, whilst others cheered those who showed courage and did not cry out. This was the first and, I am thankful to say, last, exhibition of the sort at which I had to be present, as an order was issued shortly afterwards that corporal punishment was to be administered in private. Besides their flogging, four of the culprits on this occasion were sentenced to close confinement on punishment diet for six months, and the others to wear a party-coloured dress and cross irons for the same period.

Year after year passed on without any change - the same dreary monotony, the ever-conscious feeling of being watched. Even our holidays, of which there were three in the year, were no relaxation. To be sure, we did not work, but we spent the weary hours in our lonely cells. During all this time, I never thought of escape. It never entered my head, although there were several attempts made, and one or two successful ones. It is astonishing how old housebreakers often succeed with the most insignificant means in making an escape. I know one instance where a thick iron bar was cut through with a saw made of a watch spring. How the saw itself was made, I do not I know; for prisoners manage both to preserve money and to traffic with labourers outside. An escape was always a break in the routine of our life, as, on such occurrences, all the prisoners were taken in from work, the warders being needed to scour the country in search of the runaway. On such a day as Sunday, our time was spent in our cells, except two hours exercise, which we took walking two and two in the yards.

I had been about ten years in prison, when one day I caught cold from a severe wetting. At first, I tried to work it off, but it grew worse, and I had to apply to the doctor, who sent me into the infirmary. Here I was well treated indeed; but I felt the want of kind and friendly voices, which are so comforting in sickness. My affliction proved to be inflammation of the lungs, and I did not leave the hospital for more than six weeks. I was then discharged to light labour, and shortly afterwards taken into the prison as a cleaner. This was a great relief, as the work was not so monotonous or so laborious.

The part of the prison to which I was attached was called the Separate Cells; these were rows of cells in which prisoners were confined for petty offences committed in the prison, such as fighting, stealing food, being found in possession of tobacco, and such like. A misdemeanour is very easily made out against a prisoner; an ugly look, a quick reply, an impatient manner, even silence itself is construed into an offence; there is really no way of guarding against being reported. I was brought up one day before the governor for not informing the warder of the misconduct of another prisoner. In my defence, I said that I was a prisoner myself, and that I could not be answerable for anyone else's crimes. This was called insolence; and I was told that, were it not for my previous good conduct, I should be punished on that account, and I was desired to give some other plea in justification of what was termed my connivance;

so, with shame, I pleaded fear of violence from the delinquent. This was accepted, though it was not likely that I, one of the strongest men in the prison; perhaps the strongest, should be in bodily fear of a miserable sneak, which was the character of the prisoner I should have informed against.

The crime he had committed was stealing bread, which he effected thus. Every day, at dinner hour, before the bell rings, it was part of my duty to bring round a loaf of bread and a tin of water, and leave them outside the cell door of each prisoner in separate confinement. The officer coming round shortly afterwards, opened the doors, and handed each mess in. The prisoner in question, on several occasions, had stolen bread thus placed, He used, when his cell was opened by an officer which he always managed, by some excuse or other, to have done before the loaves were deposited outside to insert a loop made of the thong of his shoe into the hole of the lock, just as the officer shut the door: these doors shut with a spring lock, and could be double-locked, in fact, always were, as a rule, but not generally before the serving of the meals. The loop thus inserted caught on the bolt, which could thus be pressed back. Waiting until the officer's back was turned, this thief would open his door, rush out in the landing, and seize three or four loaves, always leaving untouched those next to his cell; then retreating, and shutting his cell door, he ate them as fast as possible. This trick went on continually, until the unlucky day that I saw him steal no less than six loaves; unfortunately, a warder saw him also, and reported me as an accomplice, because I did not give information.

I had been about three years at indoor work as cleaner, when I caught a severe cold, with some attendant fever, which laid me up for three weeks, and left me a good deal debilitated. To recruit my health, the doctor recommended me to be sent to work on Southsea Common. I was not sorry for the change; but, at the same time, it was like opening an old sore, for on this very Common I had often ridden and walked, one amongst the crowd of seaside visitors. I had often watched, from windows in Clarence Terrace, the convicts at work, and expressed my want of pity for those outcasts of society. I recollected, now that I was there myself, how I had, one evening, compared them with the paupers, and said they were much better off. I had been at work on the Common for about twelve months, when one day I was informed that I was to be made 'a special;' that meant, that I had special privileges, of which the greatest was that I could work without an attendant warder. I could go by myself from one part of the prison to the other, and even be outside the walls, about the officers' quarters, unattended. These privileges are only granted to those who have borne a good character, and who are also near the end of their term of imprisonment. As a breach of trust would entail undergoing the entire sentence, no 'special' would attempt to escape. Whilst at my work about the yards, I used often to see Roupell, who had been in this prison about eighteen months, but whom I had never seen before; besides him, there were also at the time several of superior birth in prison, but I did not know their names. At last, the day came on which I was to be discharged.

1867 – SALE OF A BREWERY.

Mr. George Beck is instructed by the proprietor to sell by auction, at his Property Sale Rooms, No. 9, Queen Street, Portsea, Thursday, November 14, 1867, at seven o'clock in the evening, in one lot, all those admirably situate substantially erected Freehold Premises, known as the Mile End Steam Brewery, in the occupation of the proprietor, Mr. Samuel Suter, which are now in full trade, together with the leases and right of supplying several eligibly situate ale houses.

This property has very recently been erected by a builder of great repute, under the superintendence of an eminent architect, who has displayed great judgment in the construction.

The plant is of the most modern character, and fitted with all necessary steam pipes by which manual labour in brewing is nearly avoided, comprising cast iron cold and hot liquor and hop backs, Wigney's improved mashing machine, and 6-quarter tun, with first-class steam boiling vessel, sparging machine, Wigney's improved refrigerator, with 12 cases, excellent malt roller, double action patent pump, Cornish steam boiler, and powerful horizontal engine, and other appliances, the whole fitted with steam apparatus, rendering the working easy and effective.

The brewery and premises comprise a tun room, scalding and steaming ditto, loft, yard with gate entrance, also spacious store of three floors, with gate entrance, attractive retail Ale House, with bar. smoking parlour, and other necessary apartments.

The stock of ales, nearly new rolling plant, and utensils, to be taken at valuation (if desired) in the usual manner.

1867 – VISIT OF PRINCE MINBUTAIHO.

The Christmas holidays are proverbially the time for sightseeing, and country cousins from all parts are thronging to the Pantomimes and the Winter Exhibitions. A very remarkable and unusual visitor, however, is this year among the sightseers, and the results of his holidaymaking may possibly be hereafter felt by the people of a whole empire. The Japanese Prince Tokugawa Minbutaiho has been busy inspecting some of the wonders of our civilisation, and, not content with the marvels of the metropolis, he has paid a special visit to Portsmouth Harbour and Dockyard. The account of his visit is singularly interesting. The very fact of the presence of a Japanese Prince in the midst of armour-plated vessels and Palliser guns is of itself an anomaly. We have grown used to strange sights in these days of change and travel, and it does not seem much more surprising to hear of Tokugawa Minbutaiho standing in Portsmouth Dockyard watching the latest improvements in machinery and ammunition, than did our forefathers when a country squire crossed the Channel, or a travelling nobleman ventured as far as Constantinople.

It is nevertheless a striking instance of the enlightenment which is the inevitable consequence of contact with civilisation, that a Japanese dignitary should have so far forsaken the traditions of his race and country. A few years back we knew little of Japan beyond the name and its geographical situation. A rigid exclusion of foreigners was the distinguishing policy of its people. They entertained very high opinion of their own merits, abilities, and power, like most persons and nations who never submit their estimate of themselves to the test of contact with their fellows. For long years after the English had obtained footing in

Prince Tokugawa Minbutaiho, Brother of the tycoon of Japan, Visiting the Troop Ship Serapis

the neighbouring empire of China, Japan was a sealed book to them, and the Mikado, the Daimios, and all the other dignitaries had no more vitality for an English reader than the personages of the ancient mythology.

Time, however, has been too strong even for the Japanese. Events which proved irresistible have broken down the barriers which shut them out from their kind. They are naturally intelligent people, and their country bears that form of island empire which has always been favourable to national development. In most of the branches of civilised knowledge they are of course very deficient; but the young Prince who is now amongst us seems determined for his part to make up for lost time by keen and close examination of those wonders of skill and science in which modern knowledge has come to the aid of the rulers and their people throughout Europe.

The Japanese are brave people; but a very brief experience was sufficient to show them how vast were the resources of European warfare, and how hopeless was the struggle between civilisation and semi-barbarism. Their eagerness to learn our secrets proves the possession of natural intelligence, which may be turned to good account for better purposes than war, though warlike means, as exhibited in Portsmouth Dockyard, can teach a good many lessons. We are very much mistaken if the young Prince, whose intelligent inquiries surprised the officials, will rest content with the brief answers he could obtain through his interpreter, and will not speedily put himself into nearer relations with the science and the language which enfold such secrets.

Prince Tokugawa Minbutaiho, Brother of the tycoon of Japan, Visiting the Troop Ship *Serapis*

The first visit of the young Prince was to the *Serapis*, a splendid spectacle of a first-class troop transport. He then went on board the *Royal Sovereign*, and watched with curious eyes the action of the turrets. Still more strongly was his interest excited by a visit to the gunnery ships *Excellent* and the *Calcutta*. More than an hour was spent in examining the various descriptions of ordnance. The batteries were manned, and at the signal word shot and shell were poured forth with amazing accuracy. Great effect was produced by a volley of shell firing from the port broadside of the *Excellent*, at 1,200 yards range. They burst in clusters, sending up a cloud of gas which glittered prismatically under the rays of the sun. After such a display the young Prince will not be very ready to listen to the counsels of refractory Daimios when they are disposed to provoke a quarrel with the British men of war.

Later in the day the enterprising young visitor made a tour of the Dockyard, and went on board several vessels, among them the armour-plated hydraulic propelled gun vessel *Waterwitch*—which must indeed, have borne evidence of witchcraft to the eyes of the Japanese—and the armour-plated iron turret ship *Scorpion*. Afterwards he proceeded to the wood mills, and Brunel's block making machinery was exhibited with all its wonders in full play. Thence he went on to the steam factory, with its collection of machinery, and the armour plate workshop. In the latter he could see for himself the gradual process by which these leviathans afloat are "sheathed in steel." The whole process of drilling, bending, and preparing the huge plates, gripped by machines of singular shape and immense power, was explained to the Prince, whose shrewd and pertinent questions, put through his interpreter, proved that he was looking on with the attention of an intelligent student rather than the mere curiosity of an idle sightseer.

The officials of the Portsmouth Harbour and Dockyard had thus opportunity of witnessing the effect of their mechanical marvels upon "the intelligent foreigner," who is often quoted as a judge or a critic, and had reason to be satisfied with the interest which he evinced. In the great iron foundry, the Prince lingered long enough to see several lots of molten iron drawn off from the cupola furnaces and poured into a row of large moulds which stood in readiness.

Prince Minbutaiho

1868 – THE GRAND VOLUNTEER REVIEW AT PORTSMOUTH.

The Grand Volunteer Review at Portsmouth on Easter Monday was the most successful that has yet been held. The whole number in the field when the manoeuvres and sham fight took place at Portsdown, was 28,000 and 16,000 marched past the inspecting officer Lieutenant-General Sir G. Buller, on Southsea Common, at an earlier hour before going out to Portsdown. The fortifications upon that range of hills and along the Hilsea lines, with some gunboats in the creeks between Portchester lake and Portsmouth harbour, took part in the mimic battle. The entire programme was executed with equal spirit and precision, to the gratification of many thousands of spectators. The sham fight began at a quarter before two and ended a quarter before four in the afternoon. There was no hindrance and no confusion; the weather was fine, and those who had come from London went back early in the evening.

The Engraving represents the arrival at Cosham, on Good Friday, of one important portion of the volunteer forces—viz., the field batteries of the 1st Middlesex Artillery Volunteers, under the command of Lieutenant-Colonel Creed. This corps marched down from headquarters by road, and left their last halting place, Petersfield, on the Friday morning. About 2.30 p.m. the leading gun of the batteries was seen from the village of Cosham crossing the top of Portsdown by the old London road. At the entrance to the island of Portsea they were met by a strong muster of the 2nd Hants Artillery Volunteers (garrison), with their band, under the command of Lieutenant-Colonel E. Gale, accompanied by Colonel Rickards, 3rd Hants Artillery Volunteers, and a number of other officers. In the remainder of the march of the

The 1st Middlesex Artillery Passes Through Cosham

Middlesex to Portsmouth they were accompanied by a vast crowd.

All Portsmouth, Southsea, Portsea, and Landport appeared to have turned out to do honour to the strangers, and the four miles and a half of road between Portsdown and Southsea Common was as much thronged with pedestrians and vehicles of every kind as the road between London and Epsom Downs on the Derby Day. The guns of the Middlesex Artillery were admirably horsed, all the appointments being evidently in first-rate order; and men, horses, and guns, although covered with dust, looked soldierly and service-like. The headquarters of the 1st Middlesex at Portsmouth were established at the Southsea Beach Mansion, over which the regimental colours were hoisted.

Monday morning was full of promise for the success of the day. By six o'clock the sun was shining over the town and harbour, and steamers were coming across from Ryde conveying men, women, and children to witness the volunteer review, The Portsmouth people were all astir, and crowds were at the railway station to await the arrival of the volunteers from London, at the end of Cambridge Road, the main thoroughfare from Landport to the High Street, a triumphal arch had been erected. It was formed of timber, and rose 80ft. from the ground, surmounted by two lions. The sides were decorated in sections of bright colours. Spanning the pavement right and left were smaller arches, springing from the main structure. Every house along the Cambridge Road hung out banners and streamers inscribed with words of welcome to the volunteers, whom the Portsmouth people, in all sorts of festive devices, hailed, together with the Army and Navy, as "England's Defenders." At the suburban end of the High Street were another arch and four and twenty flag staffs, bearing shields with the arms of the town and various heraldic compliments addressed to riflemen. This arch was covered with evergreens, with which garlands were intertwined. Close to the Government green was a third arch of a less elaborate character, but also very handsome. But the volunteers did not march as a body under these arches, since, by a judicious arrangement, they were brought round to Southsea Common, where they marched past by a different route, not going through the town.

From the railway station there is a line of railway to the Dockyard, which passes through a large open space used as People's Park. This is opposite to the station and at the other side of the road. The station master was enabled to pass ten or a dozen of the London trains on to this park without stopping them at the ordinary terminus; so that the men descended on an open space not far from the rendezvous, and the empty trains were out of the way of those coming down after them. The result was that the arrival platforms was kept clear. No fewer than forty-eight trains arrived within the short period of two hours and a half. The first left London about half-past four, and reached Portsmouth by half-past seven o'clock. The last of the metropolitan corps was landed by ten. This result proved that to so important a point of our defences as Portsmouth, any number of men that could, under any circumstances be required, might be brought from all parts of England within a very few hours.

The rendezvous for the entire force about to take part in the day's operations was that portion of the glacis of the Portsmouth lines extending from the Cambridge Road to Southsea Common. From the station all the way were direction posts at short intervals indicating the exact spot on the glacis to which each corps was to proceed for the purpose of forming and being brigaded. In doing this none of them had to march more than a few hundred yards

Triumphal Arches at Governor's Green and Cambridge Road

on the public road. Almost as soon as they were out of the shed or of the People's Park, they were on the Government ground, from which the public was excluded; and, consequently, they were able to make all their preliminary arrangements without the slightest confusion.

Precisely at ten o'clock the gun was fired as the signal for the general body of the troops to brigade on the glacis and prepare for the march past. The arrangements on the Common were admirable. The portion occasionally used as a racecourse was railed off for the troops. Outside the rails, on each side, were lines of spectators. Half way between the point of entry from the glacis and that of the exit, at the opening of the Portsdown road, was the saluting point, with ample stands to the right and left, to which spectators were admitted by payment. To the rear of the saluting place and the stands was Spithead, and the Isle of Wight farther off, with a great expanse of sea. On the other side of the Common the flags of the Civil Service, the London Scottish, the London Irish, and several others of the metropolitan corps floated from the tops of the hotels and private residences facing the water; and every window commanding the Common was crowded with ladies, who joined in greeting the volunteers as they arrived at the ground. After the usual galloping of staff officers and orderlies here, there and everywhere, several regimental bands stationed themselves opposite to the saluting point, and immediately afterwards General Sir George Buller, the commanding officer of the day, arrived at the flagstaff, surrounded by a brilliant staff, comprising of many officers.

It had been decided that in the sham fight the enemy should be represented by the First and Second Divisions, and the defence maintained by the Third and Fourth Divisions; but a departure was subsequently made from this plan, so far as to place the regular troops in the army of defence. Just before the march past was commenced the cavalry were drawn up on the right of the guns, and at eleven o'clock the order was given to advance. First came the cavalry, entirely composed of volunteers, then the field battery of the Royal Artillery and next, two battalions of the Marine Artillery, numbering over 1,000, and after them a pontoon train. The 35th and 97th Regiments of the Line preceded the volunteers, whose appearance in marching past was creditable to their drill. They turned to the left, after passing the Grand Stand, and moved off the Common, going to Portsdown hill. It had been determined that in the case of the attacking troops the marching past should be dispensed with, and, further, that certain of the country corps should not be brought into Portsmouth at all.

To the extreme right of the battleground is a railway station at Havant, and to the extreme left

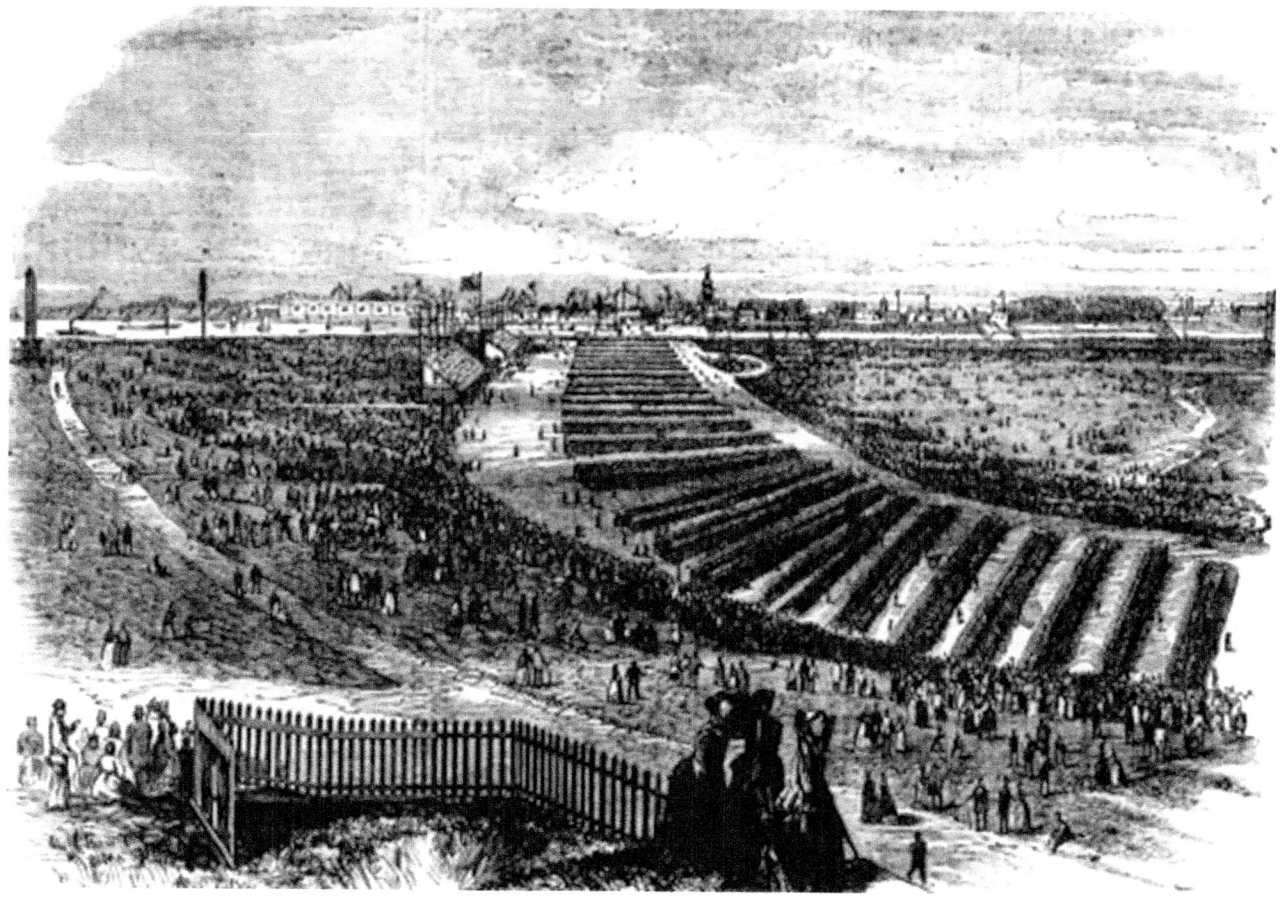

March Past on the Common

another at Fareham. At each of these, corps were landed by train, so that they were able, after a very short march, to take up their positions as a portion of the attacking force. The London riflemen had, however, all to march out from Portsmouth; but those of them who joined in the march past had only to go as far as the Hilsea lines. The scene of action was a broad, open valley, formed on one side by the Hilsea lines of Portsmouth island, and on the other by the amphitheatre of high sloping hills on which the Portsdown defences have recently been built. Between the Hilsea lines and the attacking force lay the creek communicating with the waters of the harbour beyond, and up the centre of the enemy's position on Portsdown hill ran the old London road. Between the two armies at the bottom of the valley, lay the villages of Cosham and Wymering. These were the keys of the whole position, the loss of which was to be the signal for the route of the assailants. Up near Wymering, at a place called Paulsgrove, the harbour was wider and deeper, and here the Hilsea garrison had the assistance of their gunboats in annoying the enemy's right. The enemy—that is to say, the First and Second Divisions—were supposed to have advanced from Fareham, to have taken the three great forts on Portsdown hill, and to have made the great defences of Widley and Southwick the base of their operations against the main inner lines beyond the creek at Hilsea. The theory of the defence was that the Third and Fourth Divisions were the defenders of the lines, aided by field batteries, a powerful brigade of the Royal Marine Artillery, and the 97th and 35th Regiments. These were to repulse the attack on the lines, and, under cover of their own artillery and the fire from the gunboats, make a sortie across bridges over the creek and on pontoon bridges, carry the villages of Cosham and Wymering, and so, forcing the position on the London road, entirely turn the enemy's right and drive him back over the Portsdown hills.

At a quarter before two the fight commenced. The attacking party had massed their divisions strongly on the hill, where their artillery of position was stationed on the summit of the ridge. They began by the advance of a powerful body of skirmishers in a line against Hilsea. These were too strong for the garrison outposts, which, after holding some thickets and hedges to give time for their supports within the lines to assemble to their aid, were driven back a short distance. After the first alarm had spread, the lines bristled with thousands of troops, tip and down, far and near, the line fire spread, and soon the artillery began to roar.

That of the attacking force replied, and the guns became more and more vehement as the rifles ceased. But now, from the sea and the narrow creek, in which the tide was at its full, came the *Stork* and *Fancy* gunboats, towing the large launches and cutters of the *Terrible, Gladiator, Victory, Duke of Wellington, Royal Oak*, and *Pallas*, each carrying a rifled gun at the bows. The fire which they instantly poured into

Sortie at Hilsea Lines

the right wing of the enemy at once decided matters. A hasty retreat was therefore made from the space in front of the lines back to the railway, the ridges of which they lined, holding both Cosham and as covers to their right and left flanks. No sooner had they made this movement than the garrison made a general sortie, with a vigour which drove all before it. They swarmed from all the works of the lines, and instantly as they reached the open their skirmishers were thrown out, reserves placed, and a rapid advance made against the enemy. It was wonderful to see the ease and precision with which they formed up their ranks, even while advancing. At one part of the lines the bridges were not sufficient to give egrets to the forces in the manner which the emergency demanded. A pontoon bridge was formed across the creek. This bridge was constructed and fit for the passage of infantry within ten minutes from the time of its commencement, and within fourteen minutes artillery passed over it. The sortie from all parts of the garrison now became general, and in such masses that the enemy were borne down, and had nothing left for them but to recall their skirmishers and supports, and, leaving a thin line in thickets and hedgerows to annoy the advance, concentrate their strength in the villages of Cosham and Wymering. The taking of these villages was one of the most animated parts of the whole days programme.

For the first time the volunteers fought in the streets and amid the houses. Every foot of ground was contended for in alleys, houses, and stables; and the scene as, with all the village windows crowded, the enemy was driven from point to point, was most exciting. The loss of Cosham at once necessitated a retreat of the defenders from Wymering, and change of front along the Portsdown hills to meet the attacking force, which, by the possession of the London road, had quite turned their left flank, their right had been turned by the fleet at Wymering. The enemy were ranged in masses of lines between Forts Widley and Southwick. The lines of infantry, now deployed in front of each other, maintained file fire that was absolutely deafening; and the uproar of cannon was terrific. In the midst of this great din and rush of guns and troops, the 97th and 35th Regiments of the Line, with the Royal Marine Artillery, were brought up the road on the enemy's right, and came into action against the flank of the enemy with their breech loaders. It seemed an incessant volley, under which the enemy were supposed to wither away; and it being then a quarter to four, the time agreed upon, the bugles were ordered to sound cease firing and the review was brought to a close.

The dispersal of the various brigades and corps and their breaking up to march off from all parts of the ground to their various rendezvous were among the finest sights of the day. The casualties were very few. One man had his hand injured by a cartridge; another hand was injured by a ramrod. There were two medical cases—one of palpitation of the heart, and the other of exhaustion. Twenty trains had been kept ready at the station to bring the volunteers back from Portsmouth. The first of these left at 5.35 p.m., and the last getaway by a quarter-past seven. The ordinary traffic, which had been suspended from 4.15 p.m., was resumed before half-past seven, a special train being kept ready for volunteer stragglers. Under the supervision of Mr. White, the station master, similar arrangements had been made for the management of the up trains as those which had answered so well in the morning; and the result was that, at a quarter past nine, there was no crush or difficulty, and the traffic between Portsmouth and London went on as usual.

1868 – PORTSMOUTH BOROUGH GAOL.

During the recent discussion in reference to the proposed amendment of the Camber Act it was urged by the opponents of the measure that considering the present and prospective liabilities of the borough the Council ought to be exceedingly cautious before incurring any fresh expense of any magnitude. Among the prospective engagements, likely to involve considerable cost, the erection of a new gaol was included, and judging from what we hear we fear it is almost certain that the subject will be forced upon the consideration of the local authorities before many months have elapsed.

It is whispered that a letter has been received from the Home Office, calling attention to an unfavourable report from the Government Inspector, upon the accommodation and internal arrangements of the gaol, and as the Government have compulsory powers under a recent Act of Parliament it is clear that the whole question must ere long receive the attention which its importance deserves, and at this juncture it may not be out of place if we supply a few facts in reference to this establishment.

The Borough gaol and sessions room form, as most of our readers are aware, a substantial oblong range of buildings, fronting Penny Street, and extending backward to Nicholas Street. It was commenced in 1805, and completed in 1809, at a cost of about £18,000. In 1833 the gaol was enlarged by the erection of a chapel, and additional yards, &c., on the site of

Convicts leaving York Road station for Portsmouth

Reception of Convicts at Portsmouth Prison

some old alms houses, purchased for £700. Since that period no addition has been made to the building.

The gaol contains altogether seventy-one cells, 50 being apportioned to males, and 21 to females. The staff of management consists of a governor (Mr. J. Astridge); chaplain (the Rev. A. Lowry); surgeon (Mr. J. Slight); matron (Mrs. Astridge); assistant matron, chief turnkey, and three assistants - nine persons in all. The governors of gaols are under the direction of the Magistrates, who, again, come under the supervision of the Secretary of State, to whom a report is made periodically by an Inspector.

It will be remembered that Portsmouth gaol has more than once been the subject of an adverse report. Although the gaol is in excellent order, and has an efficient governor and staff of officers, it is so ill-arranged that it is utterly impossible to effect any proper classification of the prisoners, and instead of being able to carry out the separate system (as is the case in most large gaols) the old and the young,—the hardened criminal and the juvenile offender,—are often brought into contact with each other, the result, being, we fear, that during confinement in gaol many a one who has just commenced a career of crime is encouraged to persist in his sinful course, until, at length, he becomes a regular "gaol bird."

It is a well-known fact that those who are well acquainted with the inside of a gaol would rather serve a term of imprisonment here than a shorter one in the county prison or at the gaol at Southampton, in both of which the separate and silent system is carried out in the strictest manner. It cannot be doubted that a considerable sum annually is lost to the borough in consequence of the absence of the requisite means for utilizing the labour of the prisoners. At Plymouth, for instance, we find that a quantity of the potatoes consumed by the prisoners are grown on the land connected with the gaol, at a less cost than they can be purchased, being, in fact, raised for the money cost of the manure and seed purchased for the garden. At Plymouth, too, all the clothes required for the prison are made within the prison walls—the men doing the tailoring and shoemaking, and the female prisoners the ordinary sewing and knitting of stockings, together with the washing and mangling.

In Portsmouth gaol oakum picking constitutes in practice the only productive form of labour—that is to say, it is the only work for which cash is received. It is picked at so much per ton, but in consequence of the difficulty of getting adequate supply from the Dockyard the receipts have very much decreased. Assistance is also rendered by the prisoners in cooking and keeping the establishment in a clean and proper state, and the washing and ironing is done by the females.

In gaols where there are ample means of utilizing the prison labour to the fullest extent its value is likely to suffer considerable diminution in future, the Legislature having enacted that all prisoners sentenced to hard labour shall for the first three months of their term at least, and continuously if they do not behave well be kept at what is termed first-class labour, and which may in general terms be designated unproductive. The only first-class labour in this gaol is the treadmill, and, it has, as a matter of necessity, been sanctioned by the Home Secretary, crank work, stone breaking, shot drill, &c., being unknown here.

For at least three months every hard labour prisoner in the Portsmouth gaol will be kept at the tread mill, and the labour returns will to some extent, diminish. Besides the return for labour (which, as we have shown, is here very small) there are two other sources from which contributions towards prison expenditure proceed. The Treasury pays out of the Consolidated Fund 4s. weekly for each convicted felon; and for military and naval prisoners who may happen to be incarcerated the larger sum of 1s. per day is paid, but the want of the requisite accommodation makes it necessary to limit the number of service prisoners received. The dietary in use in Portsmouth gaol is sanctioned by the Home Secretary and is believed not to be more liberal than will keep the inmates in health.

1868 – THE POST REFORM ACT GENERAL ELECTION AT PORTSMOUTH.

The party feeling and activity which have prevailed throughout the canvass for the representation of the borough gradually increased as the day approached on which the momentous issue was to be decided. Meetings which were at first comparatively few and far between, so multiplied during the last few days as to afford the residents in every district of the town an opportunity of expressing their attachment to the candidates of their choice, and every possible effort has been put forth with the view of advancing the candidature either of Messrs. Stone and Gaselee on the one hand, or that of the Tory candidate, Sir James Elphinstone, on the other.

The Liberal working men of the borough have evinced a degree of attachment to their cause, under difficulties, which is highly commendable and the contest, so far as they were concerned, has been conducted with great propriety, with a becoming regard for the importance of the cause in which they were engaged, and with the single object of legitimately enforcing those comprehensive and progressive measures which are represented by the Liberal party.

The last meeting at which the candidates were present was held in the comparatively remote neighbourhood of Eastney, and here, as elsewhere, the enthusiasm with which the late members were received warranted them and their friends in concluding that the great bulk of the constituency approved of their conduct in the past and were disposed to renew that confidence in the future by returning them triumphantly at the head of the poll. Meetings were the same evening held throughout the borough, and at these there was a large attendance, and the greatest possible enthusiasm prevailed.

On Saturday evening there was a huge torchlight demonstration - the first of the kind, we believe, which has ever been held in the borough - and although this in itself was calculated to provoke discord, those who arranged the gathering throughout scrupulously avoided any feature which was unbecoming of their position, or which was directly calculated to occasion interference with the order and comfort of the inhabitants. The whole passed off successfully with the adoption of resolutions pledging those present to exert every legitimate influence to secure the return of the Liberal candidates. The nomination, as usual, took place in St. George's Square, Portsea, at noon on Monday. The hustings were erected in the rear of the church by Mr. Lawrence, of Commercial Road, every possible care having been exercised in the arrangement with the view of affording the requisite recommendation and of avoiding accident.

The left-hand side of the building was set apart for the Liberals and the right for the Tories, the centre being barricaded for the special use of the returning officer, the candidates, and a few of their immediate friends. During the morning the greatest possible excitement prevailed in the immediate neighbourhood, and throughout the borough the most strenuous efforts were put forth with the view of securing for the Tory the "show of hands." By ten o'clock - two hours before the time announced for the commencement of the proceedings - both parties were well represented, each taking up their position in the square so as to force those of the same persuasion on the hustings, and as the hour of the proceedings approached, the crowd increased considerably. At half-past eleven the square was literally crammed, and every window commanding a view of the scene below the waving of handkerchiefs indicated the interest which was taken in the proceedings. The scene from the hustings was unusually diverting long before the arrival of the candidates.

On the Conservative side were several faces of Marylebone notoriety, and by these every conceivable trick was resorted to with the view of creating a disturbance. Fortunately, this was an eventuality which had to some extent been provided against by those upon whom the arrangements devolved, and the provision of strong barriers round the hustings, and the swearing-in of a large body of special constables, in addition to the presence of every available member of the borough police, combined to avoid consequences which might have been serious. The "roughs," with the blue and white favours, were throughout exceedingly boisterous, and to them is attributable the uproar which subsequently rendered almost inaudible the proceedings of the nomination. Considerable amusement was occasioned by the introduction of a Marylebone donkey, which was occasionally held up to the view of those on the hustings, amidst shouts of "Vote for Elphinstone, the popular candidate!" and one fellow in particular was so ludicrously grotesque in his "make-up" that the effect of it was irresistible upon the crowd. With a large cocked hat, decked with the conspicuous colours of his "friends," and otherwise dressed in character, he became at once an object of popular attraction; and his boisterous declaration, whenever a Liberal appeared, was almost beyond endurance.

But for the protection of his friends, he would doubtless have come to serious grief, and as it was, long before the proceedings were over, his cocked hat was unceremoniously tossed amongst the crowd and torn to pieces amidst cheering and great uproar. There was the usual discharge of rotten eggs and other filth from the "constitutional" part of the assembly enlivened by the throwing of a few stones, one of which very severely lacerated the eye of a gentleman who was standing on the Liberal side of the hustings. The scene in the square was further enlivened by the presence of a juvenile band of young ruffians from Marylebone, whose appearance was received by wild manifestations of delight on the part of Sir James's supporters, who were also extremely enraptured by the manner in which they kept playing their vile "music" while Mr. Stone was ineffectually endeavouring to make himself heard.

Well may the *Times* ask, in reference to similar conduct which has characterised elsewhere the behaviour in front of the hustings of the party whose chief solicitude it is to defend the Church and preserve us from a second edition of the Inquisition, whether the ancient usage which requires the public attendance of candidates on an outdoor scaffold, and the preliminary appeal to the show of hands, be not among those customs of our forefathers which might be conveniently modified. Unless it be to test the courage and strength of the candidates, we see no reason for subjecting them to a procedure which is admitted being useless and is only maintained in deference to immemorial tradition. Perhaps, even in this land of precedent, a time may come where members of parliament may be nominated in some other manner than by a gentleman shouting himself hoarse amid the buffoonery or violence of a crowd, and when a list of candidates, duly proposed and seconded in writing, may be offered to the real electors at the poll without the intervening tumult which attends the show of hands.

The only noteworthy banner on the Liberal side of the hustings on Monday was one which detailed the defeat of the Tory candidate at Greenock, Portsmouth, and Aberdeenshire, on which was the question, "Will you have him?" Occasionally the Liberals sang "Rule Britannia," in the chorus of which those of the same party in the square joined with great warmth. The words of the song not only indicated a determination on the part of the singers never, never to be slaves, but were supposed to contain a sly allusion to Sir James' achievement in securing the removal of the *Britannia*, training ship.

The Liberal candidates, Messrs. Stone and Gaselee, were the first to present themselves to the "lieges," and as the carriages in which they and their friends - including Messrs. R.E. Davies, Parson, Alderman Sheppard, Besant, Cole, Dore, Edgecombe, Alderman Wells, Baker, and others - were seated, approached the hustings a succession of cheers and hissing was indulged in. Sir James Elphinstone, with whom were Messrs. Alderman Stigant, Ford, Dr. Miller, Capt. McCoy, &c., met with a similar reception; and expressions of feeling were given upon the appearance of his worship the Mayor (E. Galt, Esq.,) accompanied by the Town Clerk (J. Howard, Esq.) and the Serjeant-at-Mace (Mr. R. Martell). The ceremony of nomination was then proceeded with.

The Mayor, in opening the proceedings, said they were assembled there that day for the purpose of exercising one of the noblest privileges of their constitution, the election of two burgesses to serve in the parliament of their country. The electors had a solemn duty to perform, and he had to ask them, and he knew he should not ask in vain, to give all parties who would address them a hearing and that amount of fairness they were entitled to on such occasions as the present. His earnest hope was that whatever might be the result of the day's proceedings, it would conduce to the true interests of the country.

Mr. E. Davies proposed the election of W.H. Stone, Esq., of Leigh Park, Havant. He (Mr. Stone) had already been in Parliament and had so faithfully represented the great Liberal party in the borough as to induce him to believe that he would again be elected by a triumphant and overwhelming majority. This, he reminded them, was not merely a question of individuals, but was a test of great and broad political principle, with the view of determining whether Mr. Gladstone retained the confidence of the country. Mr. Stone had already been for three years in the House, and during that time he had truthfully and consistently represented those Liberal and progressive principles which he expounded when he first came amongst them. He had been from the first an unceasing and uncompromising supporter of Mr. Gladstone, and they might be assured that he would continue as he had been, not merely the representative of class interest, but as a steadfast supporter of those comprehensive measures which were calculated to benefit the country at large.

Alderman Sheppard had great pleasure in seconding the nomination. He rejoiced to see before him such a large assembly of those who were for the first time called upon to exercise a vote, and he confidently believed that the result of the coming struggle would add another triumphant victory to the great Liberal party.

Mr. Parson proposed Serjeant Gaselee. After taking a retrospect of the Parliamentary career of Messrs Stone and Gaselee, and of the defeat of Sir James Elphinstone on those hustings about three years ago, he proceeded to say, "that during the last session of Parliament the most important and all-absorbing subjects have been brought forward. No page of the history of our country has ever given to the electors of England such questions for their decision, and it is in these I presume the Conservative party see, or fancy they can see, a loophole whereby they may again return their candidate to Parliament. They are basing their hope of success upon the statement that they gave to the working classes the opportunity of voting. The offer of an extension to the franchise by the Conservative Government was so encumbered, so fenced about by difficulties, so barricaded, that the offer was worth nothing, and it was by the Liberal party that the offer was rendered in any degree acceptable.

With regard to the Irish Church question the Conservative party have raised the hobgoblin cry of "No Popery." Now, gentlemen, I ask you which party is most likely to advance the interests of Roman Catholicism? the Tory party, who propose to give the Catholics pecuniary assistance in the establishment of Universities by a process which they call "levelling up," or the Liberal party, who propose to give to any religious denominations, whether Established Church, Presbyterian, Dissenter, or Roman Catholic, an equal chance. It is an insult, gentlemen, to the Liberal party to be told that Sir James Elphinstone is the only Protestant candidate, for I defy them to prove that any constituency had ever offered to them the services of any two gentlemen who have the true Protestant faith more deeply at heart. With these few remarks, I leave in your hands the decision of tomorrow, believing that Mr. Stone and Mr. Serjeant Gaselee will be returned by a triumphant majority."

Mr. Serjeant Gaselee's nomination was seconded by Mr. Dore, who referred at length to various efforts put forth by the learned Serjeant during the time he had a seat in the House and instanced particularly that which resulted in the granting of the bounty to the engineers' Widows.

Mr. Alderman Stigant next proposed Sir James Dalrymple Horne Elphinstone, and, in doing so said he was pleased to see assembled before him one of the largest assemblages that had ever met in that place on similar occasions to the present, for the purpose of electing by a show of hands two fit and proper persons to serve in the House of Commons. Their opponents took the credit for having got for the people the Reform Bill, but the electors would know to which party they were indebted for the privilege they now enjoyed. The electors had a very solemn duty to perform, and he hoped they would well consider to whom they gave their vote. The Liberal party would never have passed such an extensive measure of reform as had been carried by the Conservative party, and they were never in favour of carrying a complete measure but brought the question before the House as a rocking-horse from generation to generation. Therefore, it was the Conservatives who took the ground from under them, and brought in and passed a comprehensive measure, and Mr. Gladstone found that he had no hope or choice in the matter.

Speaking on the Irish Church question Mr. Stigant said he hoped the people would be true to their country, and not want the Queen to break her Coronation oath, which she would have to do if she gave the royal assent to the bill for disestablishment. The party who brought in the measure, if they put the matter to their own consciences, must feel that the oath was binding, and yet they wanted their sovereign, a lady who was beloved and honoured by her subjects, to break it. There was no pressure put upon the party who advocated the disestablishment more than there was many years ago, but it was brought forward for the purpose of getting the party into power. If the people returned their opponents, the Liberal candidates, they would return two members who held opinions opposed to those of all true Englishmen, whilst, on the other hand, if they returned Sir James Elphinstone, they would return one who would strenuously maintain the glorious constitution of the country in all its integrity.

He referred in strong terms to what he characterised the scandalous way in which Mr. Serjeant Gaselee had personally attacked Sir James, who was an honourable gentleman. He (Mr. Stigant) had hoped that personal disrespect and ill-feeling would not have been allowed to be mixed up with this election, and he trusted that there would be nothing of the kind on the following day. One of their opponents, it was quite certain, would be unsuccessful, and it was for the electors to say which of them they would have. With these observations he had the pleasure, as he had eleven years ago, of proposing Sir James Elphinstone, and he hoped the electors would place him in a triumphant position at the head of the poll.

Dr. Miller briefly seconded the nomination.

Mr. Stone then said, "Mr. Mayor and electors of Portsmouth. Under the circumstances in which we are placed at this moment I shall confine my remarks to a very narrow compass. If I were coming before the constituency which, by a large majority, returned myself and my learned colleague at the last election I should feel very little doubt indeed as to the result. During the time that has elapsed since then I have steadily supported the principles which I then professed, and I have kept the promises which I then made; and I have no reason to suppose that the electors who on that day returned us have changed their minds, or that they now experience any wish to vote contrary to the same Liberal principles they then so strenuously upheld. It has not been brought to my knowledge during the canvass which I have just concluded that I have done anything to forfeit the confidence placed in me three years ago. If we were, therefore, appealing to the same constituency we should feel very little hesitation as to the result. We cannot, however, for the moment, lose sight of the important fact that by the great extension of the suffrage which has just taken place the circumstances have been much altered. We cannot forget that the number of new electors is at least double that of the old, and this election might, perhaps, lead us to feel some degree of uncertainty as to the result of the present contest. I use the word uncertainty, but that is not the proper expression. We cannot but feel that those into whose hands the power in this country has just been entrusted, who have just received the political rights to which they have so long been entitled, will know how to make proper use of them. I cannot doubt that the people of England know to whom they are indebted for the granting of the privileges which have just been conferred upon them - who are the party who have always striven in defence both of the rights and the interests and welfare of the whole of the people of England. I do not believe that the electors of the borough of Portsmouth will be led away by class cries such as I see inscribed on the banner before me, or that they will be induced to vote for the so-called friend of the navy, army, or any one class as against another. I believe that they know who the true friends of the people are, and that they will vote in favour of the supporters of the party now headed by that great statesman, Mr. Gladstone, that great and distinguished patriot, who is fighting so glorious a battle for the cause of freedom and justice. I have no doubt that the enthusiasm which we see today on our behalf is but an indication of the glorious majority of tomorrow."

Mr. Serjeant Gaselee briefly addressed the electors. He congratulated them on the large increase of voters, stating that in voting for that increase he was not, like Lord Derby, taking a leap in the dark. He thanked them for their presence and was confident that they would show by their votes that he and his colleague still retained their confidence.

Sir James Elphinstone next proceeded to address the electors, and in the course of a short speech said he came before them as a supporter of the constitution of his country, and he should strenuously uphold it. If the people of Portsmouth did him the honour to return him to the House of Commons, it would give him pleasure to carry out their views as far as practicable. He would request his friends to give him a rattling show of hands and go, on the following day, as early to the poll as possible.

The Mayor then took the show of hands, and, amidst considerable signs of dissatisfaction on the part of a few declared it to be in favour of Sir James Elphinstone and Mr. Serjeant Gaselee, whereupon Mr. Cole demanded a poll on behalf of Mr. Stone.

During Monday evening considerable excitement prevailed throughout the whole borough, the Conservatives being jubilant on their alleged victory at the nomination. In some instances, acts of violence were resorted to on the part of certain roughs who professed to represent the political views of Sir James Elphinstone. The most serious of these displays took place at Landport, where party feeling has been throughout the contest exceedingly high. At the establishment of Mr. R.E. Davies considerable damage was sustained in consequence of the wanton and mischievous conduct of the mob, who entered his wholesale establishment, and, after creating a considerable disturbance, broke several large panes of glass. Other depredations were also perpetrated, and, on the whole, Sir James has no room to congratulate himself on the good behaviour of his friends.

The polling, which took place yesterday morning, caused great excitement. From an early hour it was apparent that the Conservatives were determined to muster their strength with great promptness, and the result was that a struggle ensued between the respective parties as to the right of claiming priority. A representation which was freely made early in the day to the effect that the Tories would endeavour to claim possession of the various booths, and thus deprive the Liberal electors of the right of voting was in many instances verified, and one result was that their party were in a position to claim the credit of taking the lead in the voting.

The most serious occurrence, however, of the whole was the fact that, in consequence of the large increase in the number of voters, and the absence of sufficient staff at many of the booths, a large number of the electors were compelled to retire without recording their votes, and to this circumstance, in some degree, must be attributed the great disparity between the numbers at the close of the poll.

Throughout the early part of the day the most noisy and boisterous demonstrations were indulged in on the part of those who supported Sir James. Boys from Marylebone paraded the town blowing whistle pipes and beating drums in honour of the "Protestant champion" and the "seaman's friend," while the owners of over-worked donkeys conducted themselves in a manner to show that they at least had the greatest possible confidence as to the result of the poll. By dint of Government patronage, and the exercise of every conceivable influence - even to the use of cabs and other vehicles to convey doubtful voters from their residences to the committee rooms, near the polling booth, - the Tory party succeeded in maintaining their candidate at the head of the poll, and from an early hour in the day it seemed that the great struggle would be between the Liberal candidates for second place.

In this, as in other respects, there was scarcely any variation. Mr. Stone took the lead of his learned colleague from the beginning, and throughout the day it was apparent that Serjeant Gaselee's chances of success were hopeless. Still the Liberal party - or those few, at least, upon whom the responsibility of the struggle seemed to devolve - worked zealously and after a fashion which enabled the defeated candidate to say that, although defeated, he was not disgraced. The Tories resorted to every conceivable dodge with the view of advancing their interest, the most offensive of the whole being a bill which purported to emanate from the Liberal committee, and which was to the effect that traitors were in the camp, and that it was incumbent on the liberals to plump for Mr. Serjeant Gaselee. It is scarcely necessary to add that this statement was a palpable mis-representation on the face of it, for no one who its familiar with the learned gentleman could for a moment suppose that he would be a party to any arrangement for advancing his own interest to the prejudice of a colleague. The winning party were the first to publish the returns, and from this source we gather the following as the result of the polling.

Stone – 3,797
Gaselee – 3,703
Elphinstone – 5,276

From four to five o'clock a large number of the electors assembled in the neighbourhood of the central committee rooms in Commercial Road. In the meantime, the rooms were crowded, and several speeches were delivered as to alleged cases of intimidation which had come under the notice of those who took part in the contest. Some of the speakers carried the audience with them when they stated that there were known circumstances which would lead to the unseating of Sir James, were the conduct of his party to come before the consideration of a judge. In response to frequent and enthusiastic appeals from the crowd, Messrs. Stone and Gaselee addressed the assembled electors from one of the windows of the room.

Mr. Stone said that although he had to acknowledge the honour of having been elected, as he believed, one of the members of the borough, yet he did so under circumstances which were by no means encouraging to the Liberal party. They were led to believe that they had a sufficient number of promises to warrant them in going to the poll, and he had no hesitation in saying that if those who had promised had kept their word the result would have been very different. He believed that the town was Liberal and that the present decision in no sense represented the feelings of the new electors. He therefore urged those to work steadfastly with the view of securing the return of Liberal members at the next election.

Mr. Serjeant Gaselee, who was received with the greatest possible enthusiasm, briefly addressed the electors. He said that he appeared before them as a defeated candidate but, although defeated, he was not disgraced. He had fought the battle like a man, and as such he would accept the decision at which the people had arrived, He was in no sense personally affected by the result. What he regretted was that the Liberal cause should have suffered such a defeat - what he regretted was that Portsmouth had retrograded instead of progressed. If the people of Portsmouth were content to be misrepresented in the House of Commons, it was for them to say so; but at the same time, he felt that if their friends had kept their promises, there could be no doubt, as to the two Liberal members being returned.

At the George Hotel, the headquarters of the Tories, all was bustle, noise, and excitement. Sir James Elphinstone and several of his leading supporters congregated at the centre window some time before four o'clock, all being eager to commence speaking, which they could not consistently do until four o'clock. This eagerness was manifest by the very many times the hon. Baronet pulled out his watch to look at the time, and as the minutes grew fewer his excitement became stronger. This intense eagerness did not exist only in the minds of those who were at the window, for a crowd of his supporters assembled beneath in the street and continued shouting at the top of their voices, insulting any person who was known to be of an opposite opinion, and entirely putting a stop to the ordinary traffic.

When four o'clock arrived Sir James bowed repeatedly, and as soon as some degree of order in the crowd could be obtained, he proceeded to address them amid vociferous cheering. While he was speaking, two costermongers in charge of at donkey and cart came up and took from the cart an effigy purporting to be that of Mr. Serjeant Gaselee, and this seemed to cause no end of amusement. Someone suggested that it should be burnt, and some matches having been procured, the intelligent and enthusiastic costers, with the assistance of some of their friends, proceeded to ignite the rags, which soon blazed up, and as the pieces of the effigy became burnt, they were thrown indiscriminately among the crowd, to the extreme disgust of many who had attired themselves in their holiday clothes for the occasion, and for

Sir James Elphinstone

some little time it was difficult to say whether a melee would not take place between the parties engaged in meting out (what they considered to be) justice on the learned serjeant, and the more respectable of Sir James's friends.

Sir James having retired from the window, the crowd began to disperse, and after some time had elapsed the traffic was allowed to proceed without obstruction. The "bands of music" proceeded to discourse sweet strains, the most popular tune being "Tommy Dodd," the urchins and many who should have had better sense, singing some verses of doggerel written to do honour to the hon. Baronet.

1868 – THE VOLUNTEER REVIEW AT PORTSMOUTH PART II.

A description of the great meeting of the volunteer corps at Portsmouth on Easter Monday, the inspection and "march past" on Southsea Common, before Lieutenant-General Sir George Buller, and the sham fight in the valley of Cosham and Wymering, between the Hilsea lines and Portsdown hill, was given in our last Number. We now publish several Illustrations of the mimic battle, which was one of the most interesting affairs of its kind. The battlefield extended along the northern end of Portchester Lake, from a point a little to the west of Paulsgrove, to the Hilsea lines at Portsbridge, thence northwards in a straight line beyond the village of Cosham as far as the crest of Portsdown hill, and then in a westerly direction along and including the whole of the southern slope of the Portsdown ridge as far Southwick Fort. The plan of action supposed that the British fleet had been dispatched from Spithead in search of a hostile squadron, and that an enemy had seized the opportunity to land an army in Sussex. Portsmouth was garrisoned by a mixed force of volunteers and regulars and the enemy, thinking the capture of the arsenal and Dockyard an easier task than an advance on London, had moved his whole force to the westward. He was considered to have silenced the fire of the forts on Portsdown hill for a time, to have held possession of the heights, and to be desirous of investing the town of Portsmouth. For this purpose, two strong divisions were marched round the eastern and western flanks of Portsdown hill, by night, to seize the villages of Cosham, Wymering, Paulsgrove, and the intervening farmhouses and buildings. A first parallel having thus been obtained, the enemy had intended to sap up, and, if possible, carry by assault, the Hilsea lines. He had succeeded in occupying his intended position; but

1st Hants Engineer Volunteers Constructing a Barrel Pier Bridge at Hilsea Lines

the garrison of Portsmouth, being made aware of his intention, had manned the whole of the earthworks and moved up a strong body of troops, in reserve, to resist any sudden assault, or drive the enemy from the ground.

Daylight came, and discovered the enemy with strong battalions occupying the southern slope of the hill. The operations then commenced. The two columns of the defending force, then reached the lines at Hilsea, proceeded to take their position behind the long line of strong earthworks, the third division taking the left of the position and extending from the west end of the lines to the new iron bridge, and the fourth division deploying from the new military road, across the old London road, and stretching away to the east nearly to Hilsea redoubt.

Our general view of the battle from Portsdown hill, represents an advanced period of the engagement, but it may here be referred to for the topography and plan of operations. This view looks due south, across Portchester Lake, which lies in the right-hand portion of the Engraving, with Portchester Castle on low promontory to the extreme right, and across the valley of Cosham and Wymering, with the creek in front of the Hilsea fortifications, which are shown in the middle distance of the left-hand portion. The town and shipping of Portsmouth are seen about six miles off, the farther extremity of the island formed by the Hilsea creek. Beyond Portsmouth is Spithead, with the expanse of the Solent, and the Isle of Wight in the background.

The 1st Hants Engineer Volunteers, under the command of Captain Buchan, had constructed the day before, a barrel-and-pier bridge over the water in front of Hilsea Lines. A pontoon bridge, for the use of the general public, was laid the same day by the Royal Engineers. The first mentioned bridge was designed for the sortie of the defenders in the mock conflict. The engagement was begun by the cavalry of the enemy opening communications with the two divisions advancing round the flanks of Portsdown hill. The second division was seen in columns of route, preceded by cavalry, moving about midway down the southern slope of Portsdown hill, from the direction of Havant, on to Cosham, and the first division moving in similar order from Fareham on to Paulsgrove and Wymering. This demonstration was the signal for sudden activity on the part of the defenders. The field guns and the 18-pounder guns of position of the 3rd Middlesex Artillery were dragged up the slopes of the earthworks and into the battery on the top. The Royal Engineers pontoon train at the same time began to throw over a pontoon bridge to the west of the new iron bridge, and between that and the bridge which had been thrown over the previous day. In ten minutes from the time of lashing the first saddle the creek was bridged and practicable for infantry; and in another four or five minutes the bridge was practicable for field artillery.

Now the enemy began to show his strength. From each division, as it advanced to form a junction, strong pickets were thrown out, advancing and feeling their way until they occupied the line of the railway—those from the first division in advance of Wymering and Paulsgrove, and those from the second division passing through Cosham. Before the pickets had taken their allotted positions, the junction between the two advancing divisions of the enemy was effected, and the whole force wheeled into line of columns, at deploying distance, along the face of the hill. The full force of the enemy was now displayed; and, as the strength of the defenders justified their assuming the offensive, the initiative was taken by dispatching two battalions, one from each division, across the iron bridge to drive in the enemy's pickets.

These two battalions dashed across the bridge at the double, and as soon as they had reached firm ground beyond the edge of the creek, deployed and extended skirmishing order. They rapidly closed with the pickets of the enemy, and when well within rifle range the clear notes of the bugle ran out to commence firing. A dropping fire was heard all along their line, and from behind every hillock and tuft of herbage. The pickets, almost concealed behind the line of railway, replied vigorously; but the fight had not continued many minutes before it became evident that they were on the point of being overwhelmed. To prevent this catastrophe the enemy at once threw forward several battalions in support of their pickets; at the same time guns of position, on the right and left of the enemy's forces, opened on the defenders, who at once returned the fire with interest. The skirmishers of the contending armies now closed and fought for the line of railway, the great guns on each side thundering across the valley over their heads.

While this conflict was raging a powerful reinforcement arrived to assist the defenders. Steaming up Portchester Creek came the gunboats *Stork* and *Fancy*, convoying a squadron of steam launches and towing a flotilla of pinnaces. Running up under a heavy fire from a battery of the enemy's artillery, which was brought to bear on them the moment they came into sight, the squadron took up a position opposite the village of Paulsgrove. When the right of the enemy was well in view, the *Stork* and *Fancy* cast anchor; the launches and pinnaces took up berths in regular order to the westward, and brought their guns to bear on the village and the heights behind it, but waited for the signal to commence action from the works, though severely galled by the battery from the village.

The fight between the skirmishers of the defenders and those of the enemy had been going on for some time; but the enemy were now driven from the railway, and retired to a fresh line of defence formed by the high road running through Cosham and Wymering, and including both those villages. When the enemy's skirmishers had taken up their new position, the garrison formed three columns of attack, which poured down and crossed, at the double-quick march, the two pontoon bridges and the new bridge by which the military road was carried over the creek. The fire of the gunboats drove the enemy's vedettes out of the village of Paulsgrove, and silenced the hostile battery of field artillery. The guns of the flotilla were then turned on the dense masses of the enemy's infantry, which now descended the hill, in column, to retake the position from which their cavalry had been driven. Though suffering severely, the enemy advanced at the double, reoccupied the village, intrenched themselves, and, in spite of the combined efforts of the flotilla, and, later in the day, of a supporting column of the defenders' infantry, maintained their position.

As soon as the three columns of attack of the defenders had fairly crossed the creek, some of the dense columns of the enemy deployed into line and descended the hill to meet the threatened assault. They halted above the villages of Cosham and Wymering. The defenders' columns swung round into line, advanced towards the line of the railway, which they occupied; and they also halted. Now the whole line of the enemy suddenly advanced, and, sweeping over the intervening space of ground, seized on Cosham, Wymering, Paulsgrove, and the connecting high road, a distance of nearly a mile and a half. The enemy moved up his reserves in support, and, recalling the line of skirmishers, prepared to maintain this new position. The defenders advanced over the railway, and recalled their skirmishers, taking up a position parallel to the enemy, within easy rifle range. The great struggle of the day now began. Along the whole length of this long line a furious file fire was maintained, till the low ground was shrouded in a cloud of smoke. Repeated advances of the defenders were met and repulsed with vigorous promptitude on the part of the enemy. While this main battle raged, the defenders sent brigade after brigade to try and get possession of Paulsgrove, but without success. At the other extremity of the line the enemy held the village of Cosham. The right of the defenders charged into Cosham, and a desperate battle raged in the village street, until the enemy were driven out and retreated northward up Portsdown hill.

Outflanked by this movement, the left of the enemy gave ground, but retired steadily and in good order. They held in check the fresh battalions of defenders that came up on the other side of the valley. The defenders brought up fresh reserves from behind the Hilsea earthworks. The first was a splendid battery of Armstrong 12-pounders of the Royal Artillery, followed by a battery of 9-pounder field guns of the 3rd Middlesex Artillery. Taking ground to their left, south of the village, these two batteries galloped through the open fields, and, getting into position below the extreme left of the enemy, opened up a terrible fire. The enemy's left fell back in disorder, until their whole line, yielding to the superior number of the defenders, gave ground, and then they formed column and retreated up the hill. The defenders' infantry formed column and advanced; their artillery limbered up and trotted after them; while a reserve, consisting of the Royal Marine Artillery, the 30th and 97th Regiments, advanced rapidly along the London road, and came out in overwhelming force on the left flank of the enemy.

By this time both the defenders and the enemy had again deployed into line in their new positions, and were file-firing at each other at short range. Outflanked, outnumbered, and overwhelmed by superior fire of artillery and musketry, it scarcely needed the assistance of the regular troops to complete the discomfiture of the enemy. The Royal Marine Artillery, however, were deployed full on their flanks; the snipers of the regulars delivered a few rounds of file-firing, so rapid, as compared with the muzzle-loaders, that it sounded like a continuous volley; and the battle was over. The enemy formed column and retreated, with his left thrown back. His right still maintained possession of the village of Paulsgrove; and, massing his artillery on his right and driving off the flotilla, he was able to secure the road to Fareham for an orderly and well-conducted retreat.

1868 – THE MILITARY REVIEW AS SEEN FROM WIDLEY FORT.

A correspondent has favoured us with the following graphic sketch of the review seen from this point.

"On arriving at the top of Portsdown a magnificent view presented itself. Eastward, beyond Farlington waterworks, stretched Langstone harbour, the viaduct of the Hayling railway spanning its northern extremity. Immediately below, lay Cosham and Wymering with the roads mapped out on the green parterre. The railway to Fareham ran east and west and beyond were the Hilsea lines. Portsmouth and Southsea were crowded in the distance, and beyond, separated by what seemed but a narrow channel, the Isle of Wight with its shady side presented to us, frowned upon the landscape. To the west, we looked down upon Portsmouth harbour and Portchester castle and fort.

By eleven o'clock, many thousand persons had congregated on the down, and a multitude of equipages from the aristocratic to the costermonger type were under the sheltering walks of Widley Fort; and, despite the sun, a shelter from the north wind was most enjoyable. But weary expectation could discover no traces of the coming fight save in a few red flags set here and there to indicate strategic movements.

The defenders of the Hilsea lines moat must have been asleep indeed when they allowed an enemy to reconnoitre in such close proximity. About half past eleven, the attacking party began to take positions on the side of the down, and the besieged very politely and considerately feigned not to see the threatened attack until the enemy had had ample time for luncheon. During this state of suspense, a poor unfortunate hare, scared by the troops, endeavoured to make its escape over the down. A chase after it created a few minutes' diversion for some of the spectators; hemmed in on all sides, it was obliged to succumb to its fate, doubtless, without the intervention of a license to kill.

At 1.30 the first shot was fired, and for a few moments the guns on the Hilsea lines and those on the Down had it all to themselves; but presently the rifles joined in, as well as the gunboats and launches, and the firing became pretty general. Our attention was attracted at this stage by the loud eulogies of a party snugly seated on the turf within the ramparts, indisputably enjoying the contents of their bottles and baskets. Considering that, in their position, what was going on outside could only be known to them by the evidence of their ears, it sounded somewhat oddly to hear such remarks as, "The most splendid sight I ever saw," – "pass the sandwiches" - "so well planned," - "another glass?" – "brilliant defence," – "I now feel at peace with all mankind," &c. Well, if they were content, who should quarrel with them?

The sortie from the Hilsea lines was the spectacle of the day. Company after company, battalion after battalion, poured forth, and the cry was "still they come!" Lines were thrown out to the right and left, volleys were fired into Cosham, and the enemy were compelled to evacuate it. Skirmishers were sent forward, while the main body continued to advance, and the enemy's cavalry were routed at the point of the bayonet. The defenders next brought up their guns, and dislodged the enemy from a commanding position. The enemy unlimbered again close to the fort, but had soon to make a further retreat westward, the gallant defenders still pressing on and making good use of every advantage they obtained over their opponents. From half past three to four the battle was at its height—the firing was incessant, and the roar quite indescribable; it can only be compared

View from Portsdown Hill

to continuous thunder, or thunder prolonged by repeated reverberation, as heard in a mountainous district, with ever and anon a sharper and more ringing crack.

During the engagement, the wind carried away the smoke, so that every movement and evolution could be distinctly seen; and owing to the situation, and the admirable position for overlooking the field of battle that Portsdown afforded, some ten or twenty thousand persons have seen such a review as they never saw before, and could not have seen elsewhere. But how does the field look after the battle the wheat crops and the trodden down hedges? The farmers will have something to say on the subject."

The review ball was, comparatively, as great a success as the review. The great drill shed was decorated on Tuesday night with brilliant effect, and the ball fairly rivalled that held in the same place during the visit of the French fleet. The scene was like a fairyland, so charming were the decorations and appointments. Festoons of sweet-smelling flowers hung from the bars of iron below the ceiling, flags of all nations decked the walls, medallions and mottoes, shields and armour, all contributed to a grand and novel effect. From the main hall, a large refreshment annex was entered, cool and perfumed, the flowing incline of the tent top being draped with red and white striped cloth. Two giant figures, clad in armour, from the gunboat, guarded the passage facing the ballroom, around which was also hung martial devices amidst floral designs. The company numbered about 500 ladies and gentlemen. A cold collation was admirably served in the tent, and the ball did not terminate until nearly five o'clock.

1868 – A NEW STAINED-GLASS WINDOW.

A very neat stained-glass window has recently been placed in the centre light over the communion table of St. Mary's, Portsmouth, in memory of the late Rev. Robert Stevens, who for three years preceding his death conducted the evening services in this church. At his decease, in January last, it was determined to raise some tribute to his memory in the church in which he last laboured. Accordingly, a subscription was opened amongst the congregation and their friends, the result of which was that in a few months £30 was raised, and the order was then entrusted to Messrs. Cox and Co. of Southampton Street, Strand, who have executed it with their accustomed artistic skill and finish. The window consists of a geometric pattern, with centre medallion, the subject representing "Christ blessing little children," and the whole surrounded with rich colours. At the foot of the window, in amber letters on a red ground, is the following inscription:— "In loving remembrance of the Rev. Robert Stevens, evening lecturer in this church for three years. Died 13th January, 1868, aged 30."

1868 – QUEEN'S INSPECTION OF H.M.S GALATEA.

It was mentioned in our Court news that her Majesty visited the frigate commanded by his Royal Highness the Duke of Edinburgh on Monday week. She was accompanied by the Duke and Duchess of Coburg, Prince and Princess Louis of Hesse, Prince and Princess Christian, Princess Louisa, Prince Leopold, Princess Beatrice, and the Princess of Leiningen, and attended by the ladies and gentlemen in waiting. The Queen embarked at Trinity Pier, East Cowes, on board the Royal yacht *Alberta*, and proceeded thence to the *Galatea*, where her Majesty was received on board by Captain his Royal Highness the Duke of Edinburgh, the yards being manned and the Royal Marines presenting arms.

The Queen was met on board by his Royal Highness the Prince of Wales, who arrived shortly before from London, attended by Colonel Kingscote, C.B.; and after all the officers of the *Galatea* had been presented to her Majesty by the Duke of Edinburgh, she was conducted round the ship by him, the whole ship's company being inspected at the same time. The Queen remained on board for upwards of an hour, and soon after seven o'clock landed the Duke of Edinburgh's barge at Osborne Pier, a Royal salute being fired by the *Galatea* on her Majesty's leaving the ship, H.M.S. *Hector* and the Trinity yacht paying the usual compliments as her Majesty passed to and from the frigate.

In the evening the Prince of Wales, Prince Louis of Hesse, Prince Christian, and the Prince of Leiningen, with the gentlemen attendance upon them, dined with the Duke of Edinburgh on board the *Galatea*, after which the ship was illuminated.

Inspection by the Queen

1868 – THE PORTSMOUTH GUARDIAN.

The *Portsmouth Guardian*, a penny mid-weekly paper, published in Portsea for many years past, has ceased to exist, its last number having been issued on Thursday.

1868 – DEATH OF THE VICAR OF PORTSMOUTH.

We regret to have to announce the decease of the Rev. John Paulett McGhie, the highly esteemed and respected vicar of Portsmouth, who expired at the Vicarage in the High Street, on Thursday morning, aged 64 years. The deceased succeeded to the living on the removal of the Rev. C.B. Henville, in the year 1839, stepping from the curacy to the vicarage, and during the long period he held that responsible and important position he gained the unanimous good will and esteem of his parishioners. He was ever ready to aid in every good work, but shrunk from all ostentatious display of his works of mercy and continuous efforts in promoting the well-being of the poor in the locality, by whom his loss will be felt. Mr. McGhie graduated at Queen's College, Oxford, in 1827, and took his degree in 1830. He enjoyed the friendship and confidence of his Diocesan, and for many years held the office of Rural Dean. He took a great interest in the ancient parish church of St. Thomas, and especially in the restoration of the chancel some few years since, to which he most liberally contributed. Nearly the whole of the residents in the High Street and other principal streets of the town have partially closed their shutters as a mark of respect to their late vicar. The living of Portsmouth is in the gift of the College of Winchester, and is worth about £700 per annum. The funeral will take place on Thursday morning next, at 11 o'clock. The remains will be taken into the parish church of St. Thomas, where a portion of the funeral service will be read, and thence removed to the Portsmouth Cemetery for interment. The Mayor of Portsmouth will attend the funeral.

1868 – IMPROVEMENTS TO THE FORTS AT PORTSMOUTH.

There can no doubt that the contemplated tram or railway linking Southsea Castle with Lumps Fort, Eastney Fort and Barracks, and Cumberland Fort, by means of a swing bridge at Sinah, and thus putting those important works into communication with the railway which has recently been made to South Hayling, will be an immense boon to the various departments in working connection with these forts, and as the government have, we are informed, acquired the freehold of the whole sea frontage of South Hayling, they will be enabled also to put the new fort which is proposed to construct on the south east side of Hayling at Chichester Harbour into tram or railway communication with the remaining forts and the general railway system. It is desirable now that the government should take steps to convert some 700 acres of this purchase into grass, and to have it fed with sheep in order that it may be applicable at all times as exercising, practising, or review ground for troops, for which it is well calculated.

Looking at its contiguity to all the government works at Portsmouth, and the vast number of men congregated in that neighbourhood, it is the greatest possible importance that this should be done. There can be no doubt that the government have acted wisely in purchasing the land at this time when its value is at the lowest, for there can be no doubt that if, hereafter, they should desire to alter their plans and this land should come for re-sale the exchequer would be benefited by the transaction. As land at Hayling is now selling at about £200 an acre, it is fair to assume that the government have not paid a larger price than this for their purchase; but it is to be hoped they have taken care to possess themselves of all the manorial rights in connection with the sea frontage, which in this instance we happen to know belong to the Lord of the Manor of Hayling. Only a few years since, the sea frontage land at Southsea which adjoins Hayling could have been purchased at about £1,000 an acre and the back land at £300 an acre. Now the front land is realising upwards of £4,000 an acre and the back land upwards of £500 an acre. We repeat, therefore, that we consider the government have acted wisely in the matter.

1868 – LIFE AT SOUTHSEA.

The following article, descriptive of life at Southsea, is taken from the last number of the *Queen* newspaper:-

Thirty years ago, Southsea, was a dismal little half-pay suburb, consisting of two or three straight, stiff terraces of eight-roomed houses fronting The Lines, and called then Frying Pan Row, from their generally heated condition; one poor street of starveling shops; and a considerable and odorous undrained back slum, hounded by a common and a marsh. Even twenty years ago it was utterly unknown as a watering place; but about a dozen years since it woke up one day and found that it had facilities, to wit, a magnificent beach and the finest bathing possible; and the last ten or twelve years has seen a growth and increase in Southsea such as few or no watering places can parallel.

The marsh has disappeared; the common, once little more than a huge furze thicket, has been cleared and levelled into a wide and desirable parade, cricket, and recreation ground; and where, even fifteen years ago, not a house was to be seen, there are now long rows and terraces of handsome houses looking seawards, and the great majority of which are let furnished or are lodging houses and at the present moment of writing there is not one of them to let, nor even a suite of apartments (fronting the sea) to be had, for Southsea is full, and the East Beach is a sight for parents or guardians on any fine morning or evening.

I have several times seen it literally covered with groups of well-dressed children, probably to the number of four or five hundred or more. Here sit the mammas or the nurses, chatting, tatting, and crocheting in little knots, and there roll and tumble, or dig and paddle, their precious charges by the score; and up above, on the crown of the beach, young ladies of mature age discuss absent friends and present enjoyments. It certainly is a wonderful beach for children, a wide expanse of small dry shingle for sitting, or a good belt of hard sand for walking on or digging in, as the taste of the operator may dictate, with the free bracing breezes of the Channel to air it; for opposite the East Beach the Isle of Wight ends, and the open sea comes rolling in

These advantages, while making it exceedingly desirable and healthy for children, also give perhaps the best bathing in England for their elders. On the Western Beach, which is divided from the East by Southsea Castle, and is opposite the Isle of Wight, the air is softer and milder. Along this the esplanade runs and boats ply for hire, and the visitor can either row in any kind of craft, from a six-oared galley down to the most diminutive dingy, for 6d., an hour; or he can take a sail in one of the smart little yachts which skim up and a down for hire at 2s., an hour.

Towards the end of the West Beach Stands the pier, from which a tramway runs to the railway at Landport, for the convenience of passengers, who are going and coming to and from the Isle of Wight. On this a military band plays every other afternoon through the season, when the pier is thronged with ravishing toilets and swarms of well-dressed people. Beside the pier stands the King's Rooms and the baths. These rooms for many years formed a very agreeable rendezvous and gossiping place, there being a comfortable reading and news room, and a covered promenade open on the seaside. There, too, the band played on most afternoons, and once every week there were assemblies of dancing, and once a month balls. These were always well attended, and few ballrooms could look gayer than this, brightened as the scene was by the blue and scarlet uniforms of the military and naval officers. But this season the rooms have been closed, owing to a peculiar accident, which his temporarily deprived us of the ministrations of the lessee.

Next year, I hear wonderful improvements are to be carried out, and the place will be made much more attractive. However, with the brigade day once a week, when the whole of the garrison, some four regiments of infantry, a battery of Marine Artillery, and another of Royal Artillery are exercised, to the delight of the young folks, but occasional discomposure of the old ones (for it is a startling thing to see six Armstrong guns drawn up close to you, and to be made a target of), and with an occasional inspection and review, a presentation of colours, with guard trooping and the band on the Governor's Green, we do pretty well, and get our share of military sounds and sights; and if we wish for more, why we visit the forts, of which more anon. I know that these are interesting topics for young ladies, and this is why I dwell on them; for ladies, bless them, do love to see nice uniforms, and have no objection even to walk beside them, while there is a large section who dote upon reviews and military bands; and to them, also, a ballroom so furnished is so attractive that papa must take them.

If the naval department, however, obtains our preference, then we commence with the Dockyard, and inspect, with no little wonder the huge, anchors, the vast spars, the cavernous docks, the wonderfully ingenious block machinery, the roaring foundry with its blazing furnaces and tremendous Nasmyth hammers, which can crack a nut or crush creation with equal ease; and as for ships, there is the *Royal Sovereign* to begin with, and the *Wyvern* to go on with, the two most remarkable ships in the British navy, being of the sort known as turret ships on which all the papers have been more than eloquent for ever so many months. Then there are men-of-war building, and men-of-war finished, and men-of-war fitting, and perhaps an enormous iron-clad to be launched; indeed, the Dockyard is a wonderful and unfailing resource.

Next there is the victualling yard, where all the biscuit is baked for the navy by very ingenious and interesting machinery. The corn is put in at the top of the mill, and comes out biscuit at the bottom. Here, too, all the beef, pork, tobacco, rum, potted meats, mess fittings and requisites, and other stores and provisions are supplied and served out; and then there is the Gun Wharf and the *Victory* to see, and perhaps the *Excellent*, or the *St. Vincent*, where hundreds of smart-looking sailor lads are being trained for the navy; or, better than all, the Queen's yacht, the *Victoria and Albert*. It is wonderful what interest ladies take in that spectacle, and it is not perhaps wonderful; but it is very agreeable to note with what extreme courtesy and attention they are received and treated by the attendants. And as to the ship herself, it is certainly a sight not to he missed, and the great interest displayed by our wives and daughters in the slightest thing concerning the Queen, her manners or customs, show how really deeply the example of not only a great, good, and virtuous woman, but an excellent wife and mother, can sink into and abide in the hearts of her subjects.

Then we go to church on board the *Victory*, or to the military chapel on the green, on a Sunday, and return of course duly edified. Perhaps we have a French fleet or an English fleet to review, or a Viceroy or Sultan to visit, or something of that sort, and we look for something of the kind now, at least once a year, and then what an influx of visitors we have! Beds go up to goodness knows what price, and foolish lodging-house keepers (not many though) get rid of their lodgers if they, can, to make untold hay while the brief sun shines, and very often fail to make any. Then, too, what a flurry of anxiety ensues in the bosoms of families, mammas are anxious, papas desponding. Shall we be invited to the ball? shall we get seats at the lunch? Shall we have tickets for the dinner? Will the X's or the Y's ask us round the fleet in their yacht? or shall we have to beg a seat in one of the gunboats of that horrid young Spifkin, third mate of the *Thunderbomb*? or shall we ignominiously have to subscribe our half-crowns apiece for a seat on one of the Ryde boats diverted to more profitable usage for the day? These are subjects which agitate not only the female mind, but stir even the sterner bosoms of Pater and Fraterfamilias to their inmost depths.

1868 – OPENING OF ST. MARK'S TEMPORARY CHURCH.

The opening service in connection with St. Mark's Temporary Church, North End, was held on Thursday evening, when the sacred edifice was crowded in every part. Many clergymen were present. The preliminary service was performed by the Rev. N.H. McGachen, the incumbent, and the lessons were read by the Rev. E.B.C. Churchill, incumbent of All Saints'. The building, it will be recollected, was recently used as a ballroom, the grounds adjoining being set apart as pleasure gardens, and it has since been adapted for the performance of the services of the Church of England, and has a very pretty appearance.

1868 – A POEM TO CAPTAIN KENNICOTT.

Appearing in the Portsmouth *Times and Gazette* in November 1868 is this poem dedicated to a Captain Kennicott, a contemporary of Lord Nelson at the Battle of Trafalgar in 1805.

CAPTAIN KENNICOTT.
(Received thirty-nine wounds on board the *Royal Sovereign* at Trafalgar, Oct. 21, 1805. Pining in penury at Folkestone, Nov. 1868.)

'Twas in nut-brown October,
Years sixty-three ago,
That England struck the French and Dons
Trafalgar's fatal blow!

When Nelson gave the signal
To bid the tight begin,
On board the Royal Sovereign grand
Old Collingwood led in!

That morning to his captains
The Admiral had cried,
"He can't go wrong who lays his ship
Along a foeman's side!"

Straight at the Santa Anna
The Royal Sovereign sped,
And fought till all the hostile fleet
Were captured, sunk, or fled.

Today there lives at Folkestone
A bent seafaring man.
Worn down with penury and years
Beyond life's wonted span.

Who is this white-haired skipper,
Ill-clad and pinched for food?
Tis Kennicott, once midshipman
With Nelson's Collingwood!

A bombshell at Trafalgar
The middy's eye struck out,
And gave him nine and thirty wounds,
Whose scars bears about!

Bethink you, then, kind Britons,
Of Captain Kennicott,
That he should die in want, would be
A scandal and a blot!

1868 – PROJECTED IMPROVEMENTS IN SOUTSEA.

The rescue of Southsea Common from the sea, the formation of the charming esplanade, and the erection of a number of palatial residences and beautiful streets on what was only a few years ago a marshy desert, is surprising and gratifying enough in all conscience. We hear, however, that more projected improvements and surprises are in store for us. The West of Southsea has now become so greatly separated from the East, that the desirability is, we hear, being mooted of forming an easy and rapid communication with the Eastern end and the railway not, however, by the laying down of another railway, since that would prevent the land being utilised for building purposes, but by a tramway.

It has been suggested by Mr. Pinto that a tramway worked by horse traction, and combining all the recent improvements, should be laid down communicating with the railway at the crossing at Copnor, and terminating at or near the Coast Guard Station, at the East end of Southsea Common. This line of tramway would cross three lines of roads, namely, that from Copnor to Milton on the Eastern side of the Portsea Island Union House, that which is known as Albert Road, leading from the East end of Elm Grove to Highland Road, and that from Southsea Common to Cumberland Fort. The old canal, it is proposed, should be crossed by means of a bridge, at a short distance from Hill Lane on its Western side. The communication with the railway, it is said, could be effected at a very moderate cost, as it would be only necessary to erect a small station at Copnor, at which the arrival tickets could be collected.

We hear it rumoured that a company will shortly be formed to carry out these improvements, with the title of the "East Southsea Tramway and Pier Company." The projected line for the greater portion of its length would be carried over ground which is literally "land locked," and has no communication with the highways beyond that which is afforded by occupation roads. This alone, it is believed, would induce the several owners to dispose of their land at a moderate remuneration, as by means of the new road, the remainder of their land would become much more accessible, and would be rendered immediately available for building purposes.

The tramway, however, has to form but one portion of the scheme, as it is intended to make it also a land and building speculation, for which purpose it is proposed that the new roadway should be a hundred feet in width, which would leave ample space for a carriage drive and footpath on each side of the tramway, with building land one hundred and fifty feet in depth on the East and West sides. The new road would communicate with Fratton at or near the present railway bridge by means of a road which it is proposed should be carried along the Southern bank of the old canal. A number of other innovations are promised, including an avenue of trees and a new promenade pier, but we have already mentioned enough to give our readers sufficient to think about.

1868 – ARRIVAL OF TROOPS FROM ABYSSINIA.

There was considerable excitement in Portsmouth on Monday over the reception of the 33rd Regiment, returned by the troop ship *Crocodile* from Abyssinia, and quartered in that town. The 33rd Regiment are entitled to the credit of having taken a most prominent part in the expedition. Not only has Sir Robert Napier made especial complimentary allusion to their services in his official despatches, but the Commander-in-Chief personally addressed the corps on the plains in front of Magdala, speaking in eulogistic terms of the manner in which the officers and men acquitted themselves throughout.

The regiment served in India before the Abyssinian Expedition was determined upon, and they embarked from that country at Karachi on the 21st November, arriving at Annesley Bay on the 1st of the following month. The 33rd was the first European regiment in Abyssinia, and it was upon them that the arduous task devolved of making roads up to Antalo, a distance of 300 miles.

The *Crocodile* was welcomed into Portsmouth by an immense crowd. As she neared the shore the band played successively, "See the conquering hero comes," and "Home, sweet home." The excitement on board corresponded with that on shore. The men were full of spirits, and spoke very favourably of their treatment during the expedition. They were very enthusiastic in their expressions of admiration of Sir Robert Napier and Sir Charles Staveley. The two men who first forced an entrance at the extreme end, and turned the gate— namely, No. 691, Drummer Michael Magner, and No. 942, Private James Bergin—accompanied their regiment.

Various opinions were expressed as to the fate of Theodore, but the majority on board were adverse to the conclusion that he committed suicide. The King is said to have been wounded in four places—the leg, chest, mouth, and neck—and when found he was on his face; his horse, which was gorgeously caparisoned, being by his side in his hand. He was holding a revolver —the same that was recently presented by Her Majesty—and this is now in the possession of the Commander-in-Chief, and will be brought to England. Magdala is described by the troops as a place with some pretensions to grandeur, and possessing an abundance of costly decorations, particularly in the chapel, in the rear of which, in stone tanks, was a supply of water equal to the demands of Theodore and his followers for six months.

Throughout the whole country the natives treated the troops kindly, and were ever ready to render to them the most cordial assistance. A story is told affecting the disposition of the troops before Magdala. The Commander-in-Chief, in giving directions to General Staveley, intimated that he had intended to place the 4th Regiment in the position afterwards occupied by the 33rd, but on the General saying, "I had intended to place the 33rd there," the Chief said, "Very well, as you please;" and, said one of the men, "the result of this was, that while the 4th were doing nothing on the plain, we were admiring Theodore's rupees."

1868 – LANDPORT DRAPERY BAZAAR.

George Keet, from the Landport Drapery Bazaar having taken premises as above, respectfully solicits the favour of an early inspection of his stock for the present Season, and trusts his long connection with the above firm will be a sufficient guarantee of his capabilities. The various Departments will be found replete with the latest novelties in millinery, mantles, hosiery, &c.

1868 – ALBERT COTTAGES AT LANDPORT.

The election of four candidates for admission into the Albert Cottages Alms Houses came off at the Athenaeum, Bishop Street, Portsea, on Monday last, and although the proceedings in themselves were of an encouraging and agreeable character, it is to be regretted that they revealed a decrease in that general support which the promoters have a right to expect from the general public, considering that the object of the charity is to provide 33 cottages for the occu- pation of aged members of friendly societies of the borough of Portsmouth, and to grant annuities to the occupiers.

The class for whom these benefits are sought is a provident class, composed of persons who for many years have been providing for funeral expenses or sickness, but to whom in old age, a small cottage, rent free, would be a considerable boon. It has been suggested that the members of the friendly societies would be able and willing to support the charity, but in order to be in a position to build and to maintain the cottages, the directors solicit extraneous support. The association has already received the recognition of many of the principal inhabitants, and Mr. T.P. Wills, the indefatigable secretary, is anxious to obtain an enlarged list of patrons and vice-patrons.

With the view of affording the opportunity of discussing the best means of advancing the interests of the association, the executive determined that a luncheon should precede the election, and that at this meeting the leading supporters of the Albert Cottages should be invited to attend. The reading room at the Athenaeum was selected for this purpose, and to Mr. George Wilkins, of Queen Street, were the arrangements of the table entrusted. The whole of the arrangements was perfect and satisfactory, and but one circumstance - the absence of the Mayor - occasioned any regret or disappointment on the part of the guests. His Worship had consented to preside, but in consequence of being unavoidably detained out of town he could not attend, and Mr. J.P. Pratt, J.P., presided.

During the proceedings a copy of the annual report was handed to the company. In this it was stated that during the past year the promoters of the Alms Houses carried out a drawing of prizes to aid the building fund, but in consequence of the small number of tickets sold, it entailed a loss on the promoters; another result was that many friends took tickets instead of subscribing; a further loss has arisen from the two Friendly Societies, which voted sums in the first year, having failed to do so during the past year. The promoters are glad to be able to report that some of the winners of prizes in the drawing have added their names to this year's list of subscribers, and that the annual and temporary subscriptions have both increased, whilst the amount collected by candidates is more than double. As this last, for the future, will be a very uncertain source of income until another wing can be built, the directors trust that the number of annual subscribers may be largely increased, and that the Societies which up to the present time have done little or nothing, although some of their members are amongst the occupiers of the Alms Houses, may be induced to support the charity.

At the close of the luncheon some few complimentary toasts were proposed. After the toast of the "Queen" had been duly honoured, the Chairman gave the health of is Sergeant Gaselee, M.P., which was cordially received.

Mr. Gaselee proposed "Success to the Albert Cottages," remarking that whether he was the member for the borough or not he should continue to support the undertaking.

The Secretary, Mr. Wills, responded, and, in doing so, said he regretted that during the past year the support had not been so good as was anticipated. If the Friendly Societies had nothing to do with the movement, he believed that the general public would come forward more freely, because he had known of instances in which persons had expressed an opinion that subscriptions would come in more freely if eligible candidates were not restricted to the benefit societies.

There were 20,000 persons in Portsmouth who belonged to benefit societies, and if the whole of these recognised the movement there would be no difficulty in keeping it in a flourishing condition with the additional support of more annual subscribers. When the four candidates were elected today, the whole of the sets of rooms would be filled, and their study should be to proceed with the other parts of the building. There were at present nine sets of rooms, each consisting of a comfortable bed and sitting room, closet, &c., with sufficient accommodation for man and wife; and if a husband should die, the widow was allowed to remain in the same apartments as long as she lived. He was pleased to inform the meeting that the Mayor had promised a subscription of five guineas, and subscriptions were announced from several in the room. If each member of the various Friendly Societies would give 1d. each yearly towards the funds of the institution the income would thus be increased by 100l. yearly, and this would add greatly to the usefulness of the object the promoters had in view.

Mr. Alderman Ford, in acknowledging the toast of the "vice-patrons," made a graceful appeal to those present and the public generally for increased support, and urged the propriety of endeavouring to remove the incubus referred to by Mr. Wells.

1868 – THE ELECTION OF GOVERNOR AT THE WORKHOUSE.

At a time when public attention is very closely directed to the manner in which our workhouses are managed, and the whole system may be said to be on its trial, it is of the greatest importance that those to whom the administration of the poor law is entrusted should exercise the utmost care in the appointment of officers. In an extensive borough like this, where, owing to the accident of situation and other exceptional circumstances, arising out of its position as an important naval and military station, the growth of pauperism has been in excess of the average in other places more fortunately situate, and the parishes of Portsea and Portsmouth have to maintain some sixteen hundred men, women, and children in the workhouse, irrespective of an increasing heavy out-door relief.

Strangers continually find their way into the borough, and, in too many cases, become a permanent burden to the union. Thanks, however, to the vigilance which has recently been displayed by the guardians, a large number of removals have taken place during the past year, by which a great saving will be effected. The government of a large establishment like the Portsea Island Workhouse requires the possession of numerous qualifications which are rarely found in one individual. There is no desire on the part of the ratepayers to reduce their rates, at the expense of the proper care and comfort of the poor, but there is a strong objection to the gross waste of money which often results from incompetent management. Experience teaches us, too, that large expenditure does not always secure proper treatment of the poor. In this union, however, there has never been any complaint, and in this respect, at least, it will bear favourable comparison with any other similar establishment in the United Kingdom.

But it is pretty certain that there is ample room for an improvement in the system of management, and that hitherto there has not been a staff sufficiently numerous or properly qualified to act with efficiency under the Governor. Mr. Miller has resigned, after upwards of twenty-one years' service, in consequence of failing health, finding the duties growing upon him, until at length he was fairly overweighted, and the guardians met on Wednesday for the purpose of electing his successor. Some twenty candidates presented themselves, but of these some were disqualified on account of being above the age previously fixed upon — forty — and others had retired in consequence of the salary (£150 per annum, with residence and rations for the Governor and wife), not being, in their opinion, commensurate with the duties and responsibilities of the office.

The conditions had been fixed upon a previous meeting of the Guardians, after due consideration, but, with all deference to the board, we cannot understand the reasons which guided them in drawing such a "hard and fast line" with respect to the age. We do not know of any particular virtue in the figure of 40, and, as Mr. Baker stated, there might be many men just over that age who would be well qualified to fill the office. Mr. Baker pleaded hard for delay, in order that the age might he extended and further publicity given to the advertisement for candidates, but he was outvoted, and the election proceeded.

In the course of the discussion some rather curious opinions were expressed by one or two guardians. It must be admitted that to manage properly an institution which comprises within its walls a hospital and home, a penitentiary, a reformatory, a school, and a nursery, a government far more difficult and responsible than that of our prisons, the governor ought to be thoroughly efficient in every respect. Mr. Howell thought the new governor ought, besides possessing the other necessary qualifications, to be a "philosopher," while Mr. Bayne seemed to think that the office would be sinecure. He based his opinion upon a presumed intention of the board to appoint a storekeeper, who should have the title of deputy governor. It is doubtful, however, whether this officer will be appointed, and in any case the governor will be responsible for the proper management of the establishment.

Ultimately Mr. W. Runcieman, who has for some time past acted as removal clerk (in which position he has shown intimate acquaintance with the Poor Law) was elected, and we trust that experience will prove him to be "the right man in the right place." He has the advantage of being a young man (34 years old), and, we believe, he is actuated by a desire to discharge the duties faithfully and zealously.

Many features of the present management are radically wrong and pregnant with abuses. Neither the guardians nor the public desire the deserving, though unfortunate, to be treated otherwise than kindly, but, on the other hand, they object to the union house being a kind of Elysium for the improvident, the idle, or the vicious. Let the aged and the young, and others who are deserving, be the objects of consideration, but let not the worthless obtain immunity from labour by entering the workhouse portals.

1868 – HAMPSHIRE AND ISLE OF WIGHT BLIND SCHOOL AND HOME.

The claims of the destitute blind are irresistible, and therefore it would be almost supererogatory to enlarge upon the claims of an institution the immediate mission of which is to afford relief and comfort to those who are so afflicted. Yet - from causes which must, we think, be attributable rather to inattention than to wanton indifference - the only institution or home for the poor blind in the county of Hants receives but indifferent support, and is thus cramped in its resources, and limited in its sphere of usefulness as a county charity. To say that this should not be - to urge that the promoters should at least feel themselves in a position to meet the requirements of all eligible candidates for their considerate care - and that the institution should in every respect be countenanced and supported by those who are more favoured than the existing and would-be recipients of their assistance - is to repeat an oft-told truism. And yet the occasion requires it, and the excellent services rendered by its promoters demand a much more hearty and general cooperation from the sympathising public to place the institution in that position amongst the local charities which its purpose entitles it to occupy. With this object in view, the executive and those upon whom devolves the responsibility of management have recently been endeavouring, by encouraging sales of fancy and other articles - some the gift of ladies, and others the produce of the inmates themselves - to increase the revenue, for the double purpose of extending the society's sphere of usefulness and of enlarging the Home in Park Lane, Southsea, which is at present barely sufficient to afford proper accommodation for the inmates.

A special effort was also put forth upon the occasion of the annual meeting, which was held in the Portland Hall, Southsea, on Wednesday afternoon last. During the early part of the day an elaborate assortment of fancy and other articles were arranged for sale in the hall, which was graced by the presence of several ladies; and at three o'clock a public meeting was held in the same place in the presence of a large assemblage of ladies and gentlemen, amongst whom were the elite of the neighbourhood. The chair was occupied by Admiral Sir Thomas S. Pasley, Bart., the Commander-in-Chief at the port; and amongst those who occupied positions on the platform were Mr. H.B. Norman (the honorary secretary), Mr. G. Long, J.P. (the honorary treasurer), Mr. Jacob Owen, the Rev. J.C. Martin, Rev. F. Baldy, Rev. Mr. Doudney, Rev. J.S. Blake, Rev. Mr. Drury, and Mr. Richard Marvin. The blind children in the Home were likewise on the platform, and during the proceedings sang several selections and hymns in a pleasing and creditable manner; one of the blind female scholars displayed considerable taste in her pianoforte accompaniments.

The proceedings were opened by prayer and the singing of a hymn, after which the gallant Chairman briefly introduced the business of the meeting by expressing his deep sympathy with the afflicted ones by whom they were surrounded, and his earnest desire that the objects of the institution might be still more liberally supported; and especially urging the importance of forthwith contributing towards the special fund which was being raised for the purpose of enlarging the building in accordance with plans which were lying for inspection in the hall.

The honorary secretary then read the annual report, of which the following is the substance:-

It is with no small satisfaction that at this, the fifth annual meeting of this institution, its continued and progressive usefulness and prosperity can be reported. Whereas at the end of the last year there were thirteen pupils receiving their board and education in the Home, the present number is nineteen - of whom seven have been admitted within the year. Of the thirteen pupils of last year one has left, being, both bodily and mentally, so infirm and weak that nothing could be done with him, and one who was sent home in order to recruit his health has died. The progress made by the pupils appears to be on the whole good, both in the acquisition of general learning and of the handicrafts taught, and has called forth the approbation of many of the independent observers who have visited the Home.

The funds have been maintained so as to meet the expenditure of the year, but are still obtained in many instances by much personal effort from the forgetfulness of subscribers to remit their contributions in due time. They are, therefore, kindly reminded of this circumstance, and earnestly requested to have a regular time for sending their money, and to keep it, in order, as was before stated, to the punctual payment of the rent and other outgoings, and the purchase by ready money of all goods. The house is now quite inadequate to the increased and increasing number of pupils, by whom the only large room it contains has to be used for their meals and common room, as well as for classes and music and when all are gathered together in it, it is so crowded that the smallest pupils are in danger of being hurt, nor is it large enough to be healthy under such circumstances. The house must therefore be enlarged, and a room suitable for the purposes for which the present is so unfit must be added. The best means of doing this are now under the consideration of the committee, aided by the professional advice of Mr. Pince, of Portsmouth who very kindly gives his services for the occasion. Most probably it will be needed to add a wing to the present building; for which purpose the proprietor, Mrs. Inman, is ready to afford every facility in her power.

The kind efforts of friends are earnestly requested to augment as soon as possible, the building fund, for which, to this date, above 70l. has been subscribed, and 50l. has been set aside – at the bequest of the late Mr. Wickenden, and it is thought at least 200l. more will be required.

The organ fund originated five years ago, and has been already referred to in former reports. It now amounts to 40l. 17s. 3d., mainly, collected in small sums by ladies, and has been increased this day by a donation of 5l. each from Lady Pasley and Mr. Marvin, two warm and steadfast friends of the institution. Mr. Hunter, organ builder, of London, has taken the old and useless instrument at a valuation of 40l., and undertaken to build a new organ for 115l., which will be complete and fit for the purpose of the school. 75l. more is required to make up this fund. In great measure through the kind exertions of Mr. and Mrs. Kent, of Southampton, a very successful public meeting was held there a few weeks since at the Victoria Rooms, which was most ably presided over by the Mayor, Mr. Stebbing, and very well attended. Several of the local clergy and others addressed the meeting, which resulted in largely extending the interest felt in the institution, and in an addition to its fund, by sale of goods, collection at the doors, &c., of above 25l. The report concluded by acknowledging several acts of generosity on the part of companies and individuals.

Mr. Norman next read the financial statement. The gross expenditure for the year had been 791l. 5s. 11d., and to meet that subscriptions and donations had been received to the amount of 397l. 1s. 10d., the balance last year being 19s. 8d. There were other receipts, arising principally from the sale of baskets, &c., which brought the balance exactly to the same as was represented on the opposite side of the account. One item of interest in the receipts was 4l. 9s. 4d., the produce of the sale of articles which had been contributed by ladies; and here (as observed Mr. Norman) it would be as well if he explained that it was the practice of certain lady friends to send small articles for sale in the shop in Park Lane, and that such articles would at all times be thankfully received upon delivery at that place. He should also state that a letter had just been received from an old friend to the institution, Mr. Edwin Jones, in which he promised a third 5l. note in aid of the organ fund.

An explanation was necessary to show the singular circumstance of the balance on both sides of the account being precisely alike. There was a prospect of the receipts being somewhat less than the expenditure, and as the accounts were about to be made up a friend said, "If you have not enough, say so, and then I will give you the difference, in order that you may be able to say in your report that you have made both ends meet."

It now became his (Mr. Norman's) duty to move that the report and the balance sheet be printed and circulated under the direction of the committee. And he could again assure the meeting that he had great pleasure in again standing on the platform to advocate the claims of this institution, because the objects in view were of such a high character that it was a pleasure to work with the movement in any way. It was his lot to be closely cognisant of the doings at the home, and of the care and sympathy extended towards the unfortunate inmates, and he was convinced that it was only necessary for the inhabitants to become acquainted with the objects of the charity and the working of the institution generally to secure for it a larger amount of support.

He desired to lay stress on that part of the report which urged the prompt payment of subscriptions and donations, and for a reason which he would explain. They all knew who was the life and spirit of the institution; and that lady had such a high notion of what was strictly honourable that she avoided incurring debts without the immediate prospect of paying them. It was with the view of removing her anxiety in this respect that the subscribers were earnestly desired to follow out the suggestion of the committee in the payment of their contributions.

The Rev. J.C. Martin seconded the proposition. He remarked that it was a peculiar task to have to address himself to a subject of this kind, when he knew that those on whose behalf he was about to plead were present. At the same time, it was an undoubted fact that their presence spoke with more eloquence and with greater power than any words of his could express; and there were few, he thought, who could behold what they beheld, and who were at all acquainted with the general objects of this excellent institution, who could fail to be moved to pity in their expression of sympathy towards the blind children then present. He thought there was an opinion prevalent that blindness was a kind of individual punishment from God - that it was an infliction intended to betray God's anger or displeasure towards the persons so afflicted. Far be it from him to say that God did not chastise as he pleased; but it was wrong, he urged, to conclude that afflictions of the kind to which he referred were intended as direct punishment for personal sins. If they took some of God's own people, they would see this illustrated. Take Job, for instance, of whom it was said there was none like him on the face of the earth; and yet was any man ever tried like Job? With regard to the institution itself, he was pleased that this small one - he said small because it was small as a county institution, which included the Isle of Wight - was to be found amongst them; and although small, they should not despise the day of small things. It was encouraging to know that there had been an increase by seven in the number of inmates during the past year, and by perseverance and combined influence it might be that next year the number might be doubled, and that the success of the undertaking might be still more apparent as its age increased.

The resolution was cordially agreed to.

The Rev. Mr. Drury said the duty had been committed to him of moving that the hearty thanks of the meeting be given to the committee and officers for their valuable services during the past year. He was sure that this was a motion which should be carried most heartily, because the institution was most highly favoured in the selection of its officers. In the list of officials were several good names, the first of the names being that of the lady who had worked so indefatigably in the undertaking; and he asked the meeting to show their kindly feeling, and to testify their appreciation of the services which had been so ably and disinterestedly rendered, by cordially supporting the resolution.

The Rev. Mr. Doudney seconded the resolution in a lengthy speech, during which the Rev. gentleman forcibly reminded those present of their indebtedness to God for mercies bestowed, and urging that the claims of such a society as this were sufficient to call forth their sympathies in an especial degree. At the conclusion of the address, which was listened to with great interest, the second resolution was likewise agreed to.

Mr. Marvin then directed attention more particularly to the plans and the nature of the proposed alterations at the Home. One great object in the alteration was to obtain a larger room in which the inmates could dine and have their meals. Upon some occasions there were 90 persons at one time on the premises, and the room being but 18ft. by 14ft. he thought all present would agree with him that it was entirely inadequate for the requirements of such a large body. They therefore proposed to build a large room, and to do that it was, of course, necessary that they should have funds; They had up to the present time received 120l., but the total cost of the alterations would be about 300l., and until they had received that amount it would be impossible for them to proceed with the work. There were two ways in which the money could be raised, and these he would commend to the serious consideration of the meeting. The first was for ladies and gentlemen to volunteer subscriptions, and the second was to present articles to the institution for sale in the shop in Park Lane.

The Rev. J.S. Blake proposed a vote of thanks to Sir Thomas Pasley for his kindness in presiding, and acknowledged the cordial assistance which had at all times been rendered in furtherance of the objects of the charity both by Sir Thomas and Lady Pasley during their residence in Portsmouth.

The resolution was agreed to, and briefly acknowledged in a few appropriate remarks.

Mr. Marvin said that he had been requested to urge the meeting and the public to assist in rendering the sale of articles more rapid than it had hitherto been. They now had in stock about 278l. worth of manufactured articles, and it would be of great assistance to the funds of the institution if they could be disposed of.

The sale of fancy articles was continued the same evening, and the proceeds of the day were very satisfactory.

1868 – THE FENIAN CONSPIRACY.

The swearing-in of special constables in Portsmouth continued during the week, two or more of the borough Magistrates having sat from eleven in the morning until eight in the evening daily at the Guildhall for that purpose. On Tuesday evening the members of the 2nd Hants Artillery Volunteers, under the command of Col. Galt, attended at the Guildhall, where they were, like the 5th Hants on Monday, most enthusiastically cheered by the crowd who accompanied them. The number of all ranks then added to the list of local volunteers was about 200, and during the ceremony of swearing-in the scene in and around the hall was of an animated character, most of those present uncovering their heads as a token of loyalty while the band played the National Anthem.

Up to last evening considerably over 2,000 special constables had been sworn in, and of these 600 or 700 belong to the Dockyard, and the remainder consists of other inhabitants of the borough. Since Wednesday the process of swearing-in at the Dockyard has been temporarily stopped, but the precautionary movements in other respects have been proceeded with. The authorities are endeavouring to render it impossible to carry into effect any hostile movement against the shipping, the guards and sentries being doubled, with armed boats' crews doing duty throughout the whole night.

Since Wednesday the most alarming rumours have been circulated in the neighbourhood concerning alleged Fenian movements in the locality, but so far as we can learn, none of them were founded on anything like reasonable probabilities, and the bulk of them were evidently the result of some mischief-making miscreants. Indeed, in so far as Portsmouth is concerned, these stories have been of the most flagrant and inconsistent character, and in many instances, it has been difficult to believe that they could have been received with anything like credence even on the part of the least informed portion of the inhabitants.

On Tuesday, for instance, we were informed that it was the intention of the Fenians to poison the Portsmouth water supply at its source at Farlington; and since then we heard that the gunnery ship *Excellent* was doomed, that every chapel and place of religious worship in the borough will be razed, that a violent attempt had been made to administer the Fenian oath to some workmen at the gasworks, that two men were seen ascertaining the water level near Southsea Castle, and that an attempt had also been made to effect an entrance into that stronghold. Powder, too, in casks has, according to rumour, been stopped at the station at Landport, and, more singular still, a Portsmouth tradesman has been in custody for concealing some combustibles in his cellars. These rumours are, so far as we can learn, without the slightest foundation, and another to the effect that several casks of gunpowder were recently found near the gasworks at Flathouse turns out to be another canard.

That it is still expedient, however, to continue the vigilant watch at the works referred to, we believe there can be no doubt; and we have further been credibly informed that the questionable conduct of some few of the men induced the directors, at a recent meeting, to dispense with their services.

On Wednesday, information was received from the authorities at the General Post office directing the whole of the staff at Portsmouth to be sworn-in as special constables, and the order was complied with at the Guildhall the same day. A similar communication is daily expected from the directors of the joint railway companies; indeed, such a request has already been to some extent anticipated, by several of the officials offering their services as constables. The whole of the employees of the Portsea Island Gas Light Company have been sworn in as special constables and Mr. J.L. Thorne, the superintendent of the Royal Portsmouth Sailors' Home, has also followed the initiative, and with his staff, has likewise secured, in case of emergency, the advantages of the authority conferred upon the "specials."

It is now several years since there was a military guard in the Dockyard at Portsmouth, but the present emergency has impressed the authorities with the desirability of having an increased defensive strength at this establishment, and on and after this evening Mr. Superintendent Guy will be supported by a guard of about twelve men, which will be continued every night. There are at present, exclusive of officers, about 200 of the metropolitan police in the Dockyard, and, in addition to the cutlas with which each was recently armed, it is daily expected that revolvers will be served out to them.

Mr. Superintendent Barber denies, so far as his knowledge extends, the authenticity of the rumour that meeting places of the conspirators are known to exist in Portsmouth; and it is to the credit of this officer and the men under his charge to state that they are, individually and collectively, to the extent of their ability, taking every possible precaution to avoid the consequences of such an organization, supposing it to exist. We have reason to believe that most of the local institutions of the borough are well guarded, and that, at present, there is no occasion for the extraordinary excitement which generally prevails.

A special meeting of the borough Magistrates is appointed to be held in the council chamber adjoining the police court at noon today (Saturday), for the purpose of determining upon the organisation of those constables already sworn, and of the arrangements it will be desirable to carry out next week in administering the oath to others. The present arrangement has been found very tedious, and has occasioned considerable inconvenience to the Magistrates; and, to avoid this, it will probably be arranged to meet four hours daily, say, from twelve till two, and from six to eight during the ensuing week. We are, too, almost in a position to anticipate the arrangements which will be determined upon with regard to the constables already sworn in. Districts will be formed, and the residents in each will be convened together on some convenient evening for organisation.

At Landport, the special constables will probably meet in the Landport Hall; at Portsea, in the Beneficial Society's Hall; at Southsea, in the Yorke Rooms and the St. Jude's schoolroom; and Portsmouth, in the Guildhall. The first meeting will be devoted almost exclusively, probably, to the election of the necessary officers, and upon that occasion the staves will be served out.

The Magistrates will meet at the Guildhall from three to five this (Saturday) afternoon (instead of throughout the whole day, as hitherto); and on Tuesday next the process of swearing-in will be renewed at the Dockyard.

As an illustration of the ease with which a trifle in itself may now be construed into a movement of some significances we might instance the following. On Wednesday last some soldiers were seen to leave the Guardhouse on the Grand Parade and enter the bank of Messrs. Grant Gillman, and Long and the immediate (and perhaps not unreasonable) assumption was that it indicated a precautionary movement against possible attack upon the establishment. Instead, however, of the circumstance being attributable to anything of the kind, we are informed that it was occasioned by the soldiers' removing certain articles from one place to another to suit the personal convenience of the parties immediately interested.

On Thursday some sailors were ordered from the gunship *Excellent* to proceed forthwith to the *Thunderer*, an old floating battery moored near the entrance to Portchester lake, for the purpose of affording additional protection to the neighbouring powder magazine.

It is known that several London detectives are now doing special duty in the Isle of Wight, and that a stranger is at present subjected to a surveillance, which would scarcely be tolerated in more settled times.

At a meeting for prayer held at the Circus Church, on Tuesday evening, the Rev. B.D. Aldwell, incumbent of St. Luke's, referred, in the course of an address, to Fenianism and its recent alarming spread, suggested that it might have been permitted by God as a chastisement for our national sins, to some of which he specially alluded (such as drunkenness, Sabbath-breaking, licentiousness, and the countenance given to Popery), and dwelt on the importance of prayer on the country's behalf.

At Gosport the swearing-in of special constables has been continued throughout the week, and, Captain Forrest, the chief constable of the county of Hants, will be in attendance upon the Magistrates on Monday, to assist them in determining on the details of the duties of the force, the beats, &c.

On Wednesday evening an exaggerated report was circulated that a "centre" had been taken at the "Roebuck" in High Street, where he had been endeavouring to enlist Fenians, and offered to provide them with revolvers. It turned out to be untrue; the only ground for such a report being that a member of the Hebrew persuasion had exposed a couple of pistols; but such is the excited state of feeling against anything approaching the slightest appearance of Fenianism, that information was given to the police and the dealer had a narrow escape of being imprisoned on suspicion. We pass without notice the "thousand and one" reports which have been in circulation, some of them accredited to the young sparks of the town who delight to play upon the fears of the credulous.

They possibly remember the fable of the boy and the wolf, if so, it would be as well for them to avoid following the example set by that silly flock tender; and let us hope, should the necessity arise, that they will display more courage than he did at the time of his trouble.

The following letter from the members of the "Loyal Lord Nelson Lodge" of the Independent Order of Odd Fellows Manchester Unity, was presented by a deputation to the Magistrates on Thursday last.

To the Worshipful the Magistrates acting in and for the town of Gosport and Alverstoke.

"Gentleman, We, the undersigned, being a deputation from the officers and members of the Loyal Lord Nelsen Lodge of the Independent Order of Odd Fellows, Manchester Unity, do hereby convey to you our sincere and respectful thanks for the manner in which you received a declaration of loyalty from the above lodge, presented to you on the 26th of December last, and for your courteous answer to the said declaration, which answer we read to the officers and members present on our last lodge night. And we now beg that your worships will consent to meet the assembled lodge, at our lodge room, on Tuesday evening next, the 7th inst., for the purpose of swearing us in as special constables."

We have the honour to be your worships' obedient servants,

Caleb West, H. Coasdy, Jacob Bunker, William Betts, George Chubb.

The Magistrates expressed their anxiety to comply with the request contained in the above letter, but having an appointment on Tuesday evening which would prevent their attendance upon them, they would attend at the police court on Monday evening, at half-past seven, for the swearing of the members, and the officers have since issued circulars to all the members of the Lodge, summoning a meeting at the Lodge room at half-past six on that evening, for the purpose of marching to the police station to be appointed special constables.

The most excitable news stirring in the neighbourhood of Yarmouth is "Fenians and rumours of Fenians." All the officers of the Royal Artillery stationed in the neighbourhood that were "on leave" have been ordered to join instantly. The powder that was stored in Yarmouth Castle has been moved to safer quarters, one or two parties having been about asking more questions than was thought necessary to an uninterested person.

1869 – TEMPERANCE DEMONSTRATION AT NORTH END.

On Wednesday afternoon one of the largest gatherings of children ever held in the borough assembled in the People's Park, at Landport, for the purpose of proceeding to North End to take part in a temperance fete. Before half-past one children belonging to the Bands of Hope in connection with the Wesleyan Chapel, Arundel Street, Landport; Victoria Street, Mile End; Lake Road; Alfred Terrace; Zion Chapel; St. Peter's (Wesleyan); Highbury, St. Mary Street; Kent Street; Green Row (Wesleyan); Grosvenor Street; Albert Road; Little Southsea Street (Wesleyan); and Somers Road, assembled in the park and formed themselves into a procession, which, headed by the brass band of the 3rd Hants Artillery Volunteers, and the drum and fife band belonging to the Kent Street Band of Hope, left the park by the entrance in Spring Gardens, and marched up the Commercial Road to a field opposite the Clarence Gardens, which had been kindly lent by Mr. G.E. Kent.

The procession consisted of no less than 2,600 children, all total abstainers, and the appearance they presented with their medals, sashes, and banners was very striking, and excited the admiration of the immense number of people who left their homes with the sole object of seeing them pass along the road. Arriving in the field they participated in a variety of games and sports of a rustic character, after which they were entertained with tea and cake, each society carrying out its own arrangement. After the children's wants had been attended to, the adults, of which a large number of both sexes were present, took tea in true gipsy style, the children, meanwhile, returning to their amusements.

In the course of the afternoon and evening several selections were performed by the band, and a public meeting was held, over which Mr. W.B. Robinson, of H.M. Dockyard, presided. He expressed very great pleasure at being present, and called upon all parents to encourage young children to join the Band of Hope, in order that they might be educated and informed of all the many evils to which intoxicating drink led those who used it. If children never learnt the habit of drinking, they would never want it, and it was therefore most important that they should be encouraged in every possible way in adhering to the pledge they had taken. He had done without the use of strong drink for 24 years, and he was better than he should have been had he taken it. The object of the society was to band the children together in order that they might be taught to live rightly, and to know that intemperance was morally, religiously, and physically wrong. He went on to show what good results would accrue to the nation if the people were a sober people, and in conclusion urged those present to united action, in order that the number of juvenile abstainers might be materially increased.

Mr. Wilkins, secretary, read a letter from the Rev. J.G. Gregson, regretting his inability to be present, and said that the Rev. W. Rose was also unable to be present. He was sorry he was not in a position to give the exact number of the children present, but expressed a hope that at their next meeting the numbers would be much larger. Mr. Beck followed, and in a brief speech referred to the baneful effects of drunkenness, and to the benefits total abstinence would confer on the community. He strongly advised parents to keep intoxicating beverages from the unpolluted lips of their young, and when they grew up, they would be good citizens, and would be the means of reducing the number of paupers in the country.

About 30 years ago the movement was in its infancy, but now they could count upon three or four million teetotallers, and he hoped that number would go on swelling more and more. There was a great work to be done, and let them put their shoulders to the wheel in order that it might be done successfully. Mr. Patterson, of the Central Association at Manchester, in addressing the meeting, said he saw many fathers and mothers present, and to them he wished to say one or two words. It was their duty, before God and man, to encourage their children in doing that which was right and holy, so that when they grew up, they should continue in the path they trod as children. He went on to show that moderate drinkers were the cause of drawing a great many men into habits of drunkenness, and said it was their duty to save those who could not drink moderately by abstaining themselves. He concluded by urging the children to hold fast to the principles they had adopted.

Miss Robinson, of Guildford, was next called upon. She said she was very glad to see such a large gathering, and it was the largest she had ever seen assembled for recreation. She could not help saying that she believed the children were firmer than grown up people, and as a proof of this she instanced Guildford, where, she said, some of the children of the Band of Hope adhered so strictly to their promises that they would not take strong drink even when it had been ordered by the doctor for illness. She spoke of the habit which was prevalent among adults, namely, the tempting of children to take intoxicating liquors, and urged the children present to be firm, and not to waver from their principles. The habit of self-control should be instilled into the children, and, if this were done, when they grew up, they would not be so liable to fall into the many snares by which they were surrounded. They should be taught to be provident, and it would be well if a savings bank could be started, so that they might save their money instead of spending it in trash. She referred to the pernicious habit of smoking, and recommended the youths not to commence it, or they would find it most difficult to leave it off.

At the conclusion of the meeting the children were again formed into procession, and marched back to the town by way of Buckland and Lake Road.

1869 – PORTSMOUTH CHIMES.

Now that a movement is on foot for the restoration of the Portsmouth chimes, a narrative of their origin and some few circumstances connected with the early history of St. Thomas's Church, contained in an old record of "Facts in the Life of the Worshipful the Mayor of Portsmouth, William Brandon, 1702-3," may not be without interest.

From these we learn that the original trust of the chimes, as well as certain bequests which were made at the same time for the benefit of the resident poor in the parish, were confided in the town council, upon whom all responsibility for repair, &c, devolved. The account is prefaced with the ' "hymn of the eight bells"-

"God rest thee, worthy gentleman,
Long may thy sweet chimes play,
And gentle winds thy requiem fan
Upon Saint Thomas his day."
And continues-

"Whither are hurrying these poor mid aged persons? Wot ye not? It is the high and holy festival of Saint Thomas; and as the chimes of the new tower, of the Church of Saint Thomas-a-Becket ring out the midday hour, the worshipful the Mayor, Aldermen, and Burgesses will, by their Chamberlain, distribute the Christmas alms of him whose bounty extended beyond his mortal life, and who by his wish required for his commemorative requiem the orisons of the poor and needy, and that the solemn bells should tell of his whereabouts. How arose the custom? Sit down on the bench, be patient, and I will tell it ye!

Where now is St. Thomas Street, was, in 1174, a small clear stream of fresh water, which welled out in a fair piece of meadow land, and crossing a field called Sudwede, belonging to John de Gizors, fell into the inner camber of the harbour. In later times, where the small sparkling spring burst out of the ground, rose a tall building on arches, and approached by a double flight of stone steps, built to raise the house above the level of the several springs which fed the one called Sudwede. In this noble house dwelt, at the close of the year 1702, as agent to the commissioners of the Royal Navy of Queen Anne, Wm. Brandon; who from a comparatively humble station had, by his own exertions, risen to the post he held under the Crown, and at length, in 1702, on the feast day of Saint Michael the Archangel, was, with great reverence and worship, elected and sworn into the office of Mayor of Portsmouth. Ah, those were times; when, at the reception, the Mayor in his scarlet robes, and Anne his wife, the Mayoress, daughter of Sir William and Lady Broadnox, of Godmersham, in Kent, received with all the stately etiquette of the age the congratulations of the company as they entered the room, their names being announced by the sergeants, bearing in their hands plain silver maces (still among the Corporation plate), she was a stately matron, the mother of three fine sons, Broadnox, Thomas, and Charles, and one fair daughter, Mary.

He, the Mayor, was a man of retiring habits – "austere and proud to those who knew him not; But unto such as loved him, sweet as honey!" He was a man, then, who, if he did acts of generosity, did them in his own way! Exactly so; of which I will give you some examples. Let me hear them.

When William Brandon saw that Admiral Sir George Rooke had brought from an ancient pharos, or watch tower, of Dover Castle, some noble bells, l had them re-cast at the expense of Prince George of Denmark, with most quaint devises and inscriptions, and presented them to the new tower, he determined not to be outdone in generosity; and well knowing that bells, unless they be sounded, are of no use, and that bell-ringers, tho' a very noisy, are often a very idle sort of personages, who won't ring unless they are paid, or have a leg of mutton and turnips provided for supper by mine host of the "Eight Bells," close to the Church gate, on the Collegiate land, in the High Street, with flagons of Sir Thomas Ridge's stout ales - he, at his own proper cost, by erudite and curious machinery, attached to a large clock to set St. Thomas' bells chiming every four hours, in spite of John Barkham, of Smock Alley, John Carpenter, nigh the Key gate, Benjamin Martel, of Hogmarket Street, Thomas Whiteborne, of Poynt, Edward Cleverly, of Poynt, and others, the ringers who had risen in open rebellion.

On the 21st of December, 1703, at twelve o'clock at noon, the ears of the listening townspeople were astonished and their pious feeling excited by the euphonious bells resounding in long meter the "old hundredth psalm." I can't remember this tune; but of late years we have heard "God save the King," and "The Sicilian Mariners' hymn," full many a time. In acknowledgment of the honour the town had conferred on him by electing him Chief Magistrate, as an accompaniment to their pious and patriotic strains, William Brandon gave to the Corporation, and their successors for ever, two hundred pounds, to be by them, or the major part of them, put out to interest;

and the interest therefrom arising to be by them, on every feast day of St. Thomas the Apostle, distributed among the poor and indigent persons living, and that may live, within the town and parish of Portsmouth, and that shall not be maintained at the parish charge.

For eleven years after William Brandon's death, the executors, Mr. C. Bissell and Mr. Henry Player, of Gosport, resisted the donor's charitable intentions, retaining in their own hands both the money and interest; but the money was ultimately handed over to the Corporation, and in 1722, says this authentic document in my hand, which clearly points out how this Charity should be distributed by the Corporation, as the almoners and trustees, the monies to be distributed was brought to the Guildhall in silver coins in a fair large silver dish, by Mr. Chamberlain.

The Town Clerk then read that portion of Mr. Brandon's deed, as gave the Charity into the hands of the Corporation as trustees; and after some observations by Lewis Barton, Mayor, he, with several of the Aldermen and Burgesses, in their robes of estate, in the presence of the Rev. the Vicar of Portsmouth, W. Ward, A.M., David Parker and Thomas Baker, overseers of ye poor of ye parish of Portsmouth, and Mr. Thomas Hammond, ship builder of East Street, Thomas Barton, and others the trustees of the Charity, monies paid yearly to the poor of Portsmouth on St. Thomas's day, by the hands of their Chamberlain distributed the said monies in their Town Hall.

Have no other persons given money? Oh yes! Thomas Winter, Esq., gave 200l.; John Mounsher gave 100l.; and Mr. Thomas Mills, who, with Nicholas Hedger, had retained in their possession 60l., left by Mr. J. Timbrell, gave to the Corporation the lease of a house, in Portsmouth, with power to sell, which was luckily done for 100l. - the money remaining in the hands of the Corporation, who have by a bond bearing their seal undertaken to distribute the interest yearly, with, and on the same terms as the other, on St. Thomas's day, to the poor of Portsmouth.

Nor have the poor of such portions of Portsmouth as are without the walls any claims to these monies, because at the period of the donation, by William Brandon, the waters of the Milldam, the entire extent of which was in Portsmouth, extended a long way inland, terminating at last in a broad, muddy, and marshy lake, overflowed at every tide. No trace of house was then visible, except a solitary shed belonging to Pest house Fields, and no inhabitants. Taking, therefore, the expressions of William Brandon's deed, with the state of the parish at the period of his death, these Charities must be confined to the indigent living within the walls of the town of Portsmouth.

William Brandon died in 1705; and in 1794 a mural monument, with his armorial crest, was erected to the memory of his grandfather by his grandson Philip Brandon, in the chancel of St. Thomas' Church. But as the great ball strikes! the clock of William Brandon proclaims the hour of noon! William Brandon's chimes ring out his requiem! and the Mayor, Aldermen, and Burgesses distribute William Brandon's charity.

The evil that men do lives after them;
The good is often interred with their bones.

To obviate the latter, I have from authentic sources ventured to put forth this short biography of a Portsmouth Gentleman; and as charity covereth a multitude of sins, let us trust that the hope expressed on William Brandon's monument has been realised in the words of the latter part of the 43 verse of the xxiii. chapter of St. Luke's Gospel.

The following are extracts (under date September 27th, 1701) from the records of the corporation with reference to the election of Mr. Brandon:-

Henry Maydman and William Brandon – Gents Elected Aldermen, October 24th, 1701.

This day William Brandon, Gent., who, on the 27th day of September last, was duly elected an Alderman, did duly take the oath of fidelity to His Majesty, signed the test and abjuration, and then was sworn into the office of Alderman.

Electio Major, September 21st, 1702.

Georgius Deacon, Gent. - Stant in nominee pr. offic majoris pr. Anne Sequen.

Willus Brandon' Gent. - Stant in nominee pr. offic majoris pr. Anne Sequen.

WIllus Brandon, electus est.

1869 – OPENING OF THE NEW MILITARY GYMNASIUM AT PORTSMOUTH.

One of the most beneficial of the recently introduced provisions for the recreation and amusement of the British soldier is the determination on the part of the War Office to erect and maintain a gymnasium in each of the large garrison towns. The movement was first brought into practical operation, at a comparatively recent date, at Aldershot, and for this purpose twelve men (one of whom has been sent to Portsmouth) were selected to take lessons with the view of ultimately becoming instructors, in accordance with the new

Queen's Regulations on the subject. These were supplemented by the addition of a like number in consequence of the unexpected proficiency to which the first had attained, and, as the result of their tuition, the country has now enrolled for service as instructors a body of skilled gymnasts.

The object of gymnastic institutions in the army is one which commends itself alike on national, economical, and social grounds, although it is concisely represented in official records as an undertaking for the purpose of "developing and increasing the physical powers of the soldier;" because an increase in efficiency adds proportionately to his worth, and the provision of the means for innocent and wholesome occupation will tend greatly to counteract the many pernicious influences by which he is surrounded. Although the instruction hereafter to be encouraged throughout the army will be obligatory, the exercises are so arranged that, while the most advanced are sufficient to test the powers of the strongest, the preliminary ones can be performed without damage to the weakest.

Previous to commencing any course, a strict medical examination must be made of each man, and measurements (to be repeated at the end of the course, or when the man returns to his duty) are to be taken of his chest, forearm, and upper arm, with his weight, in order to ascertain the extent of the increased development which has taken place during the course.

Several of the gymnasiums comprised in the scheme as originally proposed have been completed, and are now in satisfactory working order, whilst the delay in the completion of others - as at Portsmouth, for instance - has been wholly owing to the increase in size and the more elaborate character of the fittings which the importance of the various garrisons has rendered necessary. The site selected for the Portsmouth Gymnasium, which was inaugurated on Thursday, is familiar to our resident readers, and occupies a position which renders it of easy access from the various barracks in the garrison. The building is lofty, capacious, and well-proportioned, and has been erected with due regard to ventilation - in other words, it is constructed in compliance with the Queen's Regulation, that no smell of any kind shall be detected by a person entering it from the fresh air. In shape it is a parallelogram, with an abutting porch way or entrance, and a large square tower-like projection in the centre of the roof, which affords light and admits the high rope and other performances at an extreme elevation without the risk which would otherwise be incurred by the accumulation of dense air.

The room, which is of yellow brick, was built by the firm of Messrs. Simms and Marten, and has been elaborately fitted by Mr. Maclaren, of the University Gymnasium, Oxford. Captain French has been appointed superintendent; and Sergeant-Major Steel (of the Gymnastic Staff) senior instructor; while Sergeant McKenzie (2nd Battalion 8th Regiment), Sergeant Wharton (2nd Battalion 23rd), Sergeant Crane (35th), Sergeant Gulliver (1st Battalion 12th), Sergeant Bryant, (100th), and Sergeant Adams (2nd Battalion 2nd Regt.), have, in addition, been selected as permanent instructors.

This staff commenced the first series of gymnastic tuition shortly before ten o'clock on Thursday morning, and during the day 90 men from the 83rd, 35th, and 67th Regiments went through various preliminary movements, the whole of which were graduated so as to admit of easy progress.

A brief description of the various appliances – with which the room is furnished will not be without interest. The first consists of a padded horse, over which the operator vaults in various ways, with the assistance of a board, and when this can be attained with some degree of ease, he is conducted to a second horse, which differs in size and height, and to which no springboard is attached. An interesting experiment is next provided on a bridge ladder, which extends to a point across the centre of the room, and on which the men are taught to move in a suspended position, from one spot to another without the use of their feet. Confidence in leaving one grip and catching another is given by a few rehearsals on a row of rings (a la' Leotard) which extend along the right-hand side of the building, from which the student is taken to the elastic ladders, and submitted to a more difficult lesson with the view of adding to the confidence already attained. The men are in this way perfected sufficiently to admit of exercise on the vertical rope, which consists of climbing, and which is considered so difficult that none are allowed to go beyond the escalading plank or projecting platform from the beam without wearing the guard-belt as a preventative against accident. For the purpose of resting the arms the men are taken to the moveable beam consisting of a mast about 30 feet in length, and placed in a horizontal position across the room, the object being to give them confidence in walking along the escalading appliances which extend along the roof and to which they are introduced as they become more advanced. Other movements follow, and at the close the men are taught to ascend with rapidity the wall at the extreme rear by climbing a pole resembling an ordinary house-spout, then over small blocks resembling projecting bricks, up vertical ropes, swinging poles, &c., until the beams at the roof are reached, with which this feature in the exercise closes.

When the men have attained an average degree of efficiency, the last exercise is gone through. Each in his way is supposed to be attacking a position for the purpose of reaching the summit, and, having been placed in line, at the command of the instructor they do "the double," vaulting a bar which extends across the room about ten or twelve feet from the wall, each vying with the other to gain the credit of precedence. The whole of the arrangements for broadsword, foil, bayonet, and single-stick exercises are upon the most improved principle. The practice bayonet, by Lathan (of the firm of Wilkinson and Sons, sword makers, of Pall Mall, London), is provided, as being the most complete of the kind in use. The bayonet is capped at the point, and attached to the barrel of the rifle by means of a spring tube, which admits immediate resistance on coming in contact with an object, and as readily extends when withdrawn, thus securing the twofold advantage of avoiding accident or delay. Masks, body aprons, leg pads, fencing jackets, helmets, gloves, &c., are also provided; and there is likewise a large collection of dumb bells, weighing from 16 lbs. to 50 lbs., and bar bells from 20 lbs. in weight.

When we visited the building several very clever tricks were gone through by some of the instructors. These included an upstarting vault, an upstart front circle vault over bar, the double lock swing, the straight arm balance on bar, in addition to a flying double spring over a horse, the object of the latter being, as our guide informed us, to demonstrate the theory which teaches that even a child can stop a lion in the air. The peculiarity of the exercise was the ease with which the performer was checked when in a flying position, and thus enabled to reach the surface safely within a few feet of the object over which he vaulted.

The room, we should add, is provided with a gallery for the accommodation of visitors, and the requisite offices and ante-rooms have not been lost sight of. Throughout Thursday and Friday exercises were gone through by squads from the different regiments in the garrison, and under the personal direction of the instructors, in a manner which indicates future success. The men were supplied with properly made boots for the purpose, and with belts to avoid accidents which generally follow want of experience and care, and which will be retained by them until the completion of the whole course. It is the intention of the governing authorities, we believe, shortly to provide an entertainment, consisting of various gymnastic performances, fencing, broadsword and bayonet exercise, &c.; and from the opinion we can form of the appliances and the resources at their command, and the skill with which the instructors went through the few exercises named above, we look forward to a treat thoroughly enjoyable and one which cannot fail to be appreciated by all who may be fortunate enough to witness it.

1869 – OPENING OF THE NEW THEATRE AT EASTNEY BARRACKS.

The erection of theatres and the performance of stage plays in barracks is a comparatively recent innovation, but it is one which even now may be regarded as a complete success. It had long been felt that something was necessary, for the sake of both the mental and physical health of the men, to destroy the dull monotony of barrack life. Idleness is not only a curse in itself but leads to many other curses, of which the results are readily appreciable. Dr. Watts has told us that "Satan still some mischief finds for idle hands to do;" but it was a long time before it was fully understood that the mind of man is an essence of so essentially mercurial and active a character, that with its stupor means death.

Unless, therefore, some useful and healthful employment is found for it, it will have recourse to occupation which is neither the one nor the other, occupation, in fact, that perverts all that is noble, and crushes all that is sanguine, in man. We need scarcely animadvert upon the desirability of adding to the other reforms which have been introduced with a view of making the necessary discipline of barracks tolerable, that of wholesome mental recreation. The soldier has regular meals at regular hours, is well clothed, doctored, and exercised; but he is very much thrown upon his own resources for amusement. It is, therefore, with much pleasure that we record the opening of a new theatre at Eastney Barracks, within the walls of which the men of the Royal Marine Artillery may enjoy the luxury of a hearty laugh, and the pleasure of listening to those great moral lessons which it is the privilege of the stage to teach, and which can be in few places else so effectually inculcated.

In the above remarks we have advocated the opening of such places of amusement on the plea of utility: because they supply the men with occupation, tend to keep them from spending their time and money in a less commendable manner, and serve to reduce the length of the black list. But something might also be said on the score of equity. For if the government locate large bodies of men on the verge, we might almost say, of civilisation, and insist upon their keeping such timely hours as excludes them from the social recreations and delights of civil life, then it seems to us only fair that some compensation should be made them by promoting and encouraging unexceptionable entertainments among themselves.

Holding these opinions, we have to congratulate the officers and men of the Royal Marine Artillery on the opening of their new theatre, and on the great success which attended the inaugural performances on Wednesday and Thursday evenings last. The theatre - for which a license was readily granted - is a large and commodious building, and when completely finished and decorated it will be as handsome in its proportions and accessories as it is convenient in its approaches and arrangements. The body of the house measure 58 feet in depth and 38 feet in width, has a circular gallery at the back, and is capable of comfortably seating 650 people. The stage is 22 feet wide by 22 feet deep.

The Yankees sometimes boast that they are dependent on no country in the world; that all the necessaries and luxuries of life are to be obtained within the boundaries of their great republic. Some such boast as this may with equal veracity be made by the corps of the Marine Artillery. They comprise within themselves all the industrial elements requisite for the accomplishment of any reasonable undertaking. Not only are they capable of very creditably acting a play without extraneous aid from without, but their theatre - from top to bottom from the proscenium and stage fittings (which have been beautifully and artistically executed by Captain Bridgford) to the back seat in the gallery - has been entirely and exclusively constructed by themselves, under the management of Captain de Kantzow, to whose exertions, we understand, the success of the undertaking is mainly due. Even the placards containing the cast of the pieces bear the imprint of the corps' own press! Corporal Goss (who is also the machinist) has acted as foreman of the works; and the offices of prompter, leader of the orchestra, and property man are respectively sustained by Corporal Sullivan, Mr. Nash, and Mr. Smith.

The opening performances passed off on Wednesday with gratifying success, and were witnessed by a crowded and enthusiastic audience. After a selection of music by the admirable string band of the corps, under the direction of Mr. Smith, Corporal Sullivan stepped upon the stage and pronounced the inaugural address, which had been written for the occasion by Major Bradley Roberts.

The address was greatly applauded, and at its conclusion the curtain rose upon the initial scene of the romantic two-act drama of the "Charcoal Burner." The whole of the parts was very creditably sustained, especially those of Messrs. Hickman and Wilton, Mrs. Sullivan, and Miss Hobbs. During the interval a variety of songs were sung by Bombardier Brown and Miss Hobbs with great spirit. By the time the applause had died away the players in the second piece had been rung into their places by the prompter, and the laughable farce of "To Paris and Back far 5l." brought a pleasant evening's amusement to a close, in time for the men to attend tattoo. The performances were repeated on Thursday evening with the same gratifying result, and now that the undertaking has been fairly commenced, we may felicitate all concerned in the many pleasant evenings in store for them.

1869 – THE FUNERAL OF MR. PEABODY.

The embarkation of the coffin containing the body of the celebrated late philanthropist, Mr. Peabody, on board H.M.S. *Monarch*, specially designed for that purpose, took place on Saturday, the 11th inst. We subjoin a short summary of the ceremony.

The *Monarch* is by some considered to be our finest man-of-war of modern construction and is an armour-plated turret ship carrying seven of those immense pieces of marine artillery which have lately come into use. She will make her return voyage under canvas, so as to test her sailing qualities, and also the action of her altered balanced rudder. The coffin was conveyed by a special train direct to the railway jetty at Portsmouth, where the *Monarch* was moored in readiness to receive it. A temporary gangway had been formed from the jetty to the ship's upper deck, at the shore end of which were the Mayor and Corporation of Portsmouth. The road from the train to the ships was lined on one side with the marines and seamen of the United States corvette, *Plymouth*, which had been despatched by the President of the United States, on the receipt of the news of Mr. Peabody's decease; on the other with marines and seaman from her Majesty's ships in harbour.

Notwithstanding a steady downfall of rain, a considerable number of officers, both naval and military, in undress uniform, had assembled, as well as a large attendance of the general public.

The special train (provided free of expense, as a testimony of respect to the deceased, by the London and South Western Railway Company) arrived punctually at three o'clock. Immediately on its arrival a gun was fired from H.M.S. *Excellent* another from the *Monarch*'s bow battery, and then the *Duke of Wellington* as flagship of the Port Admiral, fired twenty minute guns, while the *Monarch* and all H.M.'s ships in harbour dipped the British ensign at their peaks to half mast, and displayed the American ensign flying, dipped to abreast of their foretopmast crosstrees. The coffin was borne by twelve men from the car to the ship and was received at the head of the gangway by Captain J.E. Commerell, who commands the *Monarch* and the ship's chaplain. Mr. Motley, the American Minister, Mr. Peabody Russell, Mr. Reed,

M.P., Sir Curtis Lampson, Mr. Morgan, Mr. Sowerby, and Captain Acomb, of the *Plymouth* accompanied the procession on board, together with a number of American and English officers.

The *Monarch* then proceeded to Spithead, the *Plymouth* and other ships dipping their ensigns as she passed, there to be swung and to take her powder on board. These necessary arrangements were completed by Monday the 13th instant, but the *Monarch* did not set sail for Portland until Tuesday last, having been detained by a heavy gale. The *Plymouth* joined her on the following day and accompanies her as consort on her voyage. This vessel was originally intended by the American Government to convey Mr. Peabody's remains to Portland, but General Grant, hearing that the Queen had given a like order to the *Monarch*, most courteously yielded. The *Plymouth* is a handsome wooden corvette, much more comely to look at than her gigantic companion, her hull being most elegantly modelled. She is reported to be a singularly fast sailer and has good steaming capacity. Both the vessels presented a most singular aspect; the masts, yards, boats, and other exposed parts having been painted a funereal grey.

On the arrival of the *Monarch* at Portland, the mortuary chapel (which during the voyage is to be closed and put under the charge of marine sentries) will be thrown open to visitors from the shore, and the body will lie in state for several days. The two vessels will proceed direct to Portland, touching only at Madeira to take in coals. Mr. Peabody Russell, a nephew of the deceased, is on board the *Monarch* where cabin accommodation has been provided for him.

Such is a brief account of the honours done to all that remained on earth of George Peabody, who, although belonging to a nation that often affects an antagonistic feeling towards England, loved the land of his forefathers so well that, not content with bestowing a large fortune on its poor, he came over in his old age to die in the "Old Country." Regretted alike by rich and poor, English and American, his name will be handed down to future generations as one of the poor's greatest benefactors. He was a self-made man, having acquired himself those riches which he so bountifully and nobly used but, unlike most *parvenus*, he was untainted with the pride so often generated by pecuniary success.

Embarkation of the Coffin

The Monarch Proceeding to Spithead

The Mortuary Chapel on Board the Monarch

1869 – SANGER'S CIRCUS.

The Messrs. Sanger, who are well known in this place as successful caterers for the amusement of the circus going public, paid us a visit on Saturday with their mammoth establishment. The announcement that a gorgeous procession would parade the principal thoroughfares every day during their stay induced an immense concourse of persons to assemble in the circus, which was located in Lake Road, Landport. The show was most brilliant, and the public not only proved their appreciation of the efforts put forth by the proprietors by loudly applauding the procession as it passed, but by crowding the enormous pavilion at each performance. The troupe of artistes is up to the highest standard in the profession, and the members were hailed with loud expressions of approval. Last (Tuesday) evening terminated their sojourn in Portsmouth.

On Sunday afternoon, an amusing incident occurred at the circus lately occupied by Messrs. Powell, Foottitt, and Clarke, in which a temperance advocate has been in the habit or preaching. It appears that Messrs. Sanger's elephant was located in the stables adjoining the building, and while the preacher was in the middle of his service the elephant broke loose, and entered the ring, much to the delight of the juvenile members of the congregation. After some time had elapsed, the keeper of the huge animal was sent for, and he (the elephant) was removed in custody.

1869 – FUNERAL OF ADMIRAL WARDEN.

The late Rear-Admiral Frederick Warden, C.B., who at his death held the office of Senior Naval Officer at Queenstown and on the coast of Ireland, was buried at Southsea Cemetery, Portsmouth, on Saturday, with all the public honours due to the rank of the deceased officer. The pallbearers were Vice-Admiral Sir S. Dacres, K.C.B., Senior Admiralty Sea Lord; Rear-Admiral A.C. Key, C.B., F.R.S., Superintendent of Portsmouth Dockyard; Captain George Hancock, her Majesty's ship *Duke of Wellington*, Flag- Captain to and representing Port-Admiral Sir James Hope, K.C.B.; Captain Willes, C.B., R.N., of Coastguard and Reserve Department, at Whitehall; Colonel Commandant G.A. Schomberg, R.M.A., C.B.; Admiral Sir Charles Talbot, K.C.B.; and Vice-Admiral Sir Baldwin Wake Walker, K.C.B.

Next to the coffin followed the immediate relatives and friends of the deceased, the latter including Rear-Admiral G.A. Halstead, Commander Hon. E.

Funeral Procession of Admiral Warden

Stanley-Dawson, Flag-Lieutenant to the deceased during the period of his command, and a large number of other officers, including the captains of all her Majesty's ships in commission in the port. The body was received at the gates of the cemetery by the Vicar of Portsmouth, the Rev. E.P. Grant, and conveyed to the church, where he read the first portion of the burial service. The service concluded, the procession proceeded to the grave, where the coffin was deposited, and the remainder of the service read by the Vicar. At the end of the prayers the naval battery fired eleven guns, in minute time, the number due to an officer of Rear-Admiral's rank dying during a period of command.

1869 – THE EASTNEY FLOWER SHOW.

The *United Service Gazette*, in a long article on "Soldiers' gardens," remarks:

"We do not recollect any paragraph that has appeared for a long time in the *United Service Gazette* the publication of which has given us more pleasure than the account of the Eastney Barracks' Flower Show. We have now a proof furnished at home at our own doors that soldiers like gardens, and know how to manage them, and that officers approve of them so much as to give their warm cooperation in bringing them to a successful issue. When it was first proposed to give little gardens to the soldiers, the wiseacres were divided as to their reasons for hostility to the alarming innovation. Some, the old "Rump" of military antiquity, were horrified at the bare idea of providing for the soldiers any amusement at all; others, a step in advance thought the notion pleasing, but chimerical; and a third took the more practical ground of objection, that the frequent moves of our regiments would destroy the interest which the men might otherwise take in their gardens. All the objectors have, however, now been put out of court, the provision of innocent means of amusing the soldier when off duty is an admitted article of the Military Code, the chimera has become a solidity, and the only objection worth anything that remains is the too frequent moves of regiments, an objection which may easily be removed, and which, no doubt, will soon be removed, to the great delight of both officers and men.

The horticulturists at Eastney Barracks appear to have availed themselves of their comparative permanence of station with complete success. The great tent in front of the officers' garden at Fort Cumberland afforded in its flower show excellent proof of what soldier-gardeners can and will do when they get only fair time and proper encouragement. We congratulate Sergeant Patterson on his first prize for "Onions, tomatoes, turnips, and devices in cut flowers." Here was a pleasant mingling of the useful with the sweet, indeed, it would be hard to tell which aroma would be the most fragrant, that of the onions and tomatoes in the pot-a-feu, or of the flowers in the flower pot.

Sergeant Francis's strength lay in carrots and peas, worthy coadjutors to the onions and tomatoes. Sergeant Lawrence had devoted himself to cabbage and lettuce, and so on to the end of the gratifying prize list, showing that here, amongst themselves and in their own small garden allotments, the sergeants and gunners of the Royal Marine Artillery were able to raise all the garden accessories of the best furnished dinner table. Why, they ought to have got prizes from the Army Medical Department as well as from their gallant Commandant, for no one knows better than Sir Galbraith Logan the inestimable advantage of a bountiful supply of good vegetables, looked at from the heights of military hygiene.

Another feature of the Eastney flower show, of which too much cannot be said in the way of commendation, was the honorary competition of the officers and their wives in the flower department, where the agency of a cultivated taste would be seen to tell in giving to the non-commissioned officers and men hints for future shows. Whilst we consider that the main object of the soldier-gardener should be to complement their rather monotonous daily bill of fare with the savour and wholesome contents of the kitchen garden, we would by no means wish to see them altogether neglect the ornamental in the pursuit of the useful. There can be nothing more civilizing, more humanising, more calculated to keep the mind pure and the love of the beautiful fresh and intense, than the cultivation of flowers, which contain within themselves the three great elements of beauty - form, colour, and fragrance. We do not allude here to the costly exotics of the conservatory, matters which we would respectfully suggest to our military florists to give themselves no trouble about. There are plenty of indigenous plants full of beauty and odour, and which should recommend themselves all the more to the soldier-gardener, because for years past they have been neglected by professional nurserymen.

For our own parts, we are sick of the modern British flower show, and would willingly make a much longer journey than to Portsmouth to see a show full of such flowers as those we have enumerated, and which have been so unfairly pushed aside for the staring, scentless, gaudy foreigners. If our soldiers want something *recherché* and out of the way, there are the native heaths in endless variety, and of which so much might be made by a little care in selection and skill in subsequent cultivation. Flower shows composed of such specimens as we have enumerated would draw immensely even in London, and their production is within the reach of every man who has a small plot of ground, or even a flower pot, or a window sill at his disposal.

We cannot take leave of the Eastney Barracks' Flower Show, without congratulating all concerned in its arrangements on the steady advance which they seem to be making from year to year. In 1868, there were 50 exhibitors, of whom 14 took prizes, whilst this year there are 68 exhibitors and 85 prize-holders a very important increase, especially in the prize-holders. We do not know whence the money comes that is distributed as prizes, but we think that a little more liberality in this department would tell advantageously in future shows. The number of allotments is 168, a number which we hope to see annually increase, for we feel quite convinced that the holders of garden allotments will give little trouble to the dispensers of military justice. The system of soldiers' gardens cannot be too widely adopted in the service, for in it is to be found the cure for that terrible *ennui* which, we believe, leads as much as anything else to the perpetration of three fourths of what are specially classified as soldiers' offences.

1869 – THE HILSEA LINES.

In commenting upon the defences of Portsmouth I have already had occasion to speak with disapprobation of the costly granite structures which frown across the Solent at Hurst Castle and Gilkicker Point, and which, in our judgment, should never have been erected. Secondly, we have been compelled to question the wisdom of expending vast sums of money upon the four water castles at Spithead, which are greatly weakened by the absence of the fort originally contemplated on the Sturbridge Sand, of which the sea has forbidden the construction. We have pointed out that these exposed masonry forts, fixed immovably upon shoals where the tide runs like the Niagara river before it shoots on the Horseshoe Fall, are liable to attack, and to the possibility of instant annihilation by chemical agents of which the force as well as man's intelligent comprehension of its application, are incessantly on the increase. Thirdly, we have felt ourselves constrained to condemn, without qualification or reserve, the mistaken policy which has led to the construction of five stupendous permanent forts upon Portsdown Hill. We have shown that all the money given to Mr. Thistlethwayte and Mr. Deverill for the surrender of their proprietary and clearance rights was, to our thinking, money thrown away; and that the better policy would have been to convert the whole of Portsdown Hill into one long earthwork whenever the hour of danger seemed near at hand.

We have not forgotten that Washington, which at the commencement of the American war was the most defenceless of cities, was within a few months protected by a cordon of earthen redoubts, which the Confederates flushed with their victories over M'Clellan and Pope never dared to attack; and that Charlestown, Fort Fisher, and Richmond, though defended only by hurried works of earth or sand, were not reduced, in spite of the enormous superiority of the attacking over the defending force, until four years had well-nigh flown, and until more than 500 million sterling had been expended upon their capture.

It is with no slight satisfaction that we find ourselves enabled today to exchange the language of censure for that of commendation. The Hilsea Lines are undoubtedly, to quote the words spoken by Colonel Jervois on the 3rd of last March, in his evidence before Sir Frederick Grey's committee, "the most formidable earthwork that was ever constructed." It is impossible for anyone who comes down from Portsdown Hill, after a melancholy inspection of its five "follies," to glance at the Hilsea Lines without mentally rejoicing!

Mistakes there have undoubtedly been in their original design, but those mistakes disappear and are forgotten in presence of the facts that the Lines are made of earth, and of the skill evinced in meeting the disadvantages which are inseparable from the "bastion trace" adopted in their construction.

It is in reference to such works as these that the truth of Sir John Burgoyne's evidence, given before the Royal Commissioners on the 12th of November 1859, becomes every day more apparent: "There is one great advantage in works of defence like the Hilsea Lines. Every £10,000 that you expend puts you in a better position than you were in before, even though you do not complete the whole. As soon as you complete any work, or, taking a line like Hilsea Line, as soon as you add two or three feet to the depth of the ditch and to the thickness of the parapets, your position is improved, even though the whole project is not completed." These words are undeniably true and wise; but, with all deference to Sir John Burgoyne's authority and experience, we may add the remark that such a defensive work is good, unless it is constructed with wrong materials and upon a faulty principle.

An earthwork in the position occupied by the Hilsea Lines is obviously what is wanted upon that spot; but can Sir John allege that every £10,000 laid out at Hurst castle is *pro tanto* a gain to the nation, in the teeth of the recorded opinion of the Defence Committee, that, "after the experiments in November, 1865, a fort of granite fitted with iron shields would be untenable after thirty shots?" It cannot be pretended that these massive stone forts, of which altogether there are some sixteen or seventeen in number, would now be erected if we had to commence again from new. No one of the least authority has ever seriously attempted to controvert the truth of the words spoken by Mr. O'Beirne in the House of Commons, when he said in August 1867, "There is nothing more clearly proved, and, I will add, more generally admitted, than that stone is perfectly worthless as a means of defence, and yet, with this knowledge in their minds, the authorities have determined to build stone basements for iron forts, and to place the forts, guns, and turrets upon that base which, once attacked, will crumble into dust, and suffer the whole structure to tumble into the ground."

In reference to such earthworks as the Hilsea Lines, nothing can be more sagacious than Sir John Burgoyne's remark; but in reference to structures like Hurst Castle, or the Drake's Island Fort at Plymouth, nothing, it seems to us can be more misleading. If, moreover, there is truth in the rumour which is universally current, that large orders for iron shields have already by given by the War Department to a Sheffield firm, it needs no prophet to foretell that a still more discreditable passage of history than that connected with the worthless Gibraltar shields awaits us in the future. It is impossible to repeat too often, that the engineers of the War Department do not know enough about iron shields to understand what manner of article they ought to order.

"We have to provide," says one of our ablest public writers on this subject, "an iron shield possessing such cohesion and resistance over a very restricted area, as shall enable that restricted space to receive and endure the concentration of the assaulting fire from the enemy's most powerful guns; and that so effectually, that no harm shall come to the gun or gunners. We must do this with the least possible amount of material, the least possible depth of structure, and the greatest economy of expense. A good shield, sufficient to resist such guns as our own artillery, could not be produced and fitted under £1,000; and there are not less than 300 shields imperatively called for at this moment for only a few of our most important works. It is evident, therefore, by reason of the problem to be solved, that the utmost skill, care, and efficiency of purposeful design is absolutely essential."

In the face of such passages as this, written, too, by men at whom it is impossible for the War Department to sneer, how will Mr. Gladstone and Mr. Cardwell hereafter face their countrymen if, while promising rigid economy and the most careful supervision of the public money that passes through their hands, they allow the Gibraltar shield episode to be repeated on a far larger scale.

Mr. Hughes, of Millwall, the constructor of the best and cheapest shield that has ever been fired at, has already transferred his mechanical ingenuity and vast experience from England to Russia. "The finest fort," said Major-General Taylor, the Inspector-General of the Artillery, in his evidence before the Grey Committee upon the 18th of May 1868, "that I have ever seen as regards material is one that I saw at Mr Hughes's Millwall manufactory. He had been making it for the Russian Government; it is intended for Krondstadt, and he showed me a model of one of its casements. That is, I think, a magnificent fort. It is all of iron, and every single bit of it is brought into its most useful bearing and position."

As it is no longer possible for the War Department to pretend that Mr. Hughes is importunate for a Government order, is it too much to hope that Mr. Cardwell will avail himself, before suffering a large order for shields to issue from his Department, of the skill and experience acquired by Mr. Hughes, which for years past he has patriotically endeavoured to place at the disposal of his native country? Nor can we forbear from adding that, before iron shields are ordered by the dozen, and in the dark, something should be done to test Mr. Crampton's proposal to make forts of iron, by casting them *in situ*, either in one solid block, weighing 5,000 tons or so, or in blocks of large size, weighing about 200 tons apiece. Mr. Ireland, of the Bolton iron and Steel works, has already shown us that anvil blocks weighing over 200 tons, can be cast without difficulty; nor does there appear to be any limit to the size of castings which can be produced on his system. If, as is generally hoped, the Moncrieff gun is destined to revolutionise our whole system of fortifications, would there not be more real economy in endeavouring to provide a solid block of cast iron, which might be made, according to Mr. Crampton, "six or seven times the thickness of a built up, wrought iron structure, and at the same total cost?"

Before committing ourselves to a large order for wrought iron shields, perforated in their centre by a port hole, which not only weakens the structure, but breaks up cast iron shot, striking on its edge, into a shower of fragments, would it not be wiser for Mr. Cardwell to give an order that the effect of shot and shell upon a 200-ton block of cast iron shall be tested at Shoeburyness? If its resistance and cohesion should prove to be what Mr. Crampton anticipates, shall we not have gone far towards solving the problem as to the nature and material of the iron forts, from the interior of which the Moncrieff gun is hereafter to spring up like a Jack in the box?

But to return to Hilsea Lines. Common sense, which, according to Vauban, is the best of engineers, has always indicted the Hilsea Channel as the right spot for the principal defence work needed to shield Portsmouth from attack on the land side. It is hardly necessary to remind our readers that the town and Dockyard of Portsmouth, and its subsidiary suburbs and villages, occupy nearly the whole surface of Portsea Island, which is some fifteen miles in circumference, and contains about 4,400 acres of excellent land. Portsea Island is washed by the deep indentations of water which run inwards from the sea on its east and west flanks, and which are called Portsmouth and Langstone Harbours. The heads of these harbours are joined by Hilsea Channel – distant some three miles from the Dockyard – which divides the Island of Portsea from the mainland of Hampshire, and which is about 2,600 yards in length. Along the natural channel, which varies in width from 50 to 1,000 feet, and of which the depth in mid-channel at the flood of ordinary spring tides, is about seven feet, it has always been felt that a permanent defensive work, or line, ought to run to shield our largest and richest marine storehouse from a sudden *coup de main*, attempted by a desperate and audacious enemy.

It must never be forgotten that there is all the difference in the world between a few shells, thrown into Portsmouth Dockyard from Portsdown Hill or from Spithead Roadway, and the simultaneous application of the torch by human hands to inflammable stores in a hundred different localities. Shells might be thrown into the Dockyard, day after day, week after week, from a distance of three of four miles, without doing us any serious injury beyond the outrage to our feelings which such an insult would imply. But if even fifty desperate men could get in to the Dockyard and be unmolested in their occupation of it for five minutes, they might inflict upon England such an amount of disaster and disgrace as is hitherto, happily, unparalleled in our rough island story.

Against such a peril as this, even Charles II, perhaps the least English of our sovereigns, strove to guard Portsmouth, by erecting a fort to command the Hilsea Channel. During the French Revolutionary War, the Government of George III deemed it advisable to purchase the land which skirted Hilsea Channel along its entire length, a purchase which they effected at a cost of £132,000. Along the 2,600 yards of water which divide Portsea Island from the mainland they then proceeded to construct field earthworks, which were considered sufficient in those days to guard the Dockyard against a *coup de main*. The field works being "of small command and weak profit," remained without alteration until, at the end of 1857, Major Jervois, the Assistant Inspector-General of Fortifications, submitted to his chief, Sir John Burgoyne, an able report, embodying a project for the better defence of Portsmouth. In this report the Hilsea Lines, nearly as they now exist, were proposed. "The plans," to quote the words employed by Sir Frederick Grey's committee in their report, "were approved by the Government, and, at the date of the report of the Defence Commission, were in progress, and received the approval of the Royal Commissioners."

It will thus be seen that the Hilsea Lines were conceived and commenced at a date anterior to the insane scare of 1859; and we defy the Royal Commissioners to point out any other work, out of nearly one hundred of which they were the initiators, which has more successfully withstood the hostile criticism to which the experience of a decennium, singularly prolific in warlike lessons, has since subjected their handiwork and sagacity. It is true, that in consequence of slips of earth which have taken place here and there, along a slope which is nearly three miles in length, and which was originally constructed at too steep an angle, there have been exaggerated rumours of failures which have assumed undue proportions in the House of Commons. "I believe," said Major J.B. Edwards, R.E., when examined on August 21st, 1868, before the Grey Committee, "that it was stated in a debate in Parliament, referring to these lines, that they were a sand covered mass of ruins. That statement is altogether incorrect. The only failure which has taken place is that of the contractor, and the only settlement that which he effected with his creditors."

If we cannot go the whole way with the enthusiastic Major, in his assertion that the "only failure" in the Hilsea Lines has been that of the contractor, we willingly concede to him that there has been much exaggeration as to the subsidence of earth and clay and sand which they have witnessed. The result promises to be, that, when the Hilsea Lines are finished, and when a quickset hedge is planted half way up their extensive slope, they will constitute the most formidable defensive earthwork that the world has ever seen.

It is difficult to describe the exact conformation of these famous lines without employing phrases which will be unintelligible to all who are not civil engineers or military men. For the benefit of those who are not unfamiliar with the technical language of military engineering, let us quote the description of the work given in the report of Sir. F. Grey's committee. "The line," it says, "lies on an arc whose chord is 2,700 yards, and versed sine 450 yards. It consists of four bastioned fronts, comprising three whole and two demi-bastions, with exterior sides of 770 yards, and lines of defence of 500 yards. There is space on the ramparts for an armament of 168 guns. The flanks were designed before the introduction of rifled artillery, with casemates for 50 guns, and were then considered out of range of fire from Portsdown Hill."

The report proceeds to say, that the merlons of earth, which covered the masonry between each embrasure that peeped out from these 50 casemates, were found to be too thin for protection, and every alternate embrasure was therefore blocked, and a larger merlon thrown up in front of it. In other words, the embrasures, in the flanks or quasi-caponieres of the bastions, were, at one *coup*, reduced from 50 to 25. We sincerely wish that, in other cases where the Royal Engineers have made a slight mistake, they would frankly confess it, and, for ourselves, at least, we promise that their explanation, if ingeniously made, will always be received with effusion.

It has been stated on many occasions that the 50 guns in the flanks of these bastions were so near together as to be unable to traverse; but this was strenuously denied by Major Edwards and Colonel Jervois, when examined before the Grey Committee. Suffice it to say that, in our judgement, the casemated guns of Hilsea Lines, which will never be brought into play until the enemy has got close enough to the double ditch, are quite sufficiently numerous, although their number has been reduced from 50 to 25. It is impossible for anyone who has ever seen war to believe that the 168 or more guns which will stand on the top of the terra plain, and which will, of course, be well protected by traverses when the hour of trial comes, will ever permit an enemy to get into a position where the casemated guns will be called upon to take any part in the sport. We have omitted to add that, such is the height of these defensive lines, as to render the general command of their parapets over the country in front some 30 feet. They will be protected in front of the rampart by a wet ditch, 130 feet wide at its surface, and containing 8 feet of water. Beyond this ditch is the tidal channel, which will eventually, though possibly not until the day when we are seriously threatened with war, from a navigable link of communication between Portsmouth and Langstone Harbours. Although it is possible that the flanks of the bastions, in which the casemated guns now stand, might with advantage have stood farther apart, and thus have crossed their fire at a greater distance than is the case as they have now been constructed, and although some carelessness seems to have been shown in making the new London Road only 9 feet wide, we have nothing but commendation to bestow upon the Hilsea Lines when viewed in their entirety.

For once, we are happy to agree unreservedly with the report of the Grey Committee, when it says that, "the Lines are adapted to a modern armament, and the enormous obstacles presented by two wet ditches, combined with the powerful flanking fire from guns both in casemates and on ramparts, render their defensive power unusually great."

Whenever Colonel Jervois wishes to impress a foreign engineer with a lofty conception of the science of military engineering, as practised in England, let him carry his visitor, not to Hurst Castle, or the No Man and Horse forts, but to the most formidable earthworks in existence, the Hilsea Lines.

1869 – THE REDUCTIONS IN THE GOVERNMENT DOCKYARDS.

In the House of Commons on Friday, our member Sir J. Elphinstone rose to call attention to the destitution at Portsmouth consequent on the discharge of men from the Dockyard, and to ask the First Lord of the Admiralty whether he intended to take any measures to alleviate that distress promoting emigration or otherwise. He expressed his concurrence in the remarks which had fallen from his Hon. friend (Sir J. Hay.) The Hon. Baronet said he now desired more particularly to call the attention of the Government to the great distress existing in several portions of the kingdom in consequence of the very large reductions which had been made in the Dockyards. Into the causes which had led to the discharge of so many of the workmen he had no desire to enter, but the result was very great and widespread distress.

At Portsmouth last year 1,118 men had been discharged. Against the character of these men nothing had been urged; they were persons of the greatest respectability; they would not go into the poor house, and after parting bit by bit with their clothing and furniture, they had to trust to the assistance of their neighbours for relief. £1,500 had been subscribed in Portsmouth for the purpose of alleviating the distress which the reductions had occasioned, and those who had been discharged were employed upon public works, the money being found by the municipality and the citizens combined.

During the continuance of the distress in Lancashire these men, then the possessors of comfortable incomes and happy homes, came forward with no sparing hand to the assistance of their brethren. He hoped that the Government might be induced to help these men in some way; and indeed, this was a duty which, in his opinion, the peremptory mode of dismissal which had been adopted rendered imperative upon them. His own acquaintance with working men was of a very intimate character, and he did not believe that it was at all consonant with the feelings or wishes of the working men of this country that so many of their brethren should be reduced to distress by being so suddenly and so unexpectedly deprived of their employment.

The Mayor of Portsmouth, in a letter which he had written, described the distress which the discharge of so many workmen had occasioned as "deep, dire, urgent, and most heartrending," and he (Sir J. Elphinstone) could support the truth of this description. It was heartrending to see gangs of men in the prime of life, standing at the corners of streets in distress, and with nothing to do. At Portsmouth there were 200 or 300 men, who, with their families, would emigrate, if they had the means; and did not think it was an unreasonable request to ask that the Government should assist them to emigrate to America, from whence they had intelligence that persons of their calling could meet with ready means of subsistence.

Mr. J. Lewis referred to the fact that 1,500 men had been discharged from Devonport Dockyard, and said he had heard with satisfaction that no further reductions were to be made either at Devonport or Portsmouth. He thought the men who had been discharged had some claim upon the consideration of the Government.

Mr. Graves said it was not one or two places that were immediately affected by the reductions in the Dockyard; these reductions affected the trade of the shipwrights throughout the kingdom. He had always been under the impression that workmen in the Dockyards entered at a lower tariff of wages than that which was obtained in private yards, and that they were entitled to some amount of pension or superannuation on leaving the service after a certain term; and if this were so, surely the men who had been discharged had a moral claim upon the consideration of the Government.

Mr. Stone was glad that his Hon. colleague, with whose sentiments he thoroughly concurred, had confined his remarks to the distress existing in Portsmouth, and that he had not gone into any matters relating to those who were responsible for this distress. It might be asked how it was that men who were discharged last year had not long before this taken steps to obtain employment elsewhere, instead of remaining a burden to the rates; but the answer had been supplied by the Hon. member for Liverpool, and it was that the depression in the shipbuilding trade was not confined to the Dockyards, but was general throughout the country.

Therefore, there was no opening for those men in their own employment in any other part of the country, and it was of no use their going elsewhere. It might be said that these men took employment with the distinct understanding that they were liable to be discharged at any moment, and therefore they had no legal claim on the Government; but there was a difference between the discharge of one or a few men from one of other establishments and wholesale discharge like this from all places where the men could find employment, which created a difficulty such as had not been foreseen.

There was another matter in reference to the position of the Government in Dockyard towns in connection with the poor rate; and the question was whether they should not contribute their fair share to the rate in crisis like this, especially as the distress affected not only the men themselves, but also shopkeepers and others who were connected with them.

During the last few years, the Government had made a contribution to the poor rate of the towns in question in respect of their premise; but this contribution, instead of varying, as did that of private individuals, was a fixed sum. Therefore, when the Government increased the rate levied upon the town by discharging their men they did not, like private employers, increase their payment to the rate. All he asked was that the Government should, in some way, recognise these facts and afford help in some way or other.

Mr. T.W. Martin spoke of the distress existing at Woolwich.

Mr. M. Chambers thought the distress might be greatly mitigated if, instead of selling our wooden ships, the men were employed to break them up.

Mr. Childers: The last time it was my duty to engage in debate of this kind, when very nearly the same speakers took part in it as have spoken this evening, was in 1866, when I think six or seven gentlemen representing Dockyards declared with one voice how absolutely necessary it was to raise the wages of the Dockyard men, because, if their wages were not raised, the men would leave the yards and the Government would get no work done. I was at the Treasury at the time, and I ventured to resist the motion, and gave good grounds for it. I must say that, having listened very patiently during the last hour to what has been said about Dockyards, and in the light of that discussion reviewed in the past, I feel grateful that the Government came to so wise a conclusion in 1866. There is no doubt that if Government had listened to the demands of the Hon. members who urged an increase of pay, the attraction of Dockyard towns would have been proportionately increased, and we should at this time have been called upon in some measure to compensate those unfortunate persons who have been thrown out of work.

Before I answer the specific questions put by the Hon. member for Portsmouth, let me say a word in reply to what has been stated by the Hon. member for Liverpool (Mr. Graves.) I thought I had answered the question he put to me when replying to a question last evening on this subject. I then stated very precisely how many men had been discharged from the Dockyards, what were their rights to compensation or superannuation and whether those rights had been respected, and I stated as clearly as I could that everybody who had rights to compensation had had those rights respected. I think I also gave the numbers of those who had been discharged with compensations, and I gave the average amount of compensation, whether in the shape of annual payment or gratuity, they had received. In reply, therefore, to my Hon. friend I would say that the persons who were discharged last year, with two exceptions, were persons who had been hired on the express condition that they would be discharged at short notice without any gratuity if their service was short, and with a certain limited gratuity if their service was long.

Having looked into the matter I believe the late Government, under whom the whole of these proceedings occurred, acted most justly with respect to these men and the terms upon which they were engaged, and therefore there is no occasion for the apprehension under which my Hon. friend (Mr. Graves) labours.

Now, Sir, I will come to the precise question which has been put to me by my Hon. friend the member for Portsmouth. He has called attention to the destitution existing at Portsmouth consequent upon the discharge of men from the Dockyards, and he has asked whether the Government is prepared to take a certain course so as to relieve it. Let me state the nature of this discharge. I have looked very carefully as far as Portsmouth is concerned into the figures with respect to these discharges, and the fact is simply this:— According to the estimates in force before 1868 there were in round numbers some 4,800 or 4,900 usually employed in the Portsmouth Dockyard. These numbers have now fallen to 4,000. The difference, therefore, is not very much if you merely look upon it as a question between the former establishment of the Portsmouth Dockyard and the present establishment; but what really happened was that towards the end of 1867 the late Government decided to engage for a specific purpose—whether wisely or unwisely I will not now inquire—an additional number of men beyond those provided for by the estimates.

Somewhere about three hundred or more were so engaged for a short time at Portsmouth, and I understand that a considerable number of these men, attracted by the chance of work, came from the north through the distress in the shipbuilding trade there; we have no official return, however, to show how many of those men came from distant parts.

During the financial year ending with March this extra employment still continued, but the Government came to a somewhat sudden decision to reduce the number of men, and the numbers in Portsmouth Dockyard between March, 1868, and June, 1868, were reduced altogether by somewhere about 1,650 men. In June, 1868, two months before the close of last session, the reduction ceased altogether, and perhaps I may, in passing, say that the questions I am now called upon to answer should have been addressed to the late Government in July last, rather than to the present Government eight months after the men have been discharged.

The distress which my Hon. friend has brought before the House was occasioned by the discharges of eight months ago, and not at all by anything which has occurred during the latter part of the year; yet Hon. members from Dockyard towns ask to consider whether the destitution is of such permanent character as to justify the Government in resorting to national measures to meet it.

Now, one word as to the cause of this destitution. I don't think the reduction in the numbers at the Dockyards such as I have described during the last 18 months before the increase, is in any respect abnormal. Reductions have been made on previous occasions quite as large but have attracted no special notice. The real fact is that the reduction in the shipbuilding trade connected with the Government is only a fraction of the reductions in the shipbuilding trade throughout the country. The number of men employed in the Government yards is very few when compared with the number in the trade as a whole, and these discharged men are very few indeed, as compared with the numbers reduced to absolute poverty by the sudden change which has come over the whole of our trade, especially the shipbuilding trade, during the last few years.

It would be altogether wrong to suppose that the former or the present Government are in the least responsible, as has been suggested, for what is really almost entirely the result of widespread and notorious distress.

With respect to Portsmouth, my Hon. friend will forgive me if I am not able to go into much detail, because although I saw him some short time ago on the matter, I received the explanatory papers from the Mayor of Portsmouth only last Tuesday. The distress at Portsmouth is by no means solely due to any reduction of the number of Dockyard men; on the contrary, I found three very distinct causes of distress at Portsmouth at this moment. Some large contract works with which the Government have nothing to do have been suspended to a very great extent during the past two months; the corporation of Portsmouth, too, has been employing a very large number of men whom they have recently discharged, and these causes have largely contributed to the destitution deplored. That is the general statement I have to make as regards Portsmouth.

Then my Hon. friend has addressed me on the subject of emigration, but I am quite sure he will not expect from me anything like a complete reply, considering the matter was brought under the consideration of the Government only three days ago. To any general system of emigration carried on by the Government I should entertain very strong objections. The colonies are coming forward themselves for that purpose. Hon. members may have seen by a letter in *The Times* this morning that there has been very considerable change of opinion on the subject of emigration in a colony of which I once knew something. But considering the whole course of our policy towards the colonies, nothing, I think, could be more unwise than that we should suddenly embark in a large emigration scheme.

At this moment the Poor Law authorities have power, under an Act of Parliament, to assist emigration; whether that system is workable or not I do not pretend to say, but the power itself exists. I must, therefore, decline giving any positive answer to the question which has been put to me, beyond pointing out the two considerations to which I have already adverted. I think it is the duty of the Government to exercise its power of discharging men in large numbers from the Dockyard with discretion and moderation, and upon some very plain principle. Whether the large discharges last year fulfilled these conditions it is not for me to say. I shall not attempt to go into that question. But my own opinion on the subject generally is perfectly clear; it is, that those who employ large bodies of men, while adhering rigidly to the terms of employment, should, on the other hand, have regard to the time, the manner, and the circumstances in which it is proposed that labour should be thrown back upon the country.

That is the only answer I can give to my Hon. friend, stating distinctly at the same time that this is the policy by which I shall be guided as long as I have anything to do with the administration of the Admiralty.

1869 – THE PORTSMOUTH VOLUNTEER REVIEW.

A review of the volunteers of the southern and western counties, with the troops in garrison, was held on Monday week, at Portsmouth, under Lieutenant-General Sir George Buller, K.C.B., the officer commanding the south-west military district. The whole force was inspected on Southsea Common, at three o'clock, Lieutenant-General Sir G. Buller, and the march past immediately followed. The volunteer cavalry led, under Colonel Bowers; two field batteries of Royal Artillery followed; with the Marine Artillery, the second battalion 13th Regiment, 101st, and 67th, making up the first division, under Brigadier-General Carey. The second division was led by the field battery of six guns of the 3rd Hants Volunteer Artillery, followed the 1st, 2nd, and 3rd Hants Volunteer Garrison Artillery. All the volunteer infantry marched very steadily, with arms at the trail. The march past occupied exactly half an hour. The sham fight then commenced.

The force was divided into two bodies, one the attacking force, under the command of Major-General Lysons, C.B., marching out to the eastward of Southsea Castle, and taking up position there preparatory to advancing to the attack; and the defending force, under the command of Major-General Carey, retiring within the walls of Portsmouth for the defence of the place. Out seaward, between Spithead and the Horse Shoal, lay the *Scorpion* turret sloop, with bulwarks down and steam up, ready to engage Southsea Castle when signalled; while further off, half hid in the haze which covered the water, lay the six screw gunboats which were ready to aid her in the attack. Captain Courtney, flag captain to Vice-Admiral Sir James Hope, commanded the flotilla. The gunboats soon began to give signs of their intention to enter into the fray, and, reply to a signal from Admiral Hope's steam yacht, the *Fire Queen* began to creep in slowly towards the castle.

A gun fired from the King's bastion of the town fortifications gave the alarm, which was immediately followed by Southsea Castle opening fire from the guns on its keep upon the *Scorpion* and her fleet of gunboats. The enemy's fleet were some time before they replied to the fire from the castle, but the six smaller craft were gradually closing up round the turret sloop which lay near the entrance to the harbour channel and right

The Defending Force Concentrating on King William's Gate

Accident at the Review at Portsmouth

under the guns of the castle. The enemy's land force the meantime was advancing against the castle along the line of sea-beach from the eastward, with the volunteer cavalry and artillery in advance, the latter opening fire upon the left flank of the castle. The gunboats had now taken a position inside the *Scorpion*, and within half a dozen cables' lengths of the seaward defences of the castle, and opened fire, the little Staunch coming up the last, with her 12-ton gun peeping out grimly through her bow-port. A reconnoitring force, while this attack was being made upon the castle by the land and sea forces of the enemy, issued from the garrison, composed of the 67th Infantry and a field battery of Royal Artillery, and felt their way towards the enemy, who advanced his cavalry, driving the sharpshooters of the 67th; but the latter formed square, threw in a heavy Snider fire, driving off the venturous horsemen, and the battery, unlimbering, hastened the cavalry in their retreat.

A second and a third charge was made by the cavalry on the left flank of the 67th; but the South Hampshires again formed square, and repulsed them just as the castle hauled down its flag in token of surrender. Again, the cavalry made a very effective charge; but the fire of rifle and artillery again proved too much for them, and drove them back. The castle

Volunteer Review at Southsea Castle

The March Past - Review of the Regulars and Volunteers at Southsea

having been taken, the enemy now made a general advance in the direction of Portsmouth, the gunboats covering his left flank and engaging the town batteries in advance.

The enemy pushed forward, a strong body of skirmishers and drove back the reconnoitring force, which retired slowly across the Common and towards the walls of the town, covered by skirmishers and artillery fire. The retreat of the 67th Regiment and the artillery over the Common and into the fortress, covered by heavy fire from the artillery mounted on the town defences, was one of the most effective events of the day. The enemy advanced with a strong line of skirmishers and field artillery in front. With the latter marched a naval officer and a body of seamen landed from the fleet, carrying the ensign of the captured castle. The third brigade of the enemy, flank movement executed simultaneously with the advance of his fourth brigade over the Common, through the streets of Southsea, debouched in front of the town defences at the centre and on the extreme left. The enemy then, uniting his entire force, prepared to assault the fortress, and attacked it throughout the whole length of its defence, his fleet redoubling their fire upon the seaward face of the defences. The naval attack failed utterly, as it was intended to do; and the fleet, succumbing to the more powerful artillery of the fortress, surrendered and was taken into the harbour. The assault of the enemy on the land face of the fortress was partially successful at the first onset, his storming columns getting possession of the Montague and King's ravelins. A heavy fire opened from the main ramparts upon the two ravelins and along the entire face of the works by the defenders soon rendered the position of the assailants untenable, and the outworks were regained. A sortie by the garrison, with the second battalion of the 13th Regiment and a battery of field artillery on the enemy's right flank, compelled him to abandon his position on the left of the defence; and a second sortie against his right, following immediately upon the first, completed his discomfiture and ended in his retreat, covered by his cavalry and artillery with lines of skirmishers.

This ended the day's proceedings. All engaged—the regular troops, as well as the volunteers seemed to enter into the afternoon's work before them in the best possible spirit. The review was got over in excellent time.

A display of fireworks came off on Southsea Common in the evening; and a grand ball was given in the great drill hall of the artillery volunteers, on the Governor's green.

1869 – WELFARE OF THE PORTSMOUTH EMIGRANTS.

The continued prosperity of the emigrants who recently went from Portsmouth to Canada, and who from thence have found their way to parts of the United States, cannot but be interesting to their friends in England and to those more especially who so kindly aided in sending them thither. The extracts given below are from a letter of a late Portsmouth Dockyard man to a friend living in Portsmouth at the present time, which is dated "Chicago, Illinois, USA Sept. 6th, 1869." It will be seen that the writer, who is a young man, and who left the Dockyard during the recent discharges, being one of the passengers who went to Canada in the *Crocodile*, appears to have gone to his new home in the true spirit of emigration, determined to do "that which his hands find to do." The apparent satisfaction expressed contrasts most favourably with same of the recent "grumblings" which have appeared in our columns.

The events of the everyday life of Chicago may be taken as a fair sample of the general life in America of the "working man," and will be read with interest as being circumstances in which those who have lived amongst us are concerned:-

"I am happy to tell you that we are in very good health, considering the extreme heat of the weather; it is much hotter here than in England. A great many people I know have been laid up through it; but, thank God, we seem to stand it pretty well. I have had a scorching job this last two weeks, on the roof of a building, exposed to the sun all day. The first day I worked with my shirt sleeves up, and the sun burnt my arms so that all the skin has come off. Trade has been very dull this summer all over the country. The people say they have not had such a bad season since the war, but I think it is on the mend now. I have been pretty fortunate in getting work, as there has been a great number of men out of employment. I have not worked at my trade for the last six weeks, as it has been very slack, and I had to stand off for a time until something came in. So, I soon began to look for something else, as men here do not trust to one trade. I went on to work at the cornice business. There is a great deal of it done here, and it is becoming a "big business" in this country. They are made of galvanized iron for the purpose of being fireproof. Most of the roofs of buildings are covered with iron or tin for the same purposes. These iron cornices are a great improvement; they are made principally for stone and brick buildings, as they come cheaper, and they can have any design they like. I worked at that a few weeks, when I left and got another job at roofing, or repairing the roofs, of the Illinois Central Railway shop. It is about a six-week job. By that time trade will be brisk again, as the fall is a busy time here. I am getting 2 dollars per day, which is pretty good just now, as there are a great many men in the market.

They have been flocking into Chicago wholesale this summer, and the consequence is that wages have gone down a little. Everything is done very different here to what it is in England. There is a great deal of machinery used here, and the work is turned out very fast. In the tin trade, which is a very extensive one, one man will do as much in one day here as he would in a week in England; everything is for speed. Mr. - is still here, and is doing pretty well; he has been in steady work all the time, at three dollars per day, at carpentering. The accounts we get from Canada are not very encouraging; there is scarcely any trade doing there. Several of the men who came from Portsmouth have come on to Chicago, and I hear that several have gone back again. You would scarcely believe what a difference there is in the two places.

In Canada they seem to be all asleep; but just across the line, in the States, it is all hurry and bustle, everybody seems to be full of business. In Chicago it is a regular rush. The Yankees are full of speculation; it is "neck or nothing" with them. They don't let money lie idle; they like to see it moving. That is one great cause of the prosperity of the country. Everybody is benefitted a little. While the Canadians are thinking whether it will pay, the Yankees have done it and got the money. This is how I just find it from observation. People in England are puzzled as to the addresses of parties here, but I will explain it. The post office system is different, and the majority of people in this country have their letters left at the post office, and call for them, as they shift about from place to place very much.

The General Post Office is a fine large building, the interior being fitted up in separate offices for different kinds of letters. The letters are sorted out and placed on racks, alphabetically; so if you wish to know if there is one for you, you go to the attendant at the window

Emigrants Embarking for Canada

and give your name, when, if there is one, you get it in a moment; but if the letter is directed to the house, the carrier will bring it to you, the same as in England.

When I wrote to you before we were in furnished rooms, and did not intend to stay very long. We have now got a very nice house and garden to ourselves. I have grown enough vegetables to keep us going without buying, and everything grows very fast. House rent is much higher than at Portsmouth, but it is much cheaper in the country than in the city. Most things are dearer than at home, with the exception of meat, bread and potatoes. Mutton ranges from six cents. (3d.) to 12 cents. (6d.) per lb. Eggs and milk are very cheap. I have visited a great many of the churches here; they are fitted up very nicely, cushioned and carpeted all over, with open pews. There are, however, very few pulpits. They have plenty of good singing, and some fine preachers; they nearly all have a collection at each service, instead of pew rents. They hold their Sunday school directly after the morning service (12.30), for about an hour and a half. The evening service does not commence until half-past seven or a quarter to eight, in consequence, I suppose, of the meal times being different.

The people here have only three meals a day - breakfast at six; dinner at twelve; supper at six. That is the general custom all over the country. It seemed rather strange to us at first, but now we are used to it we like it much better. People live much better here than in England. They generally like to see a good spread. We cannot get any beer like the English; it is not so good. We get good cider and whiskey. I often wish I could get a glass of your good English beer, as it would be a treat. I shall feel obliged if you would send me a few mignonette seeds, or any small seeds that you can put in a letter; for the seeds we brought with us, and set, have grown very fine, but have not gone to seed again. I cannot account for it in any way. This is a fine country for fruit; it is very plentiful here and cheap now, peaches in abundance. I cannot give you much political news, as this is vacation time, and not much stirring now. I guess we shall hear a little about the Alabama when Congress assembles.

I must not forget to tell you that we have seen some real, live "Fenians." There is a regiment of them close by; they generally drill on Sunday afternoons, in a piece of enclosed ground near us. I can tell you they look "awfully brave" as they parade through the streets in full uniform - and the "green flag," that is to wave over Dublin Castle someday flying. About half-a-dozen good soldiers would scare the lot of them.

With regard to religious matters, there is not so much of that blind bigotry here; the different denominations seem to be more liberal towards each other. You sometimes hear of a challenge between two parties to discuss some sectarian point; but they seem to get along pretty well, considering the mixture of people and creeds. I think the Catholics have the lead here; they have got the finest churches and schools in the city, and seem to do the "best business;" they are at it all the week, as well as on Sundays. Unitarians, too. I hold a good position here."

1869 – FUNERAL OF CAPTAIN COLIN ARTHUR CAMPBELL.

The remains of Captain Colin Arthur Campbell, R.N., were consigned to their last resting place, at the Portsmouth Cemetery, on Thursday afternoon, with all the honours usually paid to a deceased officer of his rank. The body remained on board his former ship, the *Ariadne*, frigate, now lying alongside Portsmouth Dockyard, and on board of which he died on the passage home from Malta.

Early in the afternoon the Common Hard was densely packed by inhabitants from all parts of the borough to witness the egress from the Dockyard gates, and every point commanding a view of the progress was crowded. At half-past one o'clock the Royal Marine Artillery and Light Infantry landed from the *Warrior*, *Hercules*, and *Bellerophon*, and were formed in two lines extending from the *Ariadne* at the extreme south end of the jetty, as far as the Dockyard gates. About two o'clock the coffin (which was covered with a rich pall and the Union Jack) was borne from the cabin by eight sailors of the deceased's ship and placed in the hearse on the jetty, while minute guns boomed from the *Duke of Wellington*, the ensign of every ship being lowered half-mast and continuing so until the procession had passed out of the Dockyard. The band of the *Ariadne* played the impressive "Dead March" in Saul, and the Marines (with arms reversed) and the boys and men of the ship followed, four abreast, in the rear.

The hearse, which was drawn by four horses, was beautifully furnished with plumes and appointments, and was attended on either side by the pall-bearers-namely, Captain E.P. Rice (of the *Asia*), Captain Lord Gilford (of the *Hercules*), Captain J.G. Goodenough (of the *Minotaur*), Captain A.W.A. Hood (of the *Excellent*), Captain R.R.J. Macdonald (of the *Bellerophon*), and Capt. Arthur Wilmshurst (of her Majesty's ship *Flora*); and followed by one of the cousins of the deceased, Capt. F. Campbell (aide-de-camp to the Queen, and Captain of the *Ariadne*).

The naval honours were suspended at the Dockyard gates, in consequence of the distance being too great to be marched in slow time, the band returning to the ship. In passing through the town the hearse was preceded by a carriage containing the Rev. W. Onslow, chaplain to the Prince of Wales, the Rev. Professor Main, and Dr. Holman, surgeon of the *Ariadne*; and followed by three mourning coaches. The first coach contained Major P. Campbell, R.H.A., brother of the deceased, and three cousins, namely, Colonel Fitzroy Campbell, Colonel Frederick Campbell, R.A., and Captain F. Campbell, R.N., the present captain of the *Ariadne*. The second coach contained Major Kane, Major Frith, Major Baldwin, and Captain Hodgson, commander of the *Ariadne*, and the third coach, Mr. French and the servant of the deceased. These were succeeded by a great number of private carriages and cabs.

On arriving at the cemetery some 600 men belonging to the Royal Marine Artillery were told off to keep the ground, by which means, notwithstanding the great pressure of the crowd, an uninterrupted passage was preserved to the grave. The band of the same corps, with drums muffled, played Beethoven's "Dead March" as the hearse and carriages approached the entrance, and continued during the formation of the procession, and until its arrival at the church.

The body, which, besides the mourners already mentioned, was followed to the grave by Vice-Admiral Sir James Hope, G.C.B., naval commander-in-chief, and a large number of naval and military officers, in full uniform, was borne by the deceased's boat's crew, consisting of eight sailors, the coffin being covered, as before, with a pall and Union Jack, and surmounted by the captain's hat, sword, and epaulettes.

The Rev. P. Grant, the Vicar of Portsmouth, and the Rev. Professor Main, of the Royal Naval College, conducted the procession to the church, where the first part of the burial service was gone through, the Vicar officiating. The service was concluded by the Rev. Professor Main, and the coffin having been lowered into the vault, three volleys were fired by a party of 150 men belonging to the Marine Artillery.

The whole of the arrangements, which were carried out most satisfactorily, were under the personal superintendence and direction of Mr. Henry Turner, of the firm of Messrs. G.&H. Turner, the well-known drapers and undertakers, of Queen Street, Portsea.

1869 – HER MAJESTY'S BIRTHDAY.

Wednesday being the day appointed for the celebration of Her Majesty's Jubilee birthday the different Government establishments were closed and the employees granted a holiday. The ships in commission were dressed at early morn, and the Royal Standard floated at the Saluting Battery and different forts in the garrison.

Southsea Pier and the Victoria Pier, Portsmouth, were also gaily decorated with a profusion of flags. At noon royal salutes were fired from the ships in harbour and at Spithead, led off by the *Duke of Wellington*, flagship of Vice-Admiral Sir James Hope, G.C.B.

The troops of the garrison, comprising the field battery of six guns of the Royal Artillery (11th Brigade) from Hilsea, The Royal Engineers, the 12th Brigade Royal Artillery, the Royal Marine Artillery, the 33rd, 46th, and 67th Regiments, assembled and formed a line on Southsea Common. Shortly before twelve o'clock Lieutenant-General Roller, K.C.B., commanding the South-Western district, arrived on the ground, and having rode along the line, took up his position at the saluting point attended by his staff.

At twelve o'clock a royal salute was fired from the Saluting Battery in the garrison, followed by one from the battery of the Royal Artillery, and a *feu de joie* from the infantry. The General and his staff then rode to the front, when a general salute was given, the united bands playing the National Anthem. This was followed by three cheers, led off by the General commanding. The troops afterwards marched past in review order in grand divisions, and also in two brigades, the first comprising the 33rd, 46th, and 67th Regiments, and the second a Brigade of Royal Artillery and two battalions of Royal Marine Artillery.

A few field manoeuvres were gone through at the conclusion of which the troops returned to their quarters.

The Royal Marine Light Infantry and troops at Gosport were also drawn up on the esplanade facing the sea near Haslar Hospital, and fired a *feu de joie* at twelve o'clock.